American Nationalisms

America was born in an age of political revolution throughout the Atlantic world, a period when the very definition of "nation" was transforming. Benjamin E. Park traces how Americans imagined novel forms of nationality during the country's first five decades within the context of European discussions taking place at the same time. Focusing on three case studies – Massachusetts, Pennsylvania, and South Carolina – Park examines the developing practices of nationalism in three specific contexts. He argues for a more elastic connection between nationalism and the nation-state by demonstrating that ideas concerning political and cultural allegiance to a federal body developed in different ways and at different rates throughout the nation. *American Nationalisms* explores how ideas of nationality permeated political disputes, religious revivals, patriotic festivals, slavery debates, and even literature.

Benjamin E. Park currently serves as an assistant professor of history at Sam Houston State University. He received graduate degrees in religion, politics, and history from the Universities of Edinburgh and Cambridge. He has received fellowships from the Massachusetts Historical Society, Boston University's American Political History Institute, and the University of Missouri's Kinder Institute on Constitutional Democracy. His publications have appeared in *Journal of the Early Republic, Early American Studies, Journal of American Studies*, and *American Nineteenth Century History*.

T0370633

American Nationalisms

Imagining Union in the Age of Revolutions, 1783–1833

BENJAMIN E. PARK

Sam Houston State University

CAMBRIDGE
UNIVERSITY PRESS

CAMBRIDGE
UNIVERSITY PRESS

University Printing House, Cambridge CB2 8BS, United Kingdom

One Liberty Plaza, 20th Floor, New York, NY 10006, USA

477 Williamstown Road, Port Melbourne, VIC 3207, Australia

314-321, 3rd Floor, Plot 3, Splendor Forum, Jasola District Centre, New Delhi - 110025, India

79 Anson Road, #06-04/06, Singapore 079906

Cambridge University Press is part of the University of Cambridge.

It furthers the University's mission by disseminating knowledge in the pursuit of education, learning and research at the highest international levels of excellence.

www.cambridge.org
Information on this title: www.cambridge.org/9781108414203
DOI: 10.1017/9781108333290

First published 2018
First paperback edition 2019

A catalogue record for this publication is available from the British Library

Library of Congress Cataloging in Publication data
Names: Park, Benjamin E., author.
Title: American nationalisms : imagining union in the age
of revolutions, 1783–1833 / Benjamin E. Park.
Description: New York : Cambridge University Press, 2017.
Identifiers: LCCN 2017028179 | ISBN 9781108420372 (hardback)
Subjects: LCSH: Nationalism – United States – History – 18th century | Nationalism –
United States – History – 19th century. | Regionalism – United States – History –
18th century | Regionalism – United States – History – 19th century | National
characteristics, American – History – 18th century. | National characeristics,
American – History – 18th century. | Sectionalism (United States) – History. |
United States – History – 1783–1865. | United States – Historical geography. |
United States – Territorial expansion.
Classification: LCC E301 .P35 2017 | DDC 320.540973/09033–dc23
LC record available at https://lccn.loc.gov/2017028179

ISBN 978-1-108-42037-2 Hardback
ISBN 978-1-108-41420-3 Paperback

For Michael O'Brien, a master of the historian's craft

Contents

Illustrations

Prologue

A group of ministers, lawyers, and amateur historians gathered in Boston in 1791 to form the Massachusetts Historical Society. Though political independence had only been declared fifteen years prior and the Treaty of Paris was only eight years old, some citizens of the United States were anxious to solidify the country's identity. One way to accomplish that was through the promulgation of its history. As the city of Boston, and the state of Massachusetts, had played significant roles in the nation's quest for independence, it made sense to form an organization that would track its patriotic tradition. But the state's historical society aimed to be much more than just a repository for local stories and documents. In a circular letter sent to dozens of potential "corresponding members" throughout the nation, the society was envisioned "to collect, preserve, and communicate, materials for a complete history of *this country*" and to account for "all valuable efforts of human ingenuity and industry, from the beginning of its settlement." The circular then requested documents, artifacts, histories, and general support for an institution designed to be a symbol for the nation's collaborative character.[1]

Responses were received from people scattered throughout the, by then, fourteen states in the nation. Letters came in from New York, Pennsylvania, and as far south as Georgia. Every letter was transcribed into the society's letterbook, an artifact meant to physically embody national unity. In a way, the society was a federal project that represented

---

[1] Jeremy Belknap, "Circular Letter, of the Historical Society," included in the bound volume of the Massachusetts Historical Society Letterbook, 1791–1798, MHS. (Emphasis in original.)

the federal spirit of its age: it was formed only a few years following the ratification of the Constitution. The general sentiment, especially in New England, was moving toward a more centralized location of authority, an increased sense of interdependence between the states, and a prioritization of the national over the local. It made sense, then, that a "state" historical society would reach far outside of its geographic boundaries when establishing its purpose and value.

One of the corresponding members was South Carolinian Henry William de Saussure, the Federalist politician, judge, and the second director of the United States Mint. De Saussure was honored. He immediately offered to donate a number of items including some of "the first gold coins [that] were struck under the authority of the United States." But he was even more excited about writing an important history that could then be given to the fledging organization: "I have endeavoured to procure [a history] for the Historical Society," he wrote, "respecting the Culture of Cotton & the declension of Indigo." South Carolina had recently undergone a transition in labor that catapulted the production of cotton to the center of the state's economy, and de Saussure believed it held similar potential for the rest of the United States. "The feed," he wrote, "which is now thrown into heaps, to rot as manure, might be transported in bulk to New England." De Saussure felt that "the enterprising spirit of New England will doubtless one say avail itself of this article, to open a new road to Commerce." Most importantly, this connection through the production of cotton would "add a new link to the chain which binds the Union together."[2]

In retrospect, the symbol of cotton as a link to hold the Union together seems tragically ironic. On the one hand, cotton production did indeed serve as a financial boon to not only American commerce but also an international economy that connected Charleston to London and to Boston. But cotton also, in the end, symbolized the cultural disconnect between Southern states and the rest of America due to its reliance on slave labor. As the nineteenth century progressed, Northerners increasingly viewed cotton as synonymous with slavery, a practice with which they grew increasingly uncomfortable as the decades passed. In 1830, when the

---

[2] Henry William de Saussure to the Massachusetts Historical Society, January 31, 1799, MHS. For the evolution of cotton production within South Carolina during the period, see Rachel N. Klein, *Unification of a Slave State: The Rise of the Planter Class in the South Carolina Backcountry, 1760–1808* (Chapel Hill: University of North Carolina Press, 1990).

nation faced the crisis of South Carolina threatening to nullify federal laws, Philadelphia printer Mathew Carey identified the "culture of cotton" as the wedge between Southern and Northern states that led directly to the national crisis. In the end, the culture of cotton did not lead to the Union's "binding," but rather to its deterioration.[3]

De Saussure's projection of cotton production, a staple to his state's culture, as the uniting factor of the broader American nation captures the tension located within the local cultivation of nationalism. Prior to the American Revolution, the primary tether for the thirteen colonies was an allegiance to the British crown. Once that was severed, and once they had vanquished their common tyrannical foe, they were left to construct a new sense of self that justified a shared political allegiance. Yet competing cultural traditions and a fractured print culture posed numerous problems for the production of nationalism in the young republic. This book charts how various individuals reacted to, appropriated from, and cultivated anew ideas of a national culture that transcended local borders and encompassed the entire country. Further, it demonstrates how these actions were rooted in a deeper anxiety found throughout the Atlantic world. By tracking the very impulse to define and deploy diverging visions of national union, one can see many of the catalysts that eventually led to the nation's disunion.

---

[3] Mathew Carey, *New Olive Branch: A Solemn Warning on the Banks of the Rubicon*, August 23, 1830, LCP. For cotton production as the center of an international economic market, perpetuation of slave labor, and instigator for national division, see Walter Johnson, *River of Dark Dreams: Slavery and Empire in the Cotton Kingdom* (Cambridge, MA: Harvard University Press, 2013); Sven Beckert, *Empire of Cotton: A Global History* (New York: Knopf, 2014).

Acknowledgments

This project's genesis was located at the University of Cambridge. I could not have asked for a better academic environment for intellectual development than the one provided by the university's American History Group, which included weekly scholarly seminars as well as vibrant graduate workshops. Indeed, I have been blessed to have a string of unquestionably wonderful history mentors: at Cambridge, Michael O'Brien, Sarah Pearsall, and Andrew Preston; at Edinburgh, Stewart Brown and Frank Cogliano; at Brigham Young University, Spencer Fluhman, Craig Harline, Christopher Hodson, Paul Kerry, and Grant Underwood. Pearsall and Cogliano served as my doctoral thesis examiners, and both of them offered immensely helpful critiques and suggestions for how to turn it into a monograph. My sincere thanks to the many professors and students who have made me think about history in general, and American history in particular, in new and exciting ways.

Funding and other material support for this project was provided by the University of Cambridge's Faculty of History, Hughes Hall, the Massachusetts Historical Society, Boston University's American Political History Institute, Brigham Young University's Neal A. Maxwell Institute for Religious Scholarship, the Santander Bursary Program, and the University of Missouri's Kinder Institute on Constitutional Democracy. During my many research trips, I was grateful to be provided food, lodging, and great company by Scott and Beatta Bosworth, Terryl and Fiona Givens, Sarah and Dan Gordon, Kristine Haglund, Karen Hall, Robin and Emily Jensen, Christopher and Karim Jones, Tim Nicholson, and Jonathan Wilson.

As this manuscript focused on three different states, I benefited from the collections available at and help provided by a number of different institutions and archives: in Massachusetts, the Massachusetts Historical Society, the Boston Athenaeum, the American Antiquarian Society, and Harvard University's Houghton Library; in Pennsylvania, the American Philosophical Society, the Historical Society of Pennsylvania, and the Library Company of America; and in South Carolina, the South Carolina Historical Society, the South Carolina Department of Archives and History, and the University of South Carolina's South Caroliniana Library. I also received help at the Library of Congress, Yale University's Beineke Library, the Connecticut Historical Society, the New-York Historical Society, the Virginia Historical Society, the College of William and Mary's Swem Library, and the Southern Baptist Historical Library and Archives housed at the University of Richmond.

Portions of this book were presented in different venues, including seminars, lectures, and workshops with the Massachusetts Historical Society, Boston University's American Political History Institute, the British Association for American Nineteenth Century History, and Auburn University as well as conferences for the Society for United States Intellectual History, the McNeil Center for Early American Studies, the British Association for American Studies, and the American Historical Association. At these and other events, I benefited from the advice and critiques offered by a number of wonderful friends and scholars, including Edward Blum, Mark Boonshoft, Charles Capper, Tom Cutterham, Simon Finger, Caitlin Fitz, Joanne Freeman, Cassandra Good, Sarah Barringer Gordon, Sam Haselby, Amanda Hendrix-Komoto, Woody Holton, Christopher Jones, Adam Jortner, Laurie Maffly-Kipp, Brenden McConville, Richard Newman, Mark Peterson, Jon Roberts, Sophia Rosenfeld, Bruce Schulman, Matthew Spooner, Jordan Watkins, and Conrad E. Wright. And indicative of today's digital age, I'd like to thank my fellow bloggers at *The Junto: A Group Blog on Early American History* for cultivating new understandings of what can often be staid issues.

Two institutions deserve special recognition. First, a postdoctoral fellowship with the University of Missouri's Kinder Institute for Constitutional Democracy provided an environment that was simultaneously stimulating and invigorating. Special thanks to its directors, Jeff Pasley and Justin Dyer, as well as the vast community of historians and political scientists who pushed me in new directions: Carli

Conklin, Daniel Dominguez, Jay Dow, Brandon Flint, Hunter Hampton, Armin Mattes, Jonathan Root, Jonathan Sperber, Richard Tucker, John Wigger, and Cassandra Yacovazzi. The institute is bound for great things. And I couldn't have asked for a warmer reception than what I've received at Sam Houston State University, which I am proud to call my current home. My fellow faculty, too numerous to mention, have proven to be ideal colleagues. It is an honor to work beside them.

Cambridge University Press has proven to be a fantastic collaborator. Deborah Gershenowitz was everything I could hope for in an editor, and Kristina Deusch helped me navigate the intricacies of the process. The production team made sure I avoided numerous and embarrassing errors. I also owe special thanks to the external readers who provided such helpful critiques and suggestions.

The only constant throughout this book's existence has been the unfailing love and support of my family. This work could not have been possible without my generous parents, Richard and Melanie Park, who supported me in numerous ways. I will never be able to repay them, but I hope this book stands as a testament of my appreciation for their wonderful example and extended care. My siblings, Spencer, Jared, Abraham, and, most recently, Mayu, have miraculously become even dearer to me over the last decade, a fact that I cherish and a trend that I hope continues. I am lucky to also have the support of my in-laws, Neil and Thelma Ross, who always freely shared their trust in my abilities and pride in my accomplishments.

My biggest moral support, of course, came from the three most important people in my world: Sara, Curtis, and, especially, Catherine. Though it was sometimes difficult to get work done in my office while I could hear the pitter-patter of little feet in the hallway and, at times, tiny fingers reaching beneath my door, Sara and Curtis kept me grounded and reminded me of life's purest joys. And no matter how much I suffered through writing my dissertation, I know that Catherine suffered more due to the increased duties placed upon her. She is my life, my love, and my future. To her, I owe everything.

This project began as a dissertation written under the supervision of Michael O'Brien. Michael was perhaps the harshest critic I've ever encountered, but behind every blunt comment was a sincere concern for my intellectual development. His keen attention to detail was matched only by his noted skill to connect larger arguments and contexts. He not only willingly – and efficiently! – waded through my faulty assumptions and unjustified conclusions, but also my many dangling participles and mixed prepositions. Because of his expert tutelage, I hope I have become a better reader, thinker, and writer. I cannot imagine a better teacher of the historian's craft. Sadly, he passed away between my doctoral defense and this book's publication. I therefore dedicate this work to him, one of the masters of American intellectual history.

Abbreviations

AAS   American Antiquarian Society (Worcester, MA)

APS   American Philosophical Society (Philadelphia, PA)

AC   *The Debates and Proceedings in the Congress of the United States; with an Appendix, Containing Important State Papers and Public Documents, and All the Laws of a Public Nature,* 42 vols. (Washington, DC: Gales and Seaton, 1834–1856)

DHRC   *The Documentary History of the Ratification of the Constitution.* Edited by Merrill Jensen, John P. Kaminski, Gaspare J. Salone. 26 vols. (Madison: State Historical Society of Wisconsin, 1976–present)

HSP   Historical Society of Pennsylvania (Philadelphia, PA)

HGOP   Harrison Gray Otis Papers (Massachusetts Historical Society, Boston, MA)

JBP   Jeremy Belknap Papers (Massachusetts Historical Society, Boston, MA)

LCP   Library Company of Philadelphia (Philadelphia, PA)

LDC   *Letters of Delegates to Congress, 1774–1789.* Edited by Paul H. Smith. 24 vols. (Washington, DC: 1976–1993)

LOC   Library of Congress (Washington, DC)

MHS   Massachusetts Historical Society (Boston, MA)

PHS   Pennsylvania Historical Society (Philadelphia, PA)

SCHA   South Carolina Historical Association (Charleston, SC)

SCL   South Caroliniana Library, University of South Carolina (Columbia, SC)

Introduction

The *Americans* will have no *Center of Union* among them, and no *Common Interest* to pursue, when the Power and Government of *England* are finally removed. Moreover, when the Intersections and Divisions of their Country by great Bays of the Sea, and by vast Rivers, Lakes, and Ridges of Mountains; – and above all, when those immense inland Regions, beyond the Back Settlements, which are still unexplored, are taken into the Account, they form the highest Probability that the *Americans* never can be united ... under any Species of Government whatever. Their Fate seems to be – A DISUNITED PEOPLE, till the End of Time.

        –Josiah Tucker (1781)[1]

What then is the American, this new man? ... He is an American, who, leaving behind him all his ancient prejudices and manners, receives new ones from the new mode of life he has embraced, the new government he obeys, and the new rank he holds.

        –J. Hector St. John de Crèvecoeur (1782)[2]

America was born at the very moment that the definition of "nation" was being reimagined. In an age in which such a significant word was adopting new meanings, citizens in the newly established United States cultivated novel forms of national politics and federal belonging. This new sense of

---

[1] Josiah Tucker, *Cui Bono? Or, an Inquiry, What Benefits Can Arise Either to the English or the Americans, the French, Spaniards, or Dutch, from the Greatest Victories, or Successes, in the Present War, Being a Series of Letters, Addressed to Monsieur Necker, Late Controller General of the Finances of France* (London: T. Cadell, 1781), 117–119. (Emphasis in original.)

[2] J. Hector St. John de Crèvecoeur, *Letters from an American Farmer* (1782; London: James Magee, 1783), 51–53.

political order, they believed, would introduce a stable and consistent national society. America was destined, in Thomas Paine's famous words, *"to begin government at the right end."* This was a tumultuous process of anticipation, angst, and anxiety. Casting allegiance to a broader government and conceptualizing a larger culture was a trial-and-error project that produced as much disappointment as it did success. To form "America" as a political body, many believed it was first necessary to define "Americans" as a people.[3]

Among those most concerned about national identities was printer Noah Webster. In 1787, only four years after the Treaty of Paris confirmed America's independence, Webster bemoaned how "the people of every country, but our own ... bear a patriotic preference to their own laws and national character." America's troubles stemmed from the fact that they possessed "no pride in the glorious distinction of freemen, which elevates the American beggar above the despots of Asia." Two years later, while attempting to introduce a distinctly "American" language, he wrote, "every engine should be employed to render the people of this country national, to call their attachments home to their own country, and to inspire them with the pride of national character." To Webster, the lack of this identity was the cause of, and the implementation of it the remedy to, all of America's problems. In order to "fix the commencement of national corruption," he wrote in 1787, "we must first prove the national character throughout." These ideological seeds bore political fruits. The primary reason for the federal Constitution, he explained, was because "it was found that our national character was sinking in the opinion of foreign nations." He happily quoted David S. Bogart in 1790 that an education based on America's exceptionalism would better "inform us ... of the distinguishing traits in [our] national character."[4]

Webster was far from alone in his anxiety. James Madison argued in his *Federalist* essays that a major reason for America's struggles was the "want of a due sense of national character." He queried, "What has not America lost by her want of character with foreign nations; and how many errors and follies would she not have avoided?" An anonymous poem found in

---

[3] Thomas Paine, "Common Sense" (1776), in *Paine: Political Writings*, ed. Bruce Kuklick (New York: Cambridge University Press, 2000), 1–46, p. 35. (Emphasis in original.)

[4] *The American Museum*, October 1787, LCP. Noah Webster, *Dissertations on the English Language: with Notes, Historical and Critical* (1789), in *Creating an American Culture, 1775–1800: A Brief History with Documents*, ed. Eve Kornfeld (New York: Palgrave Macmillan, 2001), 102–108, p. 106. *The American Museum*, September 1787, December 1787, December 1790, LCP.

The Columbian – another early American magazine focused on celebrating and defining "America" – wrote, "a love of liberty, a spirit of enterprise, fortitude in difficulties, and a military turn of mind, are conspicuous traits in the American character." And neither were Americans the only ones to address such a dilemma: as no less a figure than Rousseau had proclaimed, "the first rule which we have to follow is that of national character: every people has, or must have, a character; if it lacks one, we must start by endowing it with one." To advance to the status of other successful nations, America must discover and embrace its unique "character."[5]

Yet conceptions of "character" were inherently problematic. Samuel Johnson's *Dictionary of the English Language* defined it both as "personal qualities" and as a "particular constitution of the mind." Webster's own dictionary, not completed until 1828, defined it as "the peculiar qualities, impressed by nature or habit on a person, which distinguish him from others." Thus, to presume a *national* character is to assume both homogeneity and consistency within a larger group of people – a belief that the entire nation shares a "particular constitution of the mind" or "peculiar qualities" despite geographic, economic, gender, or racial differences. Such a belief promised to overlook and downplay distinctions within the broader culture, whether consciously or not. As one historian has noted, any depiction of a "national character" is an imaginative construction and "requires the constant suspension of disbelief because it is at once defined as general and as a distinctive concept of identity." This was a task bound for contestation.[6]

This was especially the case in America, where diversity was perhaps the defining feature of the early republic. Not only did geographic distance promulgate drastically competing visions of society, but deeply contextual indicators like class, race, and gender instilled varying experiences for the many residents of the new nation. Much of this diversity was masked by a fractured print culture that limited exposure to these contrasting people and voices, but it was also systematically ignored through a willful

---

[5] James Madison, "Federalist #63," in *The Federalist*, ed. Cass R. Sunstein (1788; Cambridge, MA: Harvard University Press, 2009), 411–420, p. 411. *The Columbian*, October 1786, LCP. Jean-Jacques Rousseau, *The Social Contract, or Principles of Political Right* (1762), quoted in Anthony D. Smith, *National Identity* (London: Penguin, 1991), 75.

[6] Samuel Johnson, *A Dictionary of the English Language*, Vol. 1 (London, 1766), cf. "character." Noah Webster, *An American Dictionary of the English Language* (Hartford, CT: Sidney's Press, 1828), cf. "character." Martin Brückner, *The Geographic Revolution in Early America: Maps, Literacy, and National Identity* (Chapel Hill: University of North Carolina Press, 2006), 171.

suspension of knowledge that enabled elites to imagine that they could conceptualize the best interests for all American residents. The very absence of this shared cultural character was what drove the deep anxiety to create one in the first place.[7]

These national debates had a transnational context. Ideas concerning national belonging underwent revision throughout the Atlantic world during the eighteenth century. Swiss jurist Emer de Vattel's *The Law of Nations* (1758), one of the earliest and most influential attempts to capture the shifting meaning of political bodies on the cusp of the Age of Revolutions, exemplified the nebulous relationship between society and government. "Moral persons who live together in a natural society," Vattel explained, were expected to construct sovereign governments that were based on "the law of nations" and also reflected a society's "state of nature." That is, political structures were meant to adhere to international legal codes as well as fulfill society's inherent purpose; law was exterior to but also dependent upon the body of the governed. "Whenever any form of government becomes destructive" to these inalienable rights, Thomas Jefferson penned in the Declaration of Independence, "it is the right of the people to alter or to abolish it." The idea that national allegiance and federal structures were malleable was a revolutionary concept, and it led to both political upheaval and cultural anxiety over the tenuous balance between government and society.[8]

This tension was amplified with modernity's democratic promise. This new political idea introduced an added dimension of representative government as citizens expected those who govern them to properly reflect their own interests. When a nation is meant to match the ideas, assumptions, and cultures of those within its borders, then conceptions of that government, and the principles it is meant to promulgate, are essential to its political practice. The evolution of the idea of nations from something

[7] For competing accounts of the different regional cultures in place since the colonization period, see David Hackett Fischer, *Albion's Seed: Four British Folkways in America* (New York: Oxford University Press, 1989); Daniel Richter, *Before the Revolution: America's Ancient Pasts* (Cambridge: Harvard University Press, 2011).

[8] Emer de Vattel, *The Law of Nations, or, Principles of the Law of Nature, Applied to the Conduct and Affairs of Nations and Sovereigns* (London: J. Newberry, 1760), 5–7. Thomas Jefferson, "The Declaration of Independence," in *The Portable Thomas Jefferson*, ed. Merrill D. Peterson (New York: Penguin Books, 1975), 235–241, p. 235. See also David Armitage, *The Declaration of Independence: A Global History* (Cambridge: Harvard University Press, 2007); Eric Slauter, "Rights," in Edward G. Gray and Jane Kamensky, *The Oxford Handbook of the American Revolution* (New York: Oxford University Press, 2013), 447–464.

that was inherently stable and outside the reach of the populace to something that was manmade and culturally constructed – or deconstructed – by humans through political free-will transformed the exercise of nationalism: rather than being something that vindicated the government body, it was now a tool through which citizens could assent to or protest against their national institutions. In short, nationalism became a political practice fraught with political possibilities.[9]

Given that United States independence came at the cusp of what Benedict Anderson called the origins of "imagined political communities," the development of American nationalism has been a common focus for scholars. Yet while historians have dissected and interred the notion of a homogenous identity, many have perpetuated the nationalist assumption that correlates cultural nationalism with the political nation-state. In other words, scholars have retained a connection between nationalist expression and the federal government. However, the unexamined combination of the two is a contemporary phenomenon, and it merely perpetuates an ideological construction that was certainly present, but far from dominant, in these early-modern debates. Indeed, a "nation" during this period could, at various times, describe a community, a state, a mindset, and of course, a federal body. It was hardly ever systematic and was rarely consistent. Nations emerged both within and without a federal state, and states often emerged within a coherent nationality.[10]

This was a common problem throughout the Atlantic empires during the eighteenth and nineteenth centuries. In Britain, three nations (England, Scotland, and Ireland) produced proud and competing conceptions of the "nation" within a single nation-state. In Germany, numerous independent political bodies that were stretched across different empires and sovereignties struggled to find a cultural form of nationalism that they still held in

---

[9] See David A. Bell, *The Cult of the Nation in France: Inventing Nationalism, 1680–1800* (Cambridge: Harvard University Press, 2001), 199–200. For the debate over deciphering a nation's interests, see Gordon S. Wood, "Interests and Disinterestedness in the Making of the Constitution," in *The Idea of America: Reflections on the Birth of the United States* (New York: Penguin Press, 2011), 127–170.

[10] Benedict Anderson, *Imagined Communities: Reflections on the Origin and Spread of Nationalism*, revised edition (London: Verso, 1991), 11–12. Ernest Gellner, *Nations and Nationalism*, 2nd ed. (Ithaca: Cornell University Press, 1983), 6–7. See also Armitage, *The Declaration of Independence*, 19–20. For the general trajectories of nationalisms within these various national contexts, see Linda Colley, *Britons: Forging the Nation, 1707–1837*, rev. ed. (New Haven: Yale University Press, 2009); Hagen Shulze, ed., *The Course of German Nationalism: From Federick the Great to Bismark, 1763–1867* (Cambridge: Cambridge University Press, 1985); Bell, *The Cult of the Nation in France*.

common. In France, an energetic and deadly rejection of a particular form
of nation gave way to another – and then another. Nationalities were more
often divorced from their political sovereignty than married to it.

Further, the very dichotomy between "civic" and "ethnic" nationalisms, categories which have been used to explain Western political development, has been challenged of late. "Civic" nationalism typically
focused on citizenship, political rights, and individual obligations within
a broader federal body, and had often been associated with France,
Britain, and the Netherlands. "Ethnic" nationalism, on the other hand,
often referred to myths of historical ancestry and the organizational
power of common cultures in the face of polyglot empires, and was
embodied in Germany, Italy, and Russia. Given its British political lineage
and disparate cultural communities, America has traditionally been
understood to fit within the "civic" category. Yet recent work has disin-
tegrated the distinctions between these two categories, as scholars have
located strands of ethnic capital in Western countries and sophisticated
civic commodification in Eastern nations. This book will show similar
convergences in the early American political experience. New Englanders
at the start of the nineteenth century, for instance, appealed to both
hereditary and natural rights as they tried to conceive of a national body
capable of representing their interests. In tracing the inchoate and inconsistent process of nationalism during the Age of Revolutions, the United
States thus provides a potent case study for this broader phenomenon.[11]

American Nationalisms examines how this process took place in three
specific contexts – Massachusetts, Pennsylvania, and South Carolina –
between the conclusion of the American Revolution in 1783 through the
Nullification Crisis in 1833. Though some historians have argued that the
"American Revolution, in short, gave birth to whatever sense of nationhood and national purpose Americans have had," nationalism was never
a set of static, self-dependent principles that were agreed upon by a majority
of citizens. Rather, conceptions of national identity – and even the "nation"
itself – varied dramatically during the early republic period, and
a homogenized understanding distorts a dynamic and diverse reality.
American nationalisms should therefore be understood as plural. These
theoretical constructions of nationalism were often tethered to personal
backgrounds, regional cultures, parochial concerns, and localized political

[11] For the scholarly challenge to the "ethnic" and "civic" division in nationalist studies, see
the various essays in Timothy Baycroft and Mark Hewitson, eds., *What Is a Nation?
Europe 1789–1914* (New York: Oxford University Press, 2006).

systems. While interregional and international connections indeed influenced many ideas, events, and policies, they were still interpreted, appropriated, and understood within a predominantly provincial framework. They also went through constant revision. New England was home to the earliest formulations of a sectionalized nationalism that critiqued federal control, only to witness a reversal decades later when they condemned South Carolina for doing the same thing. By focusing on the local culture for these productions, cultural continuity is more easily comprehensible.[12]

Further, by contextualizing these debates with those that were taking place across the Atlantic Ocean, both the unique and concomitant elements of America's political discourse take on a new light. These foreign examples are not used as determinative sources, but as a reminder of the porous boundaries between nations during the Age of Revolutions. Thinkers from this period may not have exemplified a cohesive "republic of letters" assumed by a previous generation of transnational historians, but they were responding to many of the same cultural tensions that urged change at the eve of modernity. Developments in Europe, the Caribbean, and Latin America provided touchstones, examples, and threats to America's sense of self.[13]

It is impossible to find examples that perfectly represent these broader cultural tensions. It is especially misguided to posit cultural elites – who are most often white, educated, and male – as indicative of wider societal ideas.

---

[12] Gordon Wood, *The American Revolution: A History* (New York, 2003), xiii. Bernard Bailyn similarly claimed that the "American Revolution not only created the American political nation but molded permanent characteristics of the culture that would develop within it." Bernard Bailyn, *Faces of Revolution: Personalities and Themes in the Struggle for American Independence* (New York, Vintage: 1992), 200.

[13] As Rachel Hope Cleves has written, "early national citizens viewed themselves as participants in a transnational community, drawn together by sinews of trade, migration, and information." Rachel Hope Cleves, *The Reign of Terror in America: Visions of Violence from Anti-Jacobinism to Antislavery* (Cambridge: Cambridge University Press, 2009), 3. See also Joyce Chaplin, "Expansion and Exceptionalism in Early American History," *Journal of American History* 89 (March 2003): 1431–1455; most especially, Chaplin notes how an Atlantic framework helps the scholar to avoid historiographical exceptionalism because "an illusion of uniqueness" is most often the result of "ignorance of what is going on in parallel fields" (1433). Rosemarie Zagarri similarly wrote that it "challenges the [early American] field's basic organizing principle: the primacy of the nation-state." Zagarri, "The Significance of the 'Global Turn' for the Early American Republic: Globalization in the Age of Nation-Building," *Journal of the Early Republic* 31 (Spring 2011): 1–37, p. 5. For the broader Atlantic context of these national discussions, see, especially, Istvan Hont, *Jealousy of Trade: International Competition and the Nation-State in Historical Perspective* (Cambridge: Harvard University Press, 2010); David Armitage, "The Declaration of Independence and International Law," *William and Mary Quarterly* 59 (January 2002): 39–64.

Historians of the past decades have successfully unearthed the practices, beliefs, and anxieties of everyday Americans through a variety of sophisticated approaches. *American Nationalisms*, however, will focus on a series of individuals and groups who, while not especially illustrative of the common citizen, are particularly adept at displaying the concerns and apprehensions of political belonging during the Age of Revolutions. Their ideas concerning the "nation" were born out of a particular political culture that was rooted in a specific societal context. Therefore, their words depicted the state cultures that simultaneously created and were created by their efforts. These individuals sought to speak for state and national bodies, an activity that required imaginative creativity and contextual sensitivity. Tracing the intricacies of this dialogue, then, while not able to capture the entirety of the early American experience, still reveals many of the deeper cultural underpinnings. Determining the mindset of a larger range of people in early America is indeed a very worthwhile project and has been ably mined by the most recent generation of nationalist scholarship, but for this book to do so would require fundamentally different interpretive and research methods. The focus of this study is to capture the *process* through which those who attempted to think nationally (and internationally) coped with these new problems posed by an important shift in American politics.[14]

The particular case studies chosen for this project are highlighted for a number of reasons. First, they were individuals who left textual remnants of their ideas. People who did not write as much are no less important, of course, for history in general or nationalist cultivations in particular. Yet for comparative purposes, it is helpful to draw from individuals who consciously participated in a political discourse captured in the evolving print culture. Further, those who receive critical engagement here, from Benjamin Rush to John C. Calhoun and from Thomas Branagan to James Forten, were either participants in or critics of a particularly nationalist dialogue that consciously engaged America's role as a federal body within a broader Atlantic network

---

[14] As Daniel Walker Howe has explained, a study of political culture looks at "not only the explicit [political] analyses and proposals ... but also the mood, metaphors, values, and style" that represents much more than just political action or belief. Daniel Walker Howe, *The Political Culture of the American Whigs* (Chicago: University of Chicago Press, 1979), 1–2. See also J. C. D. Clark, *The Language of Liberty, 1660–1832: Political Discourse and Social Dynamics in the Anglo-American World* (New York: Cambridge University Press, 1994). For works on nationalism that skillfully incorporate common Americans' perspectives, see David Waldstreicher, *In the Midst of Perpetual Fetes: The Making of American Nationalism, 1776–1820* (Chapel Hill: University of North Carolina Press, 1997); Len Travers, *Celebrating the Fourth: Independence Day and the Rites of Nationalism in the Early Republic* (Amherst: University of Massachusetts Press, 1997).

of nation-states. None of them were fully representative of their local affiliations, let alone their respective states, and though they attempted to depict a homogenized American "culture," they failed on that front, as well. But they were each influential to varying degrees, and what they do reveal is a process of struggling with national and cultural questions that was shared by a much larger number of individuals. It is in that attempt, rather than their finished products, that make them important to this story.

Nationalism was more than just cultural rhetoric, a political by-product, or a partisan tool, though it certainly played all of those roles at various times. More than that, it was also a hermeneutical springboard for thinking about community, a cultural framework for viewing political union, and an ideological instigator for policy and action. Individuals struggled to define an American nation just as they sought to implement national policies. This book, then, focuses on how specific individuals in particular contexts grappled to define America, and how the resulting definitions had tangible consequences. How one conceived America to be, or how one conceived America *should* be, led directly to political conflict and sowed the seeds for later sectional discord. Indeed, tracing the evolving notions of national union connects the "legacies" of the Revolution with the "origins" of the Civil War. How did South Carolina politicians evolve from condemning the Hartford Convention's sectionalism in 1815 to cultivating their own state-based federalism less than two decades later? While a wide array of elements or, as one historian put it, "catalysts" factored into how distinct regions within the United States moved culturally apart from each other during the early nineteenth century, a growing chasm between how various states understood "nationalism" and "union" was a crucial component. In order to understand national fracturing, then, it is important to chart the early contestations over national belonging.[15]

---

[15] Edward Ayers has argued for historians to become more conscious of cultural "catalysts" for sectionalism in *What Caused the Civil War: Reflections on the South and Southern History* (New York: W.W. Norton, 2005), 133, 138. See also Elizabeth R. Varon, *Disunion! The Coming of the American Civil War, 1789–1859* (Chapel Hill: University of North Carolina Press, 2008), 3–5. For nationalism as cultural rhetoric, see Jay Fliegleman, *Declaring Independence: Jefferson, National Language, and the Culture of Performance* (Palo Alto, CA: Stanford University Press, 1993). For nationalism as a political by-product, see Richard Beeman, Edward C. Carter, and Stephen Botein, eds., *Beyond Confederation: Origins of the Constitution and American National Identity* (Chapel Hill: University of North Carolina Press, 1987). For nationalism as a partisan tool, see Waldstreicher, *In the Midst of Perpetual Fetes*.

There is a large and expansive literature on nationalism, both on the practice and theory in general as well as the American experience in particular. No book has been more influential than Benedict Anderson's *Imagined Communities*, which argued that the growth of print culture in the mid-eighteenth century introduced "unified fields of exchange and communication below Latin and above the spoken vernaculars," which he posited as a development that laid the foundations for modern conceptions of nationalism. "The convergence of capitalism and print technology," he wrote, "created the possibility of a new form of imagined community, which in its basic morphology set the stage for the modern nation." The American Revolution was the first movement to take advantage of this development and served, as Anderson put it, as a "Creole pioneer" for the rest of modernity to follow. This connection of print culture and nationalism, what Anthony Smith has termed "classical modernism," has become the standard framework for understanding the rise of nationalist sentiments in the Western hemisphere.[16]

Yet this general thesis has been challenged of late. Understanding the nation as a collective reflection of modernity, some historians have argued, oversells the success of nationalist propaganda. It is more fruitful, explained Prasenjit Duara, to "view national identity as founded upon fluid relationships; it thus both resembles and is interchangeable with other political identities." Any conception of "nationalism," Duara continued, is "rarely the nationalism of the nation, but rather represents the site where very different views of the nation contest and negotiate with each other." Similarly, Rogers Brubaker has argued that "we should refrain from only seeing nations as substantial, enduring collectivities," but to instead "think about nationalism without nations" in order to see "nation as a category of practice, nationhood as an institutionalized cultural and political form, and nationness as a contingent event or happening." Nationalism, then, is a form of "practice" of print culture, not a result. Other historians have even questioned the centrality of print to the construction of nationalism. Such arguments force historians to

---

[16] Benedict Anderson, *Imagined Communities: Reflections on the Origin and Spread of Nationalism*, rev. ed. (London: Verso, 1991), 44, 46, 47. Anthony D. Smith, *Nationalism and Modernism: A Critical Survey of Recent Theories of Nations and Nationalism* (London: Routledge, 1998), 3. Nationalism in Eastern contexts has taken a somewhat different approach; see Kosaku Yoshino, ed., *Consuming Ethnicity and Nationalism: Asian Experiences* (Richmond, VA: Curzon Press, 1999).

examine individual and local particulars on their own terms rather than as examples of a universal whole.[17]

Further methodological developments that emphasize the practice, rather than merely the result, of nationalism highlight the cultural continuity throughout revolutionary change. The "process of nation-formation," according to Anthony Smith, is "not so much one of construction, let alone deliberate 'invention,' as of *reinterpretation* of pre-existing cultural motifs and of *reconstruction* of earlier ethnic ties and sentiments." Such a perspective helps make sense of racial and gender restrictions that are perpetuated within new nationalist conceptions, even when they are anachronistic to supposedly revolutionary national ideals. This framework is bolstered by the concept of "everyday nationalism," a scholarly approach that seeks to engage the cultural sentiment *behind* print discourse. In the most systematic defense of the approach, Jon Fox and Cynthia Miller-Idriss have argued that nationalism is produced through ordinary actions and milieu, in at least four central ways: "talking the nation" (the discourse citizens invoke), "choosing the nation" (individual choices and decisions), "performing the nation" (arts, literature, and performance), and "consuming the nation" (material and consumer goods). The categories for nationalist expressions have become varied, indeed.[18]

Further, the growing literature of postcolonial theory adds new dimensions to studies of nationalism. While most work in postcolonialism has focused on areas like the Middle East, Africa, and Asia – colonies of

---

[17] Prasenjit Duara, "Historicizing National Identity, or Who Imagines What and When," in *Becoming National: A History*, ed. Geoff Eley and Ronald Grigor Suny (New York: Oxford University Press, 1998), 151–178, p. 151–152, 161. Rogers Brubaker, *Nationalism Reframed: Nationhood and the National Question in the New Europe* (Cambridge: Cambridge University Press, 1996). For arguments that lessen the role of print culture, see Karl Deutsch, *Nationalism and Social Communication: An Inquiry into the Foundations of Nationality* (Cambridge, MA: Massachusetts Institute of Technology Press, 1966); Miroslav Hroch, "From National Movement to Fully-Formed Nation," in *Mapping the Nation*, ed. Gopal Galakrishnan (London: Verso, 1996), 78–97. For the American context, see David D. Hall, *Cultures of Print: Essays in the History of the Book* (Amherst: University of Massachusetts Press, 1996).

[18] Anthony D. Smith, *Nationalism: Key Concepts*, 2nd ed. (Cambridge: Polity Press, 2010), 90. (Emphasis mine.) Jon Fox and Cynthia Miller-Idriss, "Everyday Nationhood," *Ethnicities* 8 (December 2008): 536–563. For gender, see Anne McClintock, *Imperial Leather: Race, Gender, and Sexuality in the Colonial Context* (New York: Routledge, 1995), 352–389. For race, see Paul Gilroy, "One Nation under a Groove: The Politics of 'Race' and Racism in Britain," in *Anatomy of Racism*, ed. David Theo Goldberg (Minneapolis: University of Minnesota Press, 1990), 263–282.

exploitation, occupation, or domination – the recently emerging literature
on "settler societies" is relevant to American history. Defined as societies
settled and still populated by Europeans, often in conflict with indigenous
peoples and resulting in heterogeneous communities, settler societies have
several characteristics: the continued dominance of institutions of
European inheritance, the perpetuation of cultural and social forms, the
tensions implicit among those who were once colonized but are now
colonizers themselves, and the importance of provincial polities and identities. Rather than an abrupt break with past colonial conditions, postcolonial theory emphasizes resilience in cultural, social, and political
structures, and often points to the power and privilege bequeathed to
descendants from their colonizing ancestors. Previous systems, prejudices,
and ideas are "absorbed" into newly constructed "myths of origin and
national metaphors," even if little change has actually taken place. This
often means acknowledging a fractured response within new nations, as
various communities are left to interpret, absorb, and perpetuate nationalist tensions according to lived realities.[19]

Taken together, recent scholarship on nationalism has pushed for a more
comprehensive   and   nuanced   approach   to   nationalist   formations:
a framework that focuses on the practice, not the perceived end-result, of
nationalism; an engagement with the culture that preceded nationalist print
culture; and an acknowledgement of continuity within new national structures and the perpetuation of cultural, societal, and political norms, particularly as experienced at the local level. These are important lessons for
American historians because they help make sense of national tensions that
emerged in the late eighteenth century and continued thereafter.

Recent works on American nationalism quickly adapted these new
theoretical tools. Previously, the "idea" of America was treated as
a cogent and shared principle that spanned time and place, especially in

---

[19] Daiva Stasiulis and Nira Yuval-Davis, "Introduction: Beyond Dichotomies – Gender,
Race, Ethnicity and Class in Settler Societies," in Daiva Stasiulis and Nira Yuval-Davis,
eds., *Unsettling Settler Societies: Articulations of Gender, Race, Ethnicity and Class*
(London: Sage Publications, 1995), 1–38, p. 8. For postcolonialism, see Bill Ashcroft,
Gareth Griffiths, and Helen Tiffin, *Key Concepts in Post-Colonial Studies* (London:
Routledge, 1998); Bill Ashcroft, Gareth Griffiths, and Helen Tiffin, *The Empire Writes
Back: Theory and Practice in Post-Colonial Literatures* (London: Routledge, 2002). For
settler societies, see Stasiulis and Yuval-Davis, eds., *Unsettling Settler Societies*. For the
persistence of localist interpretations within the colonial setting, see Michael Warner,
"What's Colonial about Colonial America?" in *Possible Pasts: Becoming Colonial in
Early America*, ed. Robert Blair St. George (Ithaca, NY: Cornell University Press, 2000),
49–70.

the early republican period. Even recently, one historian has written that American nationalism was "an independent variable" detached from historical contexts. The abstract notion of what it meant to be "American" was widely assumed to be a homogenous principle that could be interpreted and analyzed. Yet the last generation of scholarship has done much to challenge this ideal. One of the more prevalent examples of this development took place in American political history. Starting in the early 1990s, historians problematized the traditional American "character" by highlighting the contested political ideas of the early republic. James Kloppenberg, for example, presented the American democratic tradition as filled with paradoxes and ironies, and mostly void of a linear development, clear pathway, or dominant identity. By demonstrating the contested nature of early American politics, then, historians have acknowledged a more diverse culture that experienced competing tensions.[20]

These lessons from political history found their way into studies of American nationalism, which in turn took a much broader and more inclusive approach. Historians have focused on public rituals, print culture, oral performance, map production, and the general construction of a cultural "other." Yet throughout this recent scholarship on America, the importance of religion remained notably absent. This is especially ironic given that religion, according to Linda Colley, "colored the way that Britons approached and interpreted their material life," determined "how most Britons viewed their politics," and was "the foundation on which their state was explicitly and unapologetically based." To put it simply, religion "gave the majority of men and women a sense of their place in history and a sense of their worth." But until recently, religion has

---

[20] Liah Greenfeld, *Nationalism: Five Roads to Modernity* (Cambridge, MA: Harvard University Press, 1992), 402. James Kloppenberg, "The Virtues of Liberalism: Christianity, Republicanism, and Ethics in Early American Political Discourse," in Kloppenberg, ed., *The Virtues of Liberalism* (New York: Oxford University Press, 1998): 21–37; Kloppenberg, *Toward Democracy: The Struggle for Self-Rule in European and American Thought* (New York: Oxford University Press, 2016); see also Alison L. LaCroix, *The Ideological Origins of American Federalism* (Cambridge, MA: Harvard University Press, 2010), 68–104. For examples of the older framework, see Richard Hofstadter, *The American Political Tradition and the Men Who Made It* (1948; New York: Vintage Books, 1956); Clinton Rossiter, *The American Quest, 1790–1860: An Emerging Nation in Search of Identity, Unity, and Modernity* (New York: Harcourt Brace Jovanovich, 1971); Paul C. Nagel, *This Sacred Trust: American Nationality, 1798–1898* (New York: Oxford University Press, 1971); Henry Steele Commager, *Jefferson, Nationalism and the Enlightenment* (New York: George Braziller, 1975).

rarely been described as a dominant factor in American identity formation. Many historians have ably pursued how nationalism affected
American religions, yet a commensurate approach has not been utilized
to determine how religion affected American nationalism.[21]

An increasing number of historians have recently utilized the tools of
postcolonial theory in their approach to early America. Kariann Yokota,
for instance, demonstrated how a cultural anxiety was central to early
American cultural practices. Similarly, Trish Loughran challenged previous articulations of the early republic being "bound" by print, and
argued instead that "there was no 'nationalized' print public sphere in
the years just before and just after the Revolution," but that "a proliferat-
ing variety of local and regional reading publics [was] scattered across
a vast and diverse geographical space." While "fragmented pieces of text
circulated haphazardly and unevenly" during the period, this was "a
world still largely dominated by the limits of the locale." Even the mindset
for most politicians failed to exceed local political borders. The American
government during its first decade, according to David Hendrickson,
"constituted not a body politic but an association of bodies politic," and
that in practice they were "far from constituting a unified nation"; though
they feigned national connectedness, their experience "confirmed the
distinctive interests and deep-rooted particularism of the several states."
Jack P. Greene has similarly noted that a "localist perspective should be
extended into the national era" due to the parochial experiences and
provincial views dominated the early republic. "What did it mean for

---

[21] Colley, *Britons*, 18, 54. For the French context, see Bell, *Cult of the Nation of France*.
The exceptions to this trend of lack of religion in nationalist discourse are recent:
Nicholas Guyatt, *Providence and the Invention of the United States, 1607–1876*
(Cambridge: Cambridge University Press, 2007); Sam Haselby, *The Origins of
American Religious Nationalism* (New York: Oxford University Press, 2015);
Amanda Porterfield, *Conceived in Doubt: Religion and Politics in the New American
Nation* (Chicago: University of Chicago Press, 2012). For public rituals, see
Waldstreicher, *In the Midst of Perpetual Fetes*; Travers, *Celebrating the Fourth*. For
print culture, see Seth Cotlar, *Tom Paine's America: The Rise and Fall of Transatlantic
Radicalism in the Early Republic* (Charlottesville: University of Virginia Press, 2011). For
oral performance, see Carolyn Eastman, *A Nation of Speechifiers: Making an American
Public after the Revolution* (Chicago: University of Chicago Press, 2009); Michael
P. Kramer, *Imagining Language in America: From the Revolution to the Civil War*
(Princeton, NJ: Princeton University Press, 1992). For maps, see Brückner, *Geographic
Revolution in Early America*. For "others," see Carroll Smith-Rosenberg, *This Violent
Empire: The Birth of an American National Identity* (Chapel Hill: University of North
Carolina Press, 2010); Philip Deloria, *Playing Indian* (New Haven: Yale University Press,
1998).

people to have parallel state and national collective identities?" Greene aptly asked. It is a good question, and digging into comparative regions provides at least some answers.[22]

Yet historians of American nationalism and identity have typically retained a larger framework that downplays region-based identities. David Waldstreicher's landmark study, for instance, while still noting how "local, regional, and national identities existed simultaneously," has maintained that a regionalist focus "draw[s] our attention away from cultural and political phenomena that transcend and transformed the local." Kariann Yokota similarly emphasized postcolonial tensions that "transcend state or other provincial boundaries" instead of focusing on either "regional, national, or even Atlantic and transnational communities." While these are important lessons that are crucial for understanding the period, they do not tell the whole story. Indeed, the recent historiographical trend against regionalism overlooks an important point: regions *mattered* to residents of early America. In short, rather than solely focusing on the whole in order better to understand the parts, it might also prove beneficial to focus on the parts in order better to understand the whole.[23]

This does not make the study of nationalism any less important, however. Nationalisms do not need be embraced by an entire nation in order to be a form of nationalism. These locally imagined nationalisms, while loosely connected through a fragmented print culture, demonstrate the process of conceptualizing divergent and at times competing forms of

[22] Kariann Akemi Yokota, *Unbecoming British: How Revolutionary America Became a Postcolonial Nation* (New York: Oxford University Press, 2011), 8–9. Trish Loughran, *The Republic in Print: Print Culture in the Age of U.S. Nation Building, 1770–1870* (New York: Columbia University Press, 2007), xix. David C. Hendrickson, *Peace Pact: The Lost World of the American Founding* (Lawrence: University of Kansas Press, 2003), 26–27, 257–258. Jack P. Greene, "Colonial History and National History: Reflections on a Continuing Problem," *William and Mary Quarterly* 64 (April 2007): 235–250, p. 235, 243, 246, 250. See also Robert Blair St. George, ed., *Possible Pasts: Becoming Colonial in Early America* (Ithaca, NY: Cornell University Press, 2000); Malini Johar Schueller and Edward Watts, eds., *Messy Beginnings: Postcoloniality and Early American Studies* (New Brunswick, NJ: Rutgers University Press, 2003); Richard C. King, ed., *Postcolonial America* (Urbana: University of Illinois Press, 2000); Amritjit Singh and Peter Schmidt, eds., *Postcolonial Theory and the United States: Race, Ethnicity, and Literature* (Jackson: University Press of Mississippi, 2000).
[23] Waldstreicher, *In the Midst of Perpetual Fetes*, 6, 10. Kariann Yokota, "Postcolonialism and Material Culture in the Early United States," *William and Mary Quarterly* 64, no. 2 (April 2007): 263–270, p. 266. For the importance of regions in European nationalist discourse at the time, see Maiken Umbach, "Nation and Region," in Baycroft and Hewitson, eds., *What Is a Nation?*, 63–80.

nationalism. Indeed, the separation of nationalism from the nation-state is a crucial element in understanding early American political culture. David Potter long ago noted that the historian "knows that there is great difference between the nation and the political state, but in a world where all the states claim to be nations and all the nations try to be states, it is difficult for him to remember that they are two things." That is, historians often consider nationalism only as it relates to the broader federal institution, rather than, to borrow again from Potter, "a tendency, an impulse, an attitude of mind." In short, nationalism was a "form of group loyalty [that] is not generically different from other forms of group loyalty." These "forms of group loyalty" were dynamic, malleable, and mutable throughout the early republic, as Americans' sense of allegiance shifted in response to evolving contexts. The study of local cultivation, then, focuses on how nationalism was practiced long before the nation-state was the dominant factor in American life.[24]

If one is to focus on the local cultivations of nationalism, it is important to choose local cultures that represent these broader anxieties. There were numerous states and regions in the early republic that witnessed robust nationalist discourse, but this book will focus on Massachusetts, Pennsylvania, and South Carolina, for several reasons. First and foremost, they provide the opportunity to examine three dynamic and diverse regions. For instance, though South Carolina was far from representative of the South, it eventually came to the forefront of creating a Southern political discourse. Second, each state provides different types of cultures and social structures based on their lived realities and discursive communities. Third, each region has produced a proud tradition of characteristics closely tethered to their sense of identities – that is, a focus on how these particular state-based cultural practices developed revises traditional ideas of the nation as a whole. And finally, each state encountered a period in which a sizeable number of their inhabitants reevaluated what it meant to be part of the American union.[25]

---

[24] David M. Potter, "The Historian's Use of Nationalism and Vice Versa," *American Historical Review* 67, no. 4 (July 1962): 924–950, p. 925, 926, 928. See also Rupert Emerson, *From Empire to Nation: The Rise of Self-Assertion of Asian and African Peoples* (Cambridge: Harvard University Press, 1960), 134, which defines the nation as "the body which legitimizes the state."

[25] Overviews of the general period include Gordon S. Wood, *Empire of Liberty: A History of the Early Republic, 1789–1815* (New York: Oxford University Press, 2009);

These three states should not be considered the most important political bodies in the nation, let alone the most representative within their own region. In the South, Virginia quickly became the dominant state power when it came to federal representation, as residents from the state held the presidential office for thirty-two of the first thirty-six years, and many of the other states, especially in New England, grew increasingly worried about a Virginian dynasty. In the mid-Atlantic, New York quickly evolved into a financial and cultural center for the broader federal body, and many political policies were geared to aid its interests. Indeed, many of the most prominent nationalist thinkers – for example, Thomas Jefferson, Alexander Hamilton, and James Madison – came from Virginia and New York. Yet their ensconced position within the Union was precisely what triggered worry from citizens in competing states, and the political cultures within New York and Virginia rarely reached the same crisis regarding federal union as in the states chosen for this study. By focusing on Massachusetts, Pennsylvania, and South Carolina, then, this project examines how citizens and communities reacted to being in the shadow of other states' interests, an anxiety that prompted more salient nationalist constructions.

Despite all three states taking part in the same revolutionary ferment and creating state constitutions at around the same time, Massachusetts, Pennsylvania, and South Carolina each produced differing political cultures that in turn influenced how local citizens both understood and

Joyce Appleby, *Inheriting the Revolution: The First Generation of Americans* (Cambridge, MA: Harvard University Press, 2001); Stanly Elkins and Eric McKitrick, *The Age of Federalism: The Early American Republic, 1788–1800* (New York: Oxford University Press, 1995). Specific treatments of individual regions include the following. For South Carolina, see Rachel N. Klein, *Unification of a Slave State: The Rise of the Planter Class in the South Carolina Backcountry, 1760–1808* (Chapel Hill: University of North Carolina Press, 1990); Maurie D. McInnis, *The Politics of Taste in Antebellum Charleston* (Chapel Hill: University of North Carolina Press, 2005); Lacy K. Ford, Jr., *Origins of Southern Radicalism: The South Carolina Upcountry, 1800–1860* (New York: Oxford University Press, 1988). For Pennsylvania, see John Smolenski, *Friends and Strangers: The Making of a Creole Culture in Colonial Pennsylvania* (Philadelphia: University of Pennsylvania Press, 2010); Andrew Shankman, *Crucible of American Democracy: The Struggle to Fuse Egalitarianism and Capitalism in Jeffersonian Pennsylvania* (Lawrence: University Press of Kansas, 2004); Albrecht Koschnik, *"Let a Common Interest Bind Us Together": Associations, Partisanship, and Culture in Philadelphia, 1775–1840* (Charlottesville: University of Virginia Press, 2007). For Massachusetts, see Stephanie Kermes, *Creating an American Identity: New England, 1789–1825* (New York: Palgrave Macmillan, 2008); Johann N. Neem, *Creating a Nation of Joiners: Democracy and Civil Society in Early National Massachusetts* (Cambridge, MA: Harvard University Press, 2008).

experienced their provincial and national identities. As Michal Rozbicki has noted, notions like "liberty" and "citizenship" were conditioned by cultural preconceptions and constructions, and thus diverged based on different settings. In Massachusetts, for instance, the influence of traditions like town participation forced the state's constitution to include an idea of democratic sovereignty and a requirement of popular approval. In South Carolina, the emphasis on land and property placed greater emphasis on ownership and representative authority. And unlike the other two states, Pennsylvania originally claimed the most radical state constitution that only became more conservative in later decades – a reversal compared to the constitutional trajectories of Massachusetts and South Carolina. Such government structures affected how local residents imagined citizenship and political union. While state – and national – legislatures were not fully representative of their constituents, they, to a large degree, constructed the boundaries in which all local residents experienced, understood, and practiced nationalism. Yet even within each state, serious disagreements and diversity remained, much to the chagrin of those who wished otherwise.[26]

The most foundational differences within the individual states is found when comparing rural and urban centers. Though political debates at the state level were meant to account for the interests of all their citizens, the reality was that the major port cities served as a hub for most of the political discussion. Communities in the backcountry were often forced to take radical action to gain an audience and invoke change. The cultures bequeathed by Puritan communities in Massachusetts and the religious and ethnically diverse populations in Pennsylvania were just as influential as the slave societies that buttressed South Carolina. While this book spends a lot of time on the political elites located in towns like Boston, Philadelphia, and Charleston, the presence of these rural conflicts often cast a lasting shadow over these ideas.[27]

---

[26] Michal Jan Rozbicki, *Culture and Liberty in the Age of the American Revolution* (Charlottesville: University of Virginia Press, 2011).

[27] For Pennsylvania, see John Smolenski, *Friends and Strangers*; Billy Gordon Smith, *The Lower Sort: Philadelphia's Laboring People, 1750–1800* (Ithaca, NY: Cornell University Press, 1990); Ronald Schultz, *The Republic of Labor: Philadelphia Artisans and the Politics of Class, 1720–1830* (New York: Oxford University Press, 1993); Thomas M. Doerflinger, *A Vigorous Spirit of Enterprise: Merchants and Economic Development in Revolutionary Philadelphia* (Chapel Hill: University of North Carolina Press, 2001). For South Carolina, see S. Max Edelson, *Plantation Enterprise in Colonial South Carolina* (Cambridge, MA: Harvard University Press, 2006); Charles Woodmason, *The Carolina Backcountry on the Eve of the Revolution* (Chapel Hill: University of North

Perhaps the most obvious difference in lived realities between these three states was the presence of enslaved African Americans. According to the 1790 census, there were 107,094 slaves in South Carolina compared to 3,707 in Pennsylvania. Massachusetts had abolished slavery in 1780. And while still small, there were growing communities of free African Americans in the Northern states. Not only did the very presence of blacks influence how others conceptualized American society, but black authors also added to this discourse by conceptualizing their own understandings of the nation. In South Carolina, slaveholding became a linchpin of their provincial identity, and blacks were invoked throughout the country as an ideological "other" in imaginative constructions of an American citizen. In Pennsylvania and Massachusetts, on the other hand, individuals like Richard Allen and Prince Hall worked to carve a form of nationalism for freed slaves. These local interactions shaped how Americans viewed themselves, their community, and their nation.[28]

Many creators of nationalism in early America utilized the growing – if still fragmented – print culture of the period. Newspapers, magazines, books, pamphlets, plays, and sermons were published with increasing frequency and often claimed a new, national voice. Philadelphia's *American Museum* and Massachusetts's *Boston Magazine*, for example, aimed to be representative of the entire nation by seeking both authors and readers throughout the states, yet their content, approach, and reach reflected regional conditions. In South Carolina, social clubs like the Society of the Cincinnati – an organization that was found throughout the nation, yet was much more active in the South – retained an aristocratic and hierarchical form of patriotism, while the Democratic-Republican societies that sprung up in Pennsylvania often envisioned a more egalitarian future. And though popular organizations like Freemasonry were found throughout all the states, the presentation and understanding of its roles were conditioned by local sensibilities.[29]

Carolina Press, 1953). For Massachusetts, see J. M. Opal, *Beyond the Farm: National Ambitions in Rural New England* (Philadelphia: University of Pennsylvania Press, 2011).

[28] For slavery and American nationalism, see David Brion Davis, *The Problem of Slavery in the Age of Emancipation* (New York: Knopf, 2014); Robert G. Parkinson, *The Common Cause: Creating Race and Nation in the American Revolution* (Chapel Hill: University of North Carolina Press, 2016).

[29] For magazines, see Robb K. Haberman, "Provincial Nationalism: Civic Rivalry in Postrevolutionary American Magazines," *Early American Studies* 10 (Winter 2012): 163–193. For social organizations, see Roland M. Baumann, "The Democratic-Republicans of Philadelphia: The Origins, 1776–1797" (Ph.D. diss., Pennsylvania State University, 1970); Steven C. Bullock, *Revolutionary Brotherhood: Freemasonry and the*

And finally, religion flourished in every region, but in different ways. While religious freedom was pronounced throughout America, Massachusetts maintained state support for the Congregationalist Church until 1818. And though South Carolina was once a stronghold for the Anglicans, and Pennsylvania was a refuge for Quakers, both states saw a dramatic increase in upstart, charismatic, and democratic religions like the Baptists and Methodists, though their success lagged in South Carolina. These religions experienced different receptions and adaptations in every region yet played an important role throughout the country in understanding what it meant to be "American." For many citizens, their American identities were formed in the pews as much as they were in the voting box.[30]

None of these states were completely representative of their particular regions, however. While New England is typically seen as a heterogeneous community, various factors led to Massachusetts producing unique concerns that separated them from neighboring states. Even more distinct was the separation between South Carolina and other Southern states. William Freehling decades ago described the "many Souths" model for Southern history during the antebellum period. More than just regional partitions – the delta, tidewater, black belt, etc. – the South in the early republic contained competing ideological, racial, and economic diversities – moderates and extremists, despots and democrats, elitists and commoners. Further, diversity within local communities exterminated the chance for unity even at the state level. Therefore, while *American Nationalisms* will trace the divergences between states, as well as maintain that there were dominant majority cultures to which most participants responded, it will also highlight the competitions within those states and the commonalities among them.[31]

All of these divergent tensions led to competing provincial cultures and, in turn, varied nationalist expressions. This book traces the various

---

Transformation of the American Social Order, 1730–1840 (Chapel Hill: University of North Carolina Press, 1998); Cotlar, *Tom Paine's America.*

[30] See Jonathan D. Sassi, *Republic of Righteousness: The Public Christianity of the Post-Revolutionary New England Clergy* (New York: Oxford University Press, 2008); Christine Leigh Heyman, *Southern Cross: The Beginnings of the Bible Belt* (New York: Alfred A. Knopf, 1997); Monica Najar, *Evangelizing the South: A Social History of Church and State in Early America* (New York: Oxford University Press, 2008); Haselby, *The Origins of American Religious Nationalism.*

[31] See the discussion of "many Souths" in William W. Freehling, *The Road to Disunion: Volume 1: Secessionists at Bay, 1776–1854* (New York: Oxford University Press, 1990), viii.

trajectories of each state through America's first five decades, and in doing so documents particularly potent moments of nationalist crisis. It points to commonalities as well as divergences. At different points, citizens in both Massachusetts and South Carolina threatened to radically alter the federal compact during the Hartford Convention and the Nullification Crisis, respectively, and each state prompted different nationalist courses: for Massachusetts, they transitioned their national allegiance away from New England and toward the federal body, whereas those in South Carolina increasingly came to understand their own state as a sovereign nation itself. Yet the focus on South Carolina's much later move toward secession overshadows the fact that New England contained the first proponents for states' rights. And while many of America's biggest national events took place in Philadelphia, a number of Pennsylvanians' conceptions of the national union were tested as debates over slavery became more strident.

In order to capture the variegated nature of these tensions, this book focuses on a different element of cultural nationalism in each chapter; and though all three states will remain in conversation, a single state will take center stage at varying times. Further, at particular moments in each chapter, one or two individual writers receive special attention. These case studies were chosen not because they were the most influential, or even that their ideas were most representative, but because they aptly embodied relevant cultural tensions and left a robust written record of those struggles. Most importantly, they engaged nationalist issues that made them think beyond their local circumstances, whatever those circumstances may have been. Even if they failed to speak for their fellow citizens, they often wrote as if they did. Frequently, it was in their *divergences* from their contemporary society that made their ideas most potent, even as society provided their cultural tools in the first place. They are poignant examples of the process of conceptualizing nationalism in the age of political experimentation.

The book is separated into two parts. The first part examines how individuals in Pennsylvania and Massachusetts originally imagined new frameworks for nationalist belonging, with those in South Carolina playing a supplemental role. Chapter 1 begins with the debates surrounding the Constitutional Convention and ratification process in 1787–1788 as the origins of American nationality. In an era when nations and states were acknowledged as products of human innovation, Americans believed that governments worked best when they matched the culture of the governed. Thus, state formation was an act of cultural invention, and debates revolved around how different states envisioned a national union. People during this period began to think nationally, but their diverging perceptions were masked by an amorphous political language. Even the term "nation" during this period was in transition, as it could mean a body of like-minded people in a particular state, a sense of belonging to a specific region, or, increasingly, an attachment to a federal institution that bound the states together. This etymological ambivalence embodied broader cultural tension. This wasn't just an American phenomenon, either, as debates over political union, federal allegiance, and national culture took place in Europe as well. Indeed, this was a moment of democratic awakenings across the Atlantic that witnessed a new birth for nationalist debates.

In Chapter 2, the discussion then moves to local ministers in the 1790s in order to examine how divergent religious contexts cultivated different frameworks for thinking about the nation. Specifically, it looks at thanksgiving sermons in Massachusetts as a case study in local appropriation: proclamations were decreed from the president and then received, interpreted, and preached in different ways by different ministers depending on their denominational traditions and theological beliefs. The preaching, in turn, both reinforced and expanded the way in which congregants interpreted the nation. And while the interchange between religious and political ideas concerning religion was an Atlantic phenomenon, the lack of a national religion made America's experiment different from that in Britain and France. The global threat of religious radicalism and skepticism challenged traditional understandings and forced new theological defenses. In Massachusetts, ministers cultivated a political theology of unionism that tethered the nation to a particular divine covenant, which ironically provided religious and cultural foundations for regional schism and dissent.

The second part of the book deals with how Massachusetts, Pennsylvania, and South Carolina each came to reconsider the terms and limits of unionism in response to competing national crises. First, in Chapter 3, we examine the buildup to and aftermath of the War of 1812, a period in which a fleeting idea of a patriotic, unified, postcolonial America was presented as the nation's future, only to fracture as debates over slavery became central components to nationalist rhetoric. As the country began to look westward with expansionist tendencies, citizens debated the implications of this expansive vision for nationalist expression. Dissecting the orations that were given on patriotic holidays, for instance, provides a lens through which to explore evolving notions of national belonging in a country whose borders were rapidly expanding. This anxiety was set against a broader context where war was seen as an increasingly global event that restructured conceptions of nations throughout Europe. It is crucial, then, to situate America's wartime nationalist rhetoric within this Napoleonic world. Ironically, politicians from New England dared to imagine a new form of ethnic and state-based nationalism that would lay the foundation for later factional debates.

War and expansion were not the only foundational events taking place in the early republic that impacted nationalist politics. Perhaps even more crucial was the debate over slavery, which had become a driving wedge between states. This was especially true in Pennsylvania, a state that had previously served as a mediating presence in America's nationalist discourse. Anti-slavery activists, including white colonizationists like Thomas Branagan and black abolitionists like James Forten, argued for new racialized notions of union that further ruptured the nationalist links between Northern and Southern states. Importantly, these debates took place at the same time that Britain was attempting to abolish slavery from its empire, which requires a comparison between these two nations and how they conceptualized slavery's role in a union. Chapter 4 examines how racial belonging became a paramount issue during a nascent age of democratic governance.

These conflicts over slavery pushed Southern states to imagine new modes of federal governance. The first climax of this divisive trajectory occurred in the 1820s and 1830s as South Carolina, for the first time, examined the possibility of nullification. As slavery and the slave economy came to dominate national discourse, Americans once again grappled with how a federal government and imagined national culture could handle such divergent interests. This tension played out on several levels, which included politicians who fought over the power and limits of a centralized government, local citizens who were left to understand how they fit into an increasingly fractured nation, and literary authors who explored issues of union and nullification through poetry and prose. In an important way, this crisis was the apex of the cultural debates concerning nationalism that had taken place in the previous five decades. Chapter 5, then, examines how politicians and authors in South Carolina appropriated nationalist myths and ideas, including the incorporation of European ideas of romantic nationalism, in their quest to validate their state as a sovereign nation. Though the crisis ended without a political severance, it laid the cultural groundwork for disunion and secession.

No individual state, throughout this entire process, ever constructed a coherent and homogenous nationalist vision, let alone a systematic political culture. Divergences remained in each community, and individuals, though they presented themselves otherwise, never stood as representative for the larger body. Neither did the events and arguments outlined here prove determinative for the decades that followed. Nationalist discourse is much too unstable for such a neat trajectory. However, these intercommunity, interstate, and intranational debates created discursive communities in which various words, arguments, and assumptions acquired specific meanings. And despite the vastly different political cultures within each states, common anxieties spread throughout. How specific individuals appropriated these ideas as they struggled to address national concerns and construct a national identity is the focus of this book. It is in *that* struggle over paradoxical meanings that the cultivation of nationalism is most revealing.

Understanding how ideas of nationalism were constructed is crucial to understanding early American political culture. From people in Massachusetts who transitioned from seeing their region as its own nation to understanding their state as the center of a broader nation, and from individuals in South Carolina who came to see their own state as a nation in and of itself, this is a story of shifting views of "nation," "Union," and "America." *American Nationalisms* examines tensions and anxieties over allegiance, patriotism, and power through a variety of sources and from a variety of perspectives. The desired result is not to recreate a homogenous nationalist discourse, but to reveal the contested and multivocal atmosphere of early American political culture during the Age of Revolutions. Charting this dynamic process offers insights into American culture in particular and cultural belonging in general.

PART I

IMAGINING UNION

Early Americans believed that the United States contained a united people. This, to many, was a crucial component for a nation's success. Statesman John Jay believed his country's homogeneity was justification for a new centralized government. "Providence has been pleased to give this one connected country to one united people," he wrote in his *Federalist* essay. Americans were "a people descended from the same ancestors, speaking the same language, professing the same religion, [and] attached to the same principles of government." Because they were "very similar in their manners and customs," they were prepared to work together in shared governance. Timothy Dwight, a minister in Connecticut, agreed. His poem, *Greenfield Hill*, praised the nation's unity:

> One blood, one kindred, reach from sea to sea;
> One language spread; one tide of manners run
> One scheme of science, and of morals one;
> And, God's own Word the structure, and the base,
> One faith extend, one worship, one praise.[1]

But these were imaginative constructions with partisan aims. In John Jay's home state of New York, three-eighths of the population were of either Dutch or French descent. They hardly shared the "same ancestors." And the entire nation's demographics proved Dwight's vision a lie: only 60 percent descended from "one kindred," the English, as the rest were German, Scottish, Irish, Dutch, French Swede, and Spanish.

---

[1] John Jay, "Federalist #2," in *The Federalist*, ed. Cass R. Sunstein (1788; Cambridge, MA: Harvard University Press, 2009), 6–11, p. 7; Timothy Dwight, *Greenfield Hill: A Poem in Seven Parts* (New-York: Childs and Swaine, 1794), 168.

Many were of indigenous and African posterity, and therefore were not even imagined as part of the political body. Even among those of similar ethnic backgrounds, political discord, religious competition, and intellectual debates were already apparent. How could a nation exist with such diversity? The following two chapters trace the way that early Americans, in the midst of a transatlantic Age of Revolutions, imagined forms of political belonging in the face of disunion. This was a new age for conceiving of nations, and a host of assorted voices were anxious to take advantage.[2]

---

[2] For demographics during the period, see Gordon S. Wood, *Empire of Liberty: A History of the Early Republic, 1789–1815* (New York: Oxford University Press, 2009), 69.

I

Imagining Nationalism in an Age of Statehood

The manner of settling a new country, exhibits a view of the human mind so foreign to the views of it which have been taken for many centuries in Europe.

–*Columbian Magazine*[1]

You will see the Constitution we have propos'd in the Papers. The Forming of it so as to accommodate all the different Interests and Views was a difficult Task.

–Benjamin Franklin[2]

The colonies had grown up under constitutions so different, there was so great a variety of religions, they were composed of so many different nations, their customs, manners, and habits had so little resemblance, and their intercourse had been so rare, and their knowledge of each other so imperfect, that to unite them in the same principles in theory and the same system of action, was certainly a very difficult enterprise.

–John Adams[3]

The Age of Revolutions cultivated novel ways to think about nations, but it also posed new problems. Nation-states were no longer considered divinely appointed structures, and politicians were forced to imagine

---

[1] *Columbian Magazine*, November 1786, LCP.
[2] Benjamin Franklin to Jane Mecom, September 20, 1787, franklinpapers.org (accessed October 2013).
[3] John Adams to Hezekiah Niles, February 13, 1818, in *The Works of John Adams, Second President of the United States: With A Life of the Author, Notes and Illustrations*, ed. Charles Francis Adams, 10 vols. (Boston: Charles C. Little and James Brown, 1851–1856), 10:238.

innovative forms of governance that would claim allegiance from a broad
range of disparate people. The political unrest found throughout Europe
and the Americas upended the traditional relationship between the citizen
and the state. This in turn left the obligation to citizens to conceive of
a new nationality that bound the political body together. How could
a nation that includes various forms of nationalities fit under one federal
structure? Americans, after achieving independence from Britain, believed
they were constructing new political approaches that reoriented their
citizens to the national government through a national culture. Yet these
arguments were not wholly new, as they drew from the ideological and
cultural tools at their disposal. This chapter uses the debates surrounding
the Constitutional Convention in 1787 to examine how Americans sought
to solve the problem of political belonging by envisioning a nationality
that was intertwined with the federal state.

Before Benjamin Rush could reform a nation, he first had to reform his
own state. Pennsylvania's original state constitution was famous in its
time for its radically democratic nature and republican form of government. Passed shortly after the Revolution commenced, it was the result of
the triumph of previously marginal voices filling a vacuum of power.
The document incorporated many of the elements presented by what
had been a radical fringe: a unicameral legislature, yearly elections, and
voting rights for all tax-paying men. Yet over the next two decades,
a movement led by political elites like Rush revised the state constitution
several times until it possessed the more conservative characteristics
shared with other American states.[4]

Rush's political views were, to a large extent, shaped by these debates
that took place in the 1780s. His arguments regarding the state constitution reveal the deeply provincial mindset with which he approached
politics. Shortly after the original state constitution was passed, he lam-
basted the document for paying "no regard ... to the ancient habits and
customs of the people of Pennsylvania in the distribution of the supreme
power of the state, nor in the forms of business, or in the stile [sic] of the
Constitution." The ideas and policies featured in the document, he

---

[4] For a general outline for Pennsylvania's constitution, see Gary B. Nash, "Philadelphia's
Radical Caucus that Propelled Pennsylvania to Independence and Democracy," in
Revolutionary Founders: Rebels, Radicals, and Reformers in the Making of the Nation,
ed. Ray Raphael, Alfred F. Young, and Gary B. Nash (New York: Alfred A. Knopf, 2011),
67–87.

argued, were not designed to "fit the people of Pennsylvania," particularly because the document "supposes perfect equality, and an equal distribution of property, wisdom and virtue, among the inhabitants of the state." To alleviate these problems Rush worked with others to create a new constitution that included, among other things, a bicameral congress, longer terms for elected officials, and a more vigorous embodiment of economic and religious diversity.[5]

While the content of Rush's critiques was significant, so too was the framing of his dissent. His disagreements were not that the principles contained in the constitution were inherently wrong, but that they failed to "fit" the people of Pennsylvania. The idea of molding a constitution to match its constituents, based on the principle that government was sufficiently malleable to match the character of the governed, was not an idea limited to Rush. Similarly, when Noah Webster explained why America's national constitution must differ from other nations, he reasoned that American "culture" was "founded on principles different from those of all nations, and we must find new bonds of union [better fit] to perpetuate the confederation." As part of a growing body of political reformers on both sides of the Atlantic, both Rush and Webster acknowledged that governments were human-made institutions that were adaptable in the hands of those in charge, and were thus to be sculpted in order to fit time and place.[6]

These ideas reflected a period of change. In the place of a government system that was previously believed to possess unchangeable parameters, political thinkers in the mid- to late eighteenth century began to imagine elastic boundaries wherein nations were fitted to their constituency. As such, the very act of creating government structures was a science of defining the habits and customs of a community and subsequently framing a constitution to match those principles. This was a phenomenon that swept across the Atlantic. Rousseau, for instance, stated that while "the constitution of man is the work of nature," the "[constitution] of the state is the work of art." Similarly, Montesquieu believed laws "should be adapted in such a manner to the people for whom they are framed that it should be a great chance if those of one nation suit another." He further stated, the "government most conformable to nature is that which best

---

[5] Benjamin Rush, *Observations upon the Present Government of Pennsylvania. In Four Letters to the People of Pennsylvania* (Philadelphia: Styner and Cist, 1777), 3, 4.

[6] Rush, *Observations*, 1–2. Noah Webster, *Sketches of American Policy* (Hartford, CT: Hudson and Goodwin, 1785), 30.

agrees with the humour and disposition of the people in whose favor it is established." These beliefs were easily translated into American culture and constitutionalism. As Eric Slauter has demonstrated, Americans at the moment of founding came to believe "that governments were fashioned by humans and subject to their control." This led them to reason "that successful political constitutions should emerge from the manners, customs, tastes, and genius of the people being constituted." Their task, then, was "to organize politics in such a way that the state would both reflect the population and reform it." This was a new age for governance.[7]

This mindset was geographically broad yet provincially bound. Coalescing cultures with constitutions revealed much about not only the person's politics, but also how a person conceived their culture. And while the state government was designed to work primarily at the local level, they were also meant to work within a web of other state governments – they were, after all, the "United States." Previously, as British subjects, residents of colonial America inherited and appropriated a sense of British nationalism that was bequeathed to them; now, they were left to construct their own sense of identity. The creation of constitutions, then, was a form of imaginative nationalism, for it forced individuals to conceptualize not only how their government was to function at both the local and national levels, but also what types of people comprised these varied communities and what type of institution – and nation – they best embodied.[8]

Yet thinking about "nations" was not a natural practice for Americans – or Europeans, for that matter. The conflation of "nation" and a federal "state" was not a prerequisite for the period, nor would it be for several decades. The "nation," in eighteenth-century political discourse, was a term in transition. Previously, it had referred to a group of people who lived within a particular territory that shared either an

[7] Jean-Jacques Rousseau, *A Treatise on the Social Compact: Or the Principles of Political Law* (London: T.Becket, 1764), 151. Montesquieu, *The Spirit of Laws*, trans. Thomas Nugent (1748; London: G. Bell & Sons, 1914), 6. Eric Slauter, *The State as a Work of Art: The Cultural Origins of the Constitution* (Chicago: University of Chicago Press, 2010), 8–9, 11.

[8] For British nationalism in North America prior to the Revolution, see T. H. Breen, "Ideology and Nationalism on the Eve of the American Revolution: Revisions *Once More* in Need of Revising," *Journal of American History* 84, no. 1 (June 1997): 13–39; Rhys Isaac, *Landon Carter's Uneasy Kingdom: Revolution and Rebellion on a Virginia Plantation* (New York: Oxford University Press, 2004); Brendan McConville, *The King's Three Faces: The Rise and Fall of Royal America, 1688–1776* (Chapel Hill: University of North Carolina Press, 2006); Richard L. Bushman, *King and People in Provincial Massachusetts* (Chapel Hill: University of North Carolina Press, 1985).

allegiance to the same crown or a common ethnicity. The body politic to which one was bound was immobile and stable; the "nation," on the other hand, was an object of nature left to be observed, not constructed. Yet throughout the eighteenth century, citizens in countries like Britain, France, and eventually America came to promote new and innovate interpretations as a result of political unrest. Noticing the change, French author François-Ignace d'Espiard declared in 1752, "the time has come to write about nations." Rather than centered on a monarchy or government institution, or as a group of ethnically homogenous and civilized individuals, the "nation" was increasingly understood as a bond between like-minded citizens and based on cultural principles. This new understanding emphasized the fact that nations were to be built by those found within its borders. The "nation," then, was both the most important as well as the most fragile aspect of political discourse. As the Abbé Sieyès wrote on the eve of the French Revolution, "The nation is prior to everything. It is the source of everything." Such a dichotomy bred political anxiety throughout these countries.[9]

The liminal nature of "national" culture was especially true in the Anglo-American context. In Britain, where English, Scottish, and Irish nations were united under a crown, national distinctiveness was assumed within the confederated state. Similarly, in America, many sought to maintain a regional sense of identity even after independence, and the nationalist imagination might have been delayed based on the weak compact of the Articles of Confederation. Yet the coming, creation, and ratification of the Constitution, however, challenged these provincial mindsets, as it forced citizens to consider what a centralized government signified for a fractured culture. Did the Constitution imply the end of a loose confederacy of societies, or was a centralized identity necessary for the nation's growth and strength? Would the federal republic be elastic

---

[9] François-Ignace d'Espiard, *L'esprit de nations* (1752; Paris: Isaac Beauregard, 1753), 4. Emmanuel-Joseph Siyès, *What Is the Third Estate?* (1789; London: Pall Mall Press, 1963), 124. For the transformation of the "nation" in general during the eighteenth century, see David A. Bell, *The Cult of the Nation in France: Inventing Nationalism, 1680–1800* (Cambridge: Harvard University Press, 2001); Geoff Eley, "State Formation, Nationalism, and Political Culture: Some Thoughts on the Unification of Germany," in *From Unification to Nazism: Reinterpreting the German Past* (London: Allen & Unwin, 1986), 50–76, p. 66; J. G. A. Pocock, "Political Languages and Their Implications," in Pocock, ed., *Politics, Language and Time: Essays on Political Thought and History* (Chicago: University of Chicago Press, 1971), 3–41; Timothy Bacroft and Mark Hewitson, eds., *What Is a Nation? Europe 1789–1914* (New York: Oxford University Press, 2006).

enough to encompass a variety of opinions and interests, or was a regenerative project necessary to homogenize the nation's cultures? The answers to these questions were multifaceted and multivocal, and the diversity of opinions belied any unifying solution.

A close examination of how individuals from the period addressed these questions of government and constitution, both at the state and federal levels, reveals how local contexts shaped how one conceptualized the new and ambiguous group of people labeled "Americans" – their customs, their attributes, and their allegiances. Not only did the responses vary throughout the nation, but they also remained fractured at the local level, as state political discourse was rife with disagreement. Indeed, the heterogeneity within each state represented, in microcosm, the broader anxieties writ large. Yet larger fissures and cultural anxieties could be found across borders. The act of state formation that took place in 1780s America, then, provides insight into the nationalist imagination, as the debates surrounding the nation's new government stretched the minds of citizens as they considered the new horizons of the country's interests and expanded the boundaries of their own allegiances.

How do you construct a united nation from a heterogeneous body? When the Treaty of Paris was signed in late 1783, Americans were left with the task of defining the relationship between thirteen political bodies whose only historical connections included bordered geographic space and a previous allegiance to the British crown. This would be a tough task. One British traveler who toured America in the 1760s wrote, "fire and water are not more heterogeneous than the different colonies in North America. Nothing can exceed the jealousy and emulation which they possess in regard to each other." The first symbol for the Continental Congress merely depicted thirteen arms holding on to the rod of liberty (Image 1.1). Yet once independence was achieved and the tether of the monarchy was gone, Americans were left to find a new connection that exceeded mere geographic convenience. The Revolution thus introduced a vacuum of political allegiances among these newly united states.[10]

America's earliest form of governance reflected this localized framework. The nation's first constitutional document, the Articles of Confederation, more closely resembled a peace treaty between

---

[10] Rufus Rockwell Wilson, ed., *Burnaby's Travels Through North America Reprinted from the Third Edition of 1798* (1798; New York: A. Wessels, 1904), 152–153.

IMAGE 1.1 Symbol of the Continental Congress, *Journal of the Proceedings of the [Continental] Congress Held at Philadelphia, September 5, 1774* (Philadelphia: William and Thomas Bradford, 1774), title page. Rare Books and Special Collections Division, Library of Congress, www.loc.gov/exhibits/us.capitol/three .jpg. A symbol of American union, the new nation was to be based solely on the conjoined attachment to the rod of liberty.

independent sovereigns than a unifying and centralized government. This structure embodied the persistent fear regarding state power and the desire for independent governance and limited federal control. When it described how "the said Colonies unite[d] themselves," the original draft of the document crossed out "one Body politic" in favor of the looser "League of Friendship." At the heart of American nationalism prior to the Constitution of 1787 was the belief in a loosely connected compact between states that retained independent sovereignty yet still allowed the states to huddle together to defend themselves against potential foreign threats. This was not a centralized body.[11]

One newspaper editorial from the period exemplified this confederate understanding of nationalism. In the inaugural 1786 issue of the

---

[11] John Dickinson's Draft Articles of Confederation, in LDC, 4:233–255. As David C. Hendrickson noted, "Americans constituted not a body politic but an association of bodies politic" during this period. Hendrickson, *Peace Pact: The Lost World of the American Founding* (Lawrence: University Press of Kansas, 2003), ix. For the predominantly local nature of American politics immediately following the Revolution, see Larry D. Kramer, *The People Themselves: Popular Constitutionalism and Judicial Review* (New York: Oxford University Press, 2004), 25–26.

Columbian Magazine, a Philadelphia-based publication edited by
Mathew Carey that intended to encourage a unified national feeling,
there appeared a column titled "Chronicle of the Year 1850." Inspired
by a recently published French book that looked ahead to the year 2500,
the anonymous author felt "strongly impressed with the idea, and threw
myself on a couch where I pursued the reflection as far as I was capable,
extending my view to this country." In his dream he "was transported to
so distant a period, as the year 1850, and, that on entering a coffee-house,
I took up a newspaper, and read some paragraphs of the following tenor,
which struck me with surprise and pleasure." The newspaper was composed of several brief dispatches from various cities and states throughout
an expanding American empire: from Philadelphia, news came that
Pennsylvania had conquered the Mediterranean; from Boston, a canal
was constructed to cross the "isthmus of Darien," sixty miles long and
a half-mile broad; from Charleston, 10,000 blacks were transported back
to Africa and settled in Goree. "Very few blacks remain in this country
now," the latter dispatch recorded, "and we sincerely hope that in a few
years every vestige of the infamous traffic, carried on by our ancestors in
the human species, will be done away." The American nation, which had
just welcomed delegates from its thirtieth state, had become a global
power.[12]

   But there were glimpses of state-based discord embedded even within
this nationalist prophesy printed in a nationalist paper. While the global
expansion took place under the umbrella of the American nation, the
achievements remained with individual states: it was Pennsylvania that
claimed dominion over the Mediterranean Sea, Massachusetts that gained
canal access through Panama, and South Carolina that exported their
human chattels. The geopolitical landscape portrayed was one of
a confederated group of states that expanded their own empires rather
than a centralized and singular body. The states may have celebrated each
other's success, but that success was predicated on their own state-
sanctioned activities. Further, the fact that the editorial could only attempt
to see sixty years in the future, rather than 650 like in the French example,
underlined the tenuous nature of the American political body at the time.
They dared not look too far into the future. The world, it seemed, was in
flux. Political prophecy was a dangerous game given the unknown nature
of the American democratic experiment.

---

[12] *Columbian Magazine*, September 1786, LCP.

Others were much more direct in expressing national uncertainty. Even before the Revolution was finished, British observer Josiah Tucker argued that any notion that the United States could produce a "rising Empire" was "one of the idlest, most visionary Notions, that ever was conceived even by Writers of Romance." This was because no nationalist bond could coalesce such "mutual Antipathies, and clashing Interests," and the nation could never "be united into one compact Empire, under any Species of Government whatever." The American fate, he concluded, was to be "A DISUNITED PEOPLE, till the End of Time." Certainly part of Tucker's complaint was bitterness over the British Empire losing her American colonies. But the feeling that America lacked a common character or interest was not peculiar to outside observers. John Adams had earlier noted that "The Characters of Gentlemen in the four New England colonies, differ as much from those in the others, as that of the Common People differs, that is as much as several distinct Nations almost." He feared that the "Consequences of this Disimilitude of Character" would lead to a "fatal" disunion and failure of war.[13] Later in his life, Adams further valorized the degree of work required to unite a disparate nation:

The colonies had grown up under constitutions so different, there was so great a variety of religions, they were composed of so many different nations, their customs, manners, and habits had so little resemblance, and their intercourse had been so rare, and their knowledge of each other so imperfect, that to unite them in the same principles in theory and the same system of action, was certainly a very difficult enterprise.[14]

These fears that there was too much difference between the states to form a coherent nation were widespread. A strong suspicion of other regions stretched down the coast. Fissures between North and South were already apparent. In South Carolina, delegate Pierce Butler complained that "The *Northern Interest* is all prevalent; their members are *firmly united*, and carry many measures disadvantageous to the *Southern interest*." He surmised that Northern states were "labouring hard *to get Vermont established as an independent State*," which would give them another vote, "by which the balance will be *quite destroyed*." North Carolinian Richard Dobbs Spaight similarly complained that the "uniform conduct"

---

[13] Josiah Tucker, *Cui Bono? Or, an Inquiry, What Benefits Can Arise Either to the English or the Americans, the French, Spaniards, or Dutch, from the Greatest Victories, or Successes, in the Present War* (London: T. Cadell, 1781), 118–19. John Adams Notes of Debates, September 6, 1774, in LDC, 1:28.

[14] John Adams to Hezekiah Niles, February 13, 1818, in *Works of John Adams*, 10:238.

of Northern states "has been to Weaken the Powers of the union as much as possible, & sacrifice our strength & dignity in hopes of rendering themselves more conspicuous as individual states." While he conceded that they probably did not "wish for a dissolution of the [con]federacy," he still claimed, "they press so extremely hard on the chain that unites us, that I imagine it will break before they are well aware of it." Disunion "may be thought distant," Spaight cautioned, but the actions of Northern states will make it happen "in a very short period." The future appeared murky indeed.[15]

The geopolitical skepticism was mutual. Massachusetts politician Samuel Osgood wondered if it was "impossible that the South" should ever be "democratic." "It is also impossible," he wrote to John Adams in 1784, "that there should be a Coincidence of political Views, in some matters of very great Importance to the [Northern] States." This fear that America was just too disparate to contain such competing interests was prevalent prior to 1787. "Time will discover," Osgood wrote to another correspondent, "whether our Union is natural; or rather whether the Dispositions & Views of the several Parts of the Continent are so similar as that they can & will be happy under the same Form of Government." Osgood's question on whether the union was "natural" implied a crucial cultural element of political allegiance. Some in Massachusetts concluded that these competing cultures made a beneficial union not only unlikely, but also undesirable. William Gordon told John Adams that the United States must "remain a collection of Republics, and not become an Empire, [because] if America becomes an Empire, the seat of government will be to the southward, and the Northern States will be insignificant provinces." Gordon believed that an "Empire will suit the southern gentry" because "they are habituated to despotism by being the sovereigns of slaves." The current union between the states and shared allegiance to the "sons of liberty" was nothing more than sheer "accident." Any form of union seemed temporary.[16]

This problem was not unique to Americans. The tension between competing interests within a broader union was far from new, though it was heightened with the struggle over self-rule that was apparent during

[15] Pierce Butler to James Iredell, April 5, 1782, in *Life and Correspondence of James Iredell*, ed. Griffith J. McRee, 2 vols. (New York: Appleton, 1857): 2:9. (Emphasis in original.) Richard Dobbs Spaight to Alexander Martin, October 16, 1784, in LDC, 21:813.

[16] Samuel Osgood to Higginson, February 2, 1784, and Samuel Osgood to John Adams, January 14, 1784, in LDC, 21:277, 326–327, respectively. William Gordon to John Adams, September 7, 1782, quoted in Hendrickson, *Peace Pact*, 204–205.

the Age of Revolutions. In many ways, the Americans inherited this problem from the very nation from whom they seceded. Indeed, the British Empire during the second half of the eighteenth-century attempted to redefine patriotism in a way that encompassed different groups with seeming divergent interests. This included the Scottish and Irish populations who claimed their own trenchant sense of nationality. Scottish political thinkers were especially adept at providing new paradigms through which to view a developing form of Britishness in response to the merging of national sovereignties and the backlash against Jacobitism and factionalism. Adam Smith, for instance, argued that national pride should be based not on geographic parameters or even a hostile enemy, but "private benevolent affections" that were cultivated through shared interests and sacrificed passions. Nationalism was not a "natural" form of love, he argued, but a developed form of political pride. David Hume similarly argued that it was "public interest" that served as the foundation for disparate people coming together within a national contract that "commences more casually and more imperfectly." Successful governments were not rigid but rather malleable enough for the "perpetual intestine struggle" of political belonging. This was an artificial construction that was dependent on particular contexts. Decades later, Scotsman Sir John Sinclair could declare that while "National peculiarities are of great use in exciting a spirit of manly emulation," it was now "in the interest of the United Kingdom to keep alive those national, *or what, perhaps, may now more properly be called local distinctions* of English, Scotch, Irish, and Welsh." The new age required a new form of national belonging to match this cultural diversity.[17]

Even the English, the supposed seat of British power, had to adapt to this evolving sense of public interests and shared nationality. This was in part accomplished through the centralization of fiscal powers within parliament, the creation of the Bank of England, and the inauguration of the modern British fiscal state. The federal union of previously disparate nations proved a usable resource for imperial power that served as an

---

[17] Adam Smith, *The Theory of Moral Sentiments*, ed. Knud Haakonssen (1759; Cambridge: Cambridge University Press, 2002), 268, 270. David Hume, "Of the First Principles of Government," in Knud Haakonssen, ed., *Hume: Political Essays* (Cambridge: Cambridge University Press, 1994), 16–19, p. 16 ("public interest"). Hume, "On the Origin of Government," in Haakonssen, ed., *Hume*, 20–24, pp. 21–22 ("casually"); Sir John Sinclair, *An Account of the Highland Society of London* (London: B. McMillan, 1813), 227. For the evolution of British patriotism, see Linda Colley, *Britons Forging the Nation, 1707–1833*, rev. ed. (New Haven: Yale University Press, 2009).

artificial umbrella for evolving nationhood. When London became the capital for British commerce, it also became the focal point for a new form of federal belonging that united profitability with patriotism. Success in international trade was determined to be the central tether through which successful nations thrived. While these economic factors were not always acknowledged as the foundation for patriotic passion, they introduced a fiscal state in which nationalist sentiment could be more broadly dispersed.[18]

These same political reverberations were felt throughout Europe, which reflected the broader relevance of these cultural concerns. At the same time the Scots and the English were uniting within a fiscal nationalism, Germany – where there was a growing desire for nationalist sentiment despite the fact that Germanic states were divided into different empires – experienced similar impulses. Friedrich Karl von Moser complained that "compared to the British, Swiss, Dutch and Swedes," the Germans lacked a "national way of thinking." Such could be expected from a culture that was split between political allegiances. But the same anxiety was also present in France on the eve of its revolution. An anonymous 1788 pamphlet published in Paris declared, "this people, assembled from a multitude of small, different nations, do not amount to a national body." One English visitor remarked that the French people "perceive quite well that they are not a nation; they want to become one." If the French nation desired to succeed, Emmanuel Sieyès declared that they needed to make "all the parts of France a single body, and all the peoples who divide it into a single Nation." In a more ominous way, Henri Grégoire declared that all citizens must be "melted into the national mass." The desire to unite disparate populations within a powerful nation was an Atlantic phenomenon.[19]

That desire to produce a culturally unified French nation led, of course, to the Reign of Terror and further instability. But their attempt reflected

---

[18] See Istvan Hont, *Jealousy of Trade: International Competition and the Nation-State in Historical Perspective* (Cambridge: Harvard University Press, 2005), 447–528; Colley, *Britons*, 55–101.

[19] Friedrich Karl von Moser, quoted in Hugh Seton-Watson, *Nations and States: An Enquiry into the Origins of Nations and the Politics of Nationalism* (London: Methuen & Co., 1977), 238–239. Anonymous, *Discours sur le patriotisme* (Paris: n.p., 1788), 88. British observer, quoted in Bell, *Cult of the Nation*, 14. Emmanuel-Joseph Sieyès, *Instructions envoyées par M. le Duc d'Orléans pour es personnes étrangères de sa procuration aux assemblées de bailliages relatives aux états-généraux* (Paris: n.p., 1789), 44. Henri Grégoire, *Essai sur la régénération physique, morale et politique de juifs*, ed. Rita-Hermon-Belot (1788; Paris: n.p., 1989), 141.

a larger development in political culture that remained long after Robespierre's fall. In a new age in which the term "nation" took on new and novel interpretations, and in which traditional states were being transformed or, in some cases, overthrown, the issue of cultural coalescing under a federal union became a paramount issue. Nation-states could no longer be taken for granted. Mere geography and hereditary overlap were not enough to maintain political allegiance. The age of democratic revolutions provoked political thinkers to re-conceptualize patriotic brotherhood, and politicians, theorists, and critics were left to construct new forms of political assent and national union. America, Britain, and France, among other nations, were faced with the modern problem of acknowledging disparate cultures throughout their political body. Many concluded that such divisions were inimical to national prosperity, and sought a way to alleviate those problems through a method of cultural regeneration. The American response to cultural and political disunity during the 1780s provided a testing ground for these new ideas. Their attempt to construct a federal state was also a pursuit to solve the problem of nationality posed by revolutionary disrupture.[20]

The anxiety over cultural disunity only became more heightened during the years following American independence. Some believed it was time to cut the cord binding the states together, as the experiment in a political confederacy that united disparate states was a misguided effort. One New York writer wonder if "instead of attempting one general government for the whole community of the United States," it would rather be preferable "to distribute the States into Three Republics"? Separating the country into like-minded bodies – New England, the middle colonies, and the South – would be the only way for nations to survive in the modern age. Another writer suggested adding a fourth republic encompassing "the lands lying on the Ohio," based on the assumption that life on the frontier would cultivate an even more different set of cultural and political beliefs. These regions could never be nationalized, they argued, because their "religion, manners, customs, exports, imports, and general interest of each" were so divergent to render a cohesive union untenable. One Massachusetts writer concurred and suggested the best hope for "a new and stronger union" would be to withdraw "the five States of New

---

[20] See also R. R. Palmer, *The Age of Democratic Revolutions: A Political History of Europe and America, 1760–1800* (1959–1964; Princeton: Princeton University Press, 2014), 347–376.

England" and construct a new nation based on shared interests. These chants became loud enough that Benjamin Rush expressed his concerns to British minister Richard Price that "some of our enlightened men who begin to despair of a more complete union of the States in Congress," he explained, "have secretly proposed an Eastern, Middle, and Southern Confederacy, to be united by an alliance offensive and defensive." Rush, however, believed this would be a lost opportunity. He hoped there could be another solution.[21]

Rush was among a group of politicians who believed the way to solve the problem of a divided-interest community was not separation, but centralization. A *Pennsylvania Gazette* editorial declared that the only way to bring the "prodigal" states back into the "their *Father's house*" was through "a VIGOROUS, EFFICIENT, NATIONAL GOVERNMENT." A strong federal structure, they believed, could serve as a regenerative force that could unite disparate states, coalesce competing cultures, and cultivate a national bond. An energetic nation solved the problems of a confederate union. Noah Webster argued that it was time for "a revolution in the form of government," just as there had been a revolution in the form of liberty. This new political architecture, he believed, would cause "a change of principles and manners, which are the springs of government." The reciprocal relationship between society and government promised both a political and cultural bond. Robert Davidson, a Presbyterian minister in Pennsylvania, stated that a federal government, "being connected with the constitutional taste and manners of a people," would introduce "the progress of refinement" required to blend disparate societies. Disunion was not the only option.[22]

These anxieties climaxed with the Constitutional Convention in 1787. Importantly, the convention's attempt to establish a rigorous federal government coincided with the broader movement to define a united national culture. The 1780s witnessed the growing popularity of

---

[21] *New York Daily Advertiser*, March 24, 1787; *New York Daily Advertiser*, April 2, 1787; *Boston Independent Chronicle*, February 15, 1787 (all sourced from loc.chroniclingamerica.gov). Benjamin Rush to Richard Price, October 27, 1786, in *The Letters of Benjamin Rush*, ed. Lyman H. Butterfield, 2 vols. (Princeton, NJ: Princeton University Press, 1951), 1:408.

[22] *Pennsylvania Gazette*, August 15, 1787, loc.chroniclingamerica.org. Noah Webster, "Remarks on the Manners, Government and Debt of the United States" (1787), in Webster, *A Collection of Essays and Fugitiv Writings: On Moral, Historical, Political and Literary Subjects* (Boston: I. Thomas and E. T. Andrews, 1790), 81–117, p. 87. Robert Davidson, *An Oration, on the Independence of the United States of America* (Carlisle, PA: Kline and Reynolds, 1787), 14.

sentimentalism and its concomitant strain to connect citizens together through a strong sense of belonging. Through newspapers, magazines, tracts, and, increasingly, novels, Americans believed there could be a unified form of thinking "American." This, in turn, encouraged individuals to believe that state and national interests could not only be balanced, but that they overlapped. Or, at the very least, it would enable them to produce citizens who could dispassionately identify the nation's best course of action, which would be suitable for all citizens and states. By cultivating a strong sense of centralized culture, interests, and identity, America could be unified and appear to the world as a solid country worthy of global interaction.[23]

These voices for consolidation became increasingly loud. It eventually resulted in the calls for a new federal constitution. Yet one especially potent example of this impulse was displayed in a long essay that was published serially in a handful of Philadelphia newspapers while the Constitutional Convention was still in session. Written by Nicholas Collin and titled "An Essay on the Means of Promoting Federal Sentiments in the United States, by a Foreign Spectator," the essay argued for a unified federal culture that would match a centralized federal government. Collin, a Swedish Lutheran minister and member of the American Philosophical Society, sat on the board of trustees for the University of the State of Pennsylvania. Though he presented himself in the essays as a "foreign spectator," he had actually lived in America for nearly two decades. Collin believed political federalism could only succeed in a society that embraced cultural federalism, by which he meant a unified culture in which Americans shared the same interests, customs, and habits. "A national taste has a near connection with principles, sentiments, and manners," he proclaimed, "and is therefore more or less congenial with the established mode of government." If American politicians adopted a more centralized government, then it was up to the American people to cultivate a concomitant culture where social cohesion justified the energetic federal system. This included an emphasis not only on shared republican principles, but also shared elements of civility,

[23] See John Murrin, "A Roof Without Walls: The Dilemma of American National Identity," in *Beyond Confederation Origins of the Constitution and American Identity*, ed. Richard Beeman, Stephen Botein, and Edward C. Carter (Chapel Hill: University of North Carolina Press, 1987), 333–348; Sarah Knott, *Sensibility and the American Revolution* (Chapel Hill: University of North Carolina Press, 2008); G. J. Barker-Benfield, *Abigail and John Adams: The Americanization of Sensibility* (Chicago: University of Chicago Press, 2010).

politeness, and even social practices like dancing. Cultural nationalism was all-encompassing.[24]

Collin acknowledged that the connection between "refined" practices and "political" policies might "appear nonsense" to some readers. Yet he maintained that that cultural practices like "social amusements . . . are of great consequence to manners and national felicity." A spread of uniquely "American" practices would ensure a strong citizenship and shared sense of unity. "Laws have a near connexion with manners," he explained, "and thereby a great influence on government." This implied that the more American society shared "cultivated manners," the less likely it would suffer societal ills and cultural fracturing. Of course, the possibility of cultural disjointedness was exacerbated as America looked westward and considered national expansion. An introduction of new cultures, he reasoned, would mean a "multiplicity of laws" and a fracturing of society. "What idea must this give a reflecting person of the government," he warned, if there was no shared "sense or power" found throughout the expanding nation? The only solution, he believed, was to be found in the cultivation of "Federal Sentiments" within a "SENTIMENTAL POLITICAL UNION." America's future depended on it.[25]

Throughout the many parts of his essay, Collin expressed a fear that the continuity of regional difference would mean "a dissolution of the union." Only a nation of overlapping interests and customs, he believed, could share a strong, centralized, federal government. America's westward expansion was both the nation's strength and a potential weakness. From a geopolitical perspective, expansion raised numerous concerns of competing jealousies and regional dissent. As a solution, Collin argued for, among other things, a federal university that would cultivate a national culture meant to spread across the entire continent and match

---

[24] *Pennsylvania Gazette*, September 5, 1787, LCP. Kate Haulman has noted that this essay was just one example of a broader cultural movement during the period that aimed to make the republic balance "local, national, and international" interests; Haulman, *Politics of Fashion in Eighteenth-Century America* (Chapel Hill: University of North Carolina Press, 2011), 181, 204–209. See also Knott, *Sensibility and the American Revolution*, 250–252.

[25] *Pennsylvania Gazette*, September 12, 1787, LCP. *Pennsylvania Gazette*, September 26, 1787, LCP. *Independent Gazetteer*, September 17, 1787, LCP. John L. Brooke argued that culture often served as an "internal police" throughout the various states during this period; "Patriarchal Magistrates, Associated Improvers, and Monitoring Militias: Visions of Self-Governments in the Early American Republic, 1760–1840," in *State and Citizen: British America and the Early United States*, ed. Peter Thompson and Peter S. Onuf (Charlottesville: University of Virginia Press, 2013), 178–217.

the soon-to-be-realized constitution. "The public education throughout the states," he reasoned, "is a great federal concern, as without it no state can ... act its part in the confederation with dignity, honor and a federal spirit." Specifically, a federal education that was focused on "the belles letters or elegant literature" would be "extremely useful by innobling [sic] those affections which are the bands of civil society." More importantly, this shared education would be utilized "under the patronage of Federal Power," because it extended federalism's reach to more than just the political sphere. "In proportion as elegant learning is cultivated" and shared, he concluded, "it will structure manners, religion, laws, and government." These purposes were intimately intertwined, and the success of federalism could only be achieved through the cultivation of a shared education. For a centralized federal government, there must be a unified American people.[26]

Collin's proposals were part of a larger Atlantic discussion concerning the state's role in regenerating society. They are thus best understood in conversation with European proponents of similar solutions. This was a political question that transcended local contexts. For instance, the French during the 1780s were simultaneously debating the importance of national sentiment and political belonging at the very moment they were redefining their federal structure. One author asked this very question in the title of his 1787 pamphlet, *Qu'est-ce que la nation e quest-ce que la France?* (What Is the Nation, and What Is France?). The terms that were most popular in describing this political project were words like "revival," "restoration," "recovery," and, most often, "regeneration." Robespierre hauntingly declared, "Considering the depths to which the human race has been degraded by the vices of our former social system, I am convinced of the need to effect a complete regeneration, and, if I may so express it, to create a new people." Such a project both implied the lack of cultural unity and need for artificial cohesion, as well as the faith in a governmental structure that could properly construct a society fit for stability. Thus, when journalist Pierre-Nicolas Chantreau declared that France was indeed a nation, he qualified that it had only "really been so"

[26] *Independent Gazetteer*, September 7, 13, 15, and 17, 1787, LCP; for the national plans for a federal university, see Adam R. Nelson, "The Perceived Dangers of Study Abroad, 1780–1800: Nationalism, Internationalism, and the Origins of the American University," in *The Founding Fathers, Education, and "The Great Contest": The American Philosophical Society Prize of 1797*, ed. Benjamin Justice (New York: Palgrave Macmillan, 2013), 175–200; for the interconnected issues of political union and geopolitical security, see Hendrickson, *Peace Pact*.

since 1789, when the National Convention attained power and regenerating the broader society.[27]

The incessant quest to cultivate a pure French culture and political body eventually culminated in perpetual violence. This in turn shaped how many European nations dealt with the problem in the future. But the hope of using a strong federal structure to reform society and cultivate a shared national body remained. A few decades later, when the German states faced a similar dilemma of uniting under a single national government, an anonymous article published in the political newspaper *Deutsche Blätter* complained that Germany, even with a centralized government, would not be "a country, not a nation, but a mixture of lesser peoples with one language" housed under a loose federal umbrella. Such a temporary fix would be nothing more than positioning them "at the same state that France and Spain were at" prior to their revolutions. Germans, the author warned, were attempting to skip too many steps in making a German nation-state. "Neither in Nature, however, nor in politics, is it possible to jump" from political conglomerate to national body. There was a process to follow in constructing a nationality through societal regeneration. "Individuals, like peoples, must first have mounted that educational step, which for the middling sort to climb is one higher still, before they can hope to reach the last one," the essay reasoned. Germany was not ready to be a nation because they lacked a national culture, and a national culture could only be achieved through a regenerating project meant to blend society together. The anxiety to overcome cultural and political disunity was difficult to overcome.[28]

Yet the more pertinent context for the American debates was what had been taking place in the British Empire. The multinational allegiance of English, Scottish, Irish, and Welsh people under the British crown

---

[27] Robespierre, speech, July 13, 1793, in James Guillaume, ed., *Procès-verbaux du Comité d'instruction publique de la Convention*, 6 vols. (Paris, 1891–1907), 2:35. Pierre-Nicolas Chantreau, quoted in Bell, *Cult of the Nation in France*, 14. See also Alyssa Goldstein Sepinwall, *The Abbé Grégoire and the French Revolution: The Making of Modern Universalism* (Berkeley: University of California Press, 2005). David A. Bell noted that there "arrived an extraordinary moment in the history of French national sentiment" where "unprecedented claims on behalf of the *nation* together with unprecedented doubts about it, all in a context in which leaders of the nascent revolutionary movement were also loudly lamenting France's failure to constitute a true *patrie*." Bell, *Cult of the Nation in France*, 75.

[28] *Deutsche Blätter*, November 10, 1814, in Hagen Schulze, ed., *The Course of German Nationalism: From Frederick the Great to Bismarck, 1763–1867* (Cambridge: Cambridge University Press, 1991), 120.

bequeathed a creative yet fraught tradition of balanced interests and unified nationalism. This was one of the primary concerns that led to the Revolution in the first place, as Americans believed that parliament did not seriously consider their interests nor properly understand the cultural differences inherent in their community. "The addition of new states to the British empire," Thomas Jefferson complained in his *Summary View*, "has produced an addition of new, and sometimes opposite interests." It was left to the king "to resume the exercise of his negative power, and to prevent the passage of laws by any one legislature of the empire, which might bear injuriously on the rights and interests of another." Britons responded with their established doctrine of parliament's sanctity and ability to decipher the best interests of the entire empire. So persuaded were they that parliament could unify the disparate cultural bodies that they scoffed at American pleas for either colonial representation or the monarch to step in and adjudicate the disjointed factions. These same questions would reemerge within an independent America during the late 1780s and early 1790s as new political debates arose that critiqued the empire's structure. The entire Atlantic world seemed to be in flux.[29]

Many European onlookers hoped Americans could solve this problem that was plaguing Atlantic nations. François Barbé-Marbois, part of the French legation to the United States during the Revolution who stayed in America as *chargé d'affaires* in 1784, attempted to visually depict America's nationalist potential. In his sketch, "Allegory of the American Union," the marquis de Barbé-Marbois depicted America as an adult Hercules perched on top of thirteen stones. These cornerstones represented how each state, though small and weak on its own, could join together and create a powerful arch that soared above the natural world and supported a powerful national hero (Image 1.2). This sketch, drawn by a French emissary, ably captured how the American political body was seen by some as a national solution to an international problem. They would build the bridge to span the chasm of cultural disunity.

All of these tensions fed into American debates about the Constitution's creation and adoption in 1787–1788. The Constitution aimed to solve the problem of national disruption. The results, however,

---

[29] Thomas Jefferson, *A Summary View of the Rights of British America* (Williamsburg: Clementinarind, 1774), 16. For the constitutional debates over cultural interests and parliamentary representation, see Jack P. Green, *The Constitutional Origins of the American Revolution* (New York: Cambridge University Press, 2011), 104–148; Eric Nelson, *The Royalist Revolution: Monarchy and the American Founding* (Cambridge: Harvard University Press, 2014), 29–107.

IMAGE 1.2 Marquis de François Barbé-Marbois, *Allegory of the American Union*, 1784, American Philosophical Society. Each of the blocks represented a state in the new American nation. Together they represented a newly forged union that bridges the chasm of anarchy.

were mixed. On the one hand, the new federal document was based on compromised interests, which in turn left many unsatisfied. On the other, its policies gave a framework for shared political values and an energetic federal structure. The ratification debates over the next year, then, provided the opportunity for these ideas to take root in the particular political cultures of each state, which enabled citizens from different backgrounds and contexts to struggle with the ideas of political nationalism. Thus, the seeds for both union and disunion were sown within the very fabric of America's founding document.

––––––––––

These tensions played different roles in different locations. Pennsylvania, which hosted the Constitutional Convention and soon became the temporary home for the nation's capital, provides a potent example of how local cultures shaped the reception of and debate over federal government during this period. One of the first states to confirm the new federal system in late 1787 – indeed, when the Constitution was ratified by their state convention, they thought they *were* the first – their rushed debates set many precedents for the states that followed. They also demonstrated the limitations of one state's rhetoric. Though the Constitution possessed federal intentions and was crafted with many states in mind, its ability to pass in Pennsylvania depended on its proponents being able to demonstrate how, in the words of Benjamin Rush, it "fit" the people of the state. This necessitated the appropriation of local political language and assumptions in crafting the federal message.[30]

The state also provides a potent example of the deeply divided nature of the Constitution's reception. Support for the new government came predominantly from the more urban areas near Philadelphia, while rural populations near the western border were much more hesitant concerning this new energetic federalism. Despite an attempt by elites to appear otherwise, Pennsylvania did not present a united front. Federalists held control over most of the newspapers, and they suppressed anti-federalist arguments. The published proceedings from their state convention only included eloquent defenses of the Constitution. The *Pennsylvania Herald* editor who attempted to provide space for dissenting voices lost his job as a result of elite backlash. Cultural and political heterogeneity within the state's mixed community could only go so far. Even the most elastic conceptions of nationalism required the silencing of opinions that did not fit a particular ideological framework.[31]

---

[30] For the general narrative of the Constitution's passage in the state, I have relied upon Pauline Maier, *Ratification: The People Debate the Constitution, 1787–1788* (New York: Alfred A. Knopf, 2010), 97–124.
[31] See Maier, *Ratification*, 99–101.

Once in control of the message, federalist elites argued that Pennsylvania possessed a history of governing mechanisms that were not dependent upon a single or isolated ideology, religion, or ethnicity. Immigration left the state without a dominant ethnic group – a third were German, a third were English, and nearly a third were Scottish or Irish. And, while Philadelphia remained the hub of activity for the state (not to mention, as far as it could be identified at the time, the nation), inland communities like Harrisburg, Pittsburgh, and Lancaster presented divergent voices that expressed the state's heterogeneity. As such, their notions of cultural authority were shaped by the fact that there were different points of influence and opinion. In both Massachusetts and South Carolina, centralized locations of cultural, political, and intellectual dominance framed understandings of authority and control. Since it was impossible to delineate a dominant culture in Pennsylvania, federalists argued that it was necessary to base political authority upon a system in which representation and participation enabled the voice of diverse communities. To envision a central government that could "fit" all the governed, then, was an experiment in imaginative political construction, a willful deference to the reality of deep cultural heterogeneity. Yet that background also framed how political discourse would take shape.[32]

In part due to their cultural background, most Pennsylvanians believed that government could only be removed from the power of the people when fundamentally necessary. And even on those rare occasions, many argued the government still had to be as representative of the governed as possible. Citizens were expected to actively participate through meetings, committees, pamphlets, and electoral organizations – the only way to gain their rights was to fulfill their obligations. Popular activism was not only allowed, but expected, and political participation shaped an understanding of not only local government but also federal authority. The state offered more opportunity for class mobility as well as the cultural associations that provided means through which popular politics could be arranged. This expectation for participation engendered a close association between the government and the governed. While there certainly remained a class-based hierarchy for political power, the discourse of

---

[32] See R. Eugene Harper, *The Transformation of Western Pennsylvania, 1770–1800* (Pittsburgh, PA: University of Pittsburgh Press, 1991); John B Frantz and William Pencak, eds., *Beyond Philadelphia: The American Revolution in the Pennsylvania Hinterland* (University Park: Pennsylvania State Press, 1998).

citizenship in Pennsylvania reflected their cultural framework of balancing citizen and state.[33]

Much of this philosophy was found in the state's governing documents. Pennsylvania's constitution had gone through several revisions since its passage in 1776, with most of its most radical elements being stripped by 1787. While the historical narrative of the state's politics during this period has depicted the state as moving away from populist politics toward a more conservative model, much of the debates were over *how* popular power was to be harnessed, rather than whether it should be harnessed at all. Indeed, the political discourse that shaped the state's 1776 constitution still played an important role in the debates over the federal Constitution's ratification in 1787. Those in Pennsylvania who fought hard for the Constitution's passage utilized a populist rhetoric that endorsed popular activism. The battle between federalists and anti-federalists in the state, just as it was over the state constitution, was not a fight between elite and popular authority, but how that authority was to be wielded. As such, the debates surrounding the Constitution took place within a different cultural framework than those that took place in states to the north and south, as its success and failure depended on an argument's ability to appropriate the state's political history. In South Carolina, for instance, federalist rhetoric focused on the importance of sacrifice and order, two principles that were dominant themes in the state's political discourse. David Ramsay, though raised in Pennsylvania, knew how to package the Constitution for South Carolinians: "In society," he explained during the debates over ratification, "every individual must sacrifice a part of his natural rights; the minority must yield to the majority, and the collective interest must control [sic] particular interests." In the Deep South, stability claimed priority over populism.[34]

---

[33] For popular associations and their connection to participatory politics, see Albrecht Koschnik, *Let A Common Interest Bind Us Together: Associations, Partisanship, and Culture in Philadelphia, 1775–1840* (Charlottesville: University of Virginia Press, 2007); Jessica Chopin Roney, *Governed by the Spirit of Opposition: The Origins of American Political Practice in Colonial Philadelphia* (Baltimore: Johns Hopkins University Press, 2014). For the perpetuation of social class in revolutionary Pennsylvania, see Billy G Smith, *The "Lower Sort": Philadelphia's Laboring People, 1750–1800* (Ithaca, NY: Cornell University Press, 1990); Charles Olton, *Artisans for Independence: Philadelphia Mechanics and the American Revolution* (Syracuse, NY: Syracuse University Press, 1975).

[34] *American Museum*, May 1788, LCP. For the political background for South Carolina's debate over the Constitution, see Robert M. Weir, "'The Harmony We Were Famous

But populism held more political capital in Pennsylvania. James Wilson, one of the predominant voices in favor of the Constitution in the state – and one of the few convention delegates whose speeches made it into the official proceedings – maintained the state's traditional rhetoric concerning populist politics. "Representation is made necessary only because it is impossible for the people to act collectively," he stated during the Constitutional Convention. Later, he argued that the only way that the "national pyramid" of America was to reach its highest point was to have "as broad a basis [of the people's support] as possible." This was a rhetorical shift that muted the Constitution's increased federal sovereignty while at the same time shaping its understanding within a framework of popular representation and participation. The Constitution was not only constructed in Philadelphia, he implied, but it was also framed by Pennsylvanian tradition. Wilson nearly filibustered most of the convention meetings with his long speeches declaring that the Constitution fit within Pennsylvania's republican legacy. That the federalists felt they had to silence dissenting voices from the state in order to validate a particular populist message was a calculated tool of the ratification process.[35]

When James Wilson defended the new Constitution to his fellow Pennsylvanians, he invoked many of the principles that were connected to the state's notion of a political community. He even couched the document's appeal in terms of popular sovereignty. "The people at large will acquire an additional privilege in returning members to the House of Representatives," he explained, "whereas, by the present Confederation, it is the legislature alone that appoints the delegates to Congress." Wilson argued that it was those who opposed the Constitution who "pursue[ed] their] own interest, in preference to the public good," since the latter was

For': An Interpretation of Pre-Revolutionary South Carolina Politics," *William and Mary Quarterly* 26 (October 1969): 473–501; Mark D. Kaplanoff, "How Federalist was South Carolina in 1787–88?" in *The Meaning of South Carolina History: Essays in Honor of George C. Rogers, Jr.*, ed. David R. Chesnutt and Clyde N. Wilson (Columbia: University of South Carolina Press, 1991), 67–103. For the general narrative of Pennsylvania's constitution from progressive to conservative, see Nash, "Philadelphia's Radical Caucus"; Eric Foner, *Tom Paine and Revolutionary America* (1976; New York: Oxford University Press, 2004), 183–210; Gordon Wood, *The Creation of the American Republic, 1776–1787*, 2nd ed. (Chapel Hill: University of North Carolina Press, 1998), 445–495.

[35] James Wilson, June 6, 1787, in *The Records of the Federal Convention of 1787*, ed. Max Ferrand, 11 vols. (New Haven, CT: Yale University Press, 1911–1937), 1:142. James Wilson, quoted in Peter Onuf, *Origins of the Federal Republic: Jurisdictional Controversies in the United States, 1775–1787* (Philadelphia: University of Pennsylvania Press, 1983), 202–203.

the true purpose of the newly proposed government. This political theme became a popular one for federalists in the coming year, though with different results in each location based on the regional discourse. In response, many anti-federalists argued that the popular will was not being heard. Philadelphia's *Independent Gazetteer*, for instance, claimed that "in a month's time there will not remain 500 people in all Pennsylvania in favor of the new government, except those who expect offices under it." The only people who supported the new government were those in line to benefit from it, and they were therefore rigging the system in order to procure the necessary votes. Both sides accused the other of ignoring the voice of the people.[36]

These themes continued into Pennsylvania's ratification convention itself. When Wilson delivered the opening speech, he emphasized Pennsylvania's tradition of multiple and, at times, competing interests. This had prepared them for a form of federalism that embraced "the wide and almost unbounded jurisdiction of the United States." The state of Pennsylvania, he argued, was better adjusted for the new form of government than any other in the nation. He explained that "the true chain between the people and those to whom they entrust the administration of the government" was more apparent in the federal Constitution than the Articles of Confederation. In its "principles," he concluded, the Constitution "is purely democratical," and "when we take an extensive and accurate view of the streams of power that appear through this great and comprehensive plan . . . we shall be able to trace them to one great and noble source, THE PEOPLE." Wilson was certainly exaggerating the Constitution's "democratical" elements, but he did so knowing that such language was necessary to gain local support. It was important to base the Constitution's power not in federal control but in the common people. Their ability to appropriate the principles of the state's political discourse was a primary reason they were able to ratify the Constitution so quickly and easily.[37]

---

[36] James Wilson, in DHRC 2:167–172. *Indepedendent Gazeteer*, December 5, 1787, in DHRC 2:264–265. Pauline Maier notes how this line of defense worked well in New York while it mostly fell flat in Virginia, which was based on the latter's diverging framework for representative politics. Maier, *Ratification*, 255–270, 380–395.

[37] James Wilson, in DHRC 2:341, 350. See Kenneth Owen, "Political Community in Revolutionary Pennsylvania, 1774–1800" (D.Phil. diss.: University of Oxford, 2011). For debates over the meaning of "the people" during the period, see Michal Jan Rozbicki, *Culture and Liberty in the Age of the American Revolution* (Charlottesville: University of Virginia Press, 2011), 114–126. For these debates leading to a fracturing in Pennsylvania politics, see Andrew Shankman, *Crucible of American Democracy: The Struggle to Fuse*

This traditional political framework shaped both sides of the debate. The anti-federalists concurred that it was a contest over the power of the people, but they concluded that the Constitution came down on the wrong side of that divide. One writer claimed the prevailing attitude of the federalists was that "COMMON PEOPLE HAVE NO BUSINESS TO TROUBLE THEMSELVES ABOUT GOVERNMENT." The series of essays written by "Centinel," published in the *Independent Gazateer*, agreed with the critique and accused the "northern states" of maintaining an "aristocratic junto" that preferred "the *well-born few*, who had been zealously endeavouring since the establishment of their constitutions, to humble that offensive *upstart, equal liberty*; but all their efforts," the essay continued, "were unavailing, the *ill-bred churl* obstinately kept his assumed station." Those pushing the Constitution "desired their delegated power, and assumed sovereignty." They were trying to establish a union "constituted on the most *unequal* principles, destitute of accountability to its constituents, and as despotic in its nature, as the Venetian aristocracy." The "Centinel" concluded by claiming that "a government that will give full scope to the magnificent designs of the *well-born*; a government where tyranny may glut its vengeance on the *low-born*, unchecked by *an odious bill of rights*." The Constitution's primary fault, according to this logic, was that it failed to acknowledge the importance of the common citizen and the necessary connection between delegates and those they represented.[38]

The accusation by "Centinel" that this federal context for government came from the "northern states" was important to the anti-federalist argument in Pennsylvania. Their task was to prove that the Constitution did not match the culture of the state and that it was "foreign" in the sense that it was imported from outside their culture. The proud tradition of populist politics in the state, they argued, did not match what was being forced by the cultural and political colonists of the North. New England, they believed, failed to acknowledge a difference of opinion and, importantly, a difference of lived realities for those in the middle states. As such, the Constitution was not only ill equipped for Pennsylvania's culture, but the former was a direct threat to the latter. Another Pennsylvanian anti-federalist, after noting that "the excellent Montesquieu himself observes, that 'the manners and customs of the people have an intimate connection

Egalitarianism and Capitalism in Jeffersonian Pennsylvania (Lawrence: University Press of Kansas, 2004).
[38] *Independent Gazetteer*, October 12, November 8, 1787, LCP. (Emphasis in original.)

with their laws,'" argued that the state should reject the Constitution because it did not reflect their cultural values. The question "which should be agitated is not whether the proposed constitution be better or worse than those that have from time to time existed," but instead, "whether it be in every respect adapted to secure our liberty and happiness at the *present state* of the world." To promote a "national" government that did not match the character of the governed implied a cultural imperialism that muted society's differences. A truly representative government, claimed the *Pennsylvania Herald*, would take into account all the rights "which the states hold sacred." Though it was framed in Philadelphia, the Constitution did not, according to anti-federalists, mirror its immediate environment.[39]

Not all politicians and critics interpreted their state culture the same way, yet they maintained this tension between competing federal and state interests. Massachusetts delegate Elbridge Gerry, for instance, one of three convention participants who did not sign the Constitution, claimed that "the eastern States will soon rebel against [the Constitution], for it is not a Government adapted to their Genius, Habits, or aversion to arbitrary power." But, he then added, "if they are of a different opinion, I have no objection to their trying on the federal Chains, for I am persuaded they will find the bonds of this constitution eventually to be [beneficial]." In Gerry's mind, the Constitution did not even "fit" the people of New England, the bastion of centralized political authority. This opinion demonstrates the elasticity of how different people in different states not only interpreted particular documents, but also interpreted their own local context. Importantly, though, while Gerry believed the Constitution did not match his state's character, he left open the option that he could be mistaken, which others argued to be the case.[40]

Not all were as humble in their diagnosis. The anti-federalists in Pennsylvania recognized what was at stake. "It is beyond a doubt," wrote one editorial, "that the new federal constitution ... will in great measure destroy, if not totally annihilate, the separate governments of several states." The result, he warned, was that "we shall, in effect, become one great Republic. Every measure of any importance, will be Continental." That the writer characterized the nation becoming "one

---

[39] *A Review of the Constitution, Proposed by the Late Convention ... By a Federal Republican* (Philadelphia: Robert Smith and James Prang, 1787), 7–8. (Emphasis in original.) *Pennsylvania Herald*, October 27, 1787, in DHRC 2:203–205.

[40] Elbridge Gerry to John Wendell, November 16, 1787, Elbridge Gerry Papers, MHS.

great Republic" as a negative development demonstrates his recognition of various political cultures within the United States. The fact that the measurement of government and culture would be "Continental" was to be feared. The adoption of the Federal Constitution, according to this reasoning, necessitated the destruction of the state's political tradition.[41]

In response, federalists cultivated a new view of popular authority. Pelatiah Webster, a Philadelphia merchant, claimed that each state would retain their own sovereignty and interests in most cases, "except where great and manifest *national purposes and interests* make that controul necessary." The federal government, Webster explained, recognized the existence of multifaceted states that encompassed contrasting cultures and customs, but still maintained that "each State derives strength, firmness, and permanency from its compact with the other states." Webster saw Pennsylvania's culture in the same terms: numerous communities with various beliefs and practices who were nevertheless able to come together and became stronger as a union rather than they would as distinct bodies. The energetic blending of divergent interests through a centralized union incorporated to promote the common good was a lived reality in Pennsylvania. Federalism, that is, was a state tradition.[42]

Pennsylvania federalists countered the anti-federalist message by claiming the new Constitution was "more a government *of the people*, than the present Congress ever was, because, the members of Congress have been hitherto chosen by the legislatures of the several states." Under the new Constitution, on the other hand, "the proposed Representatives are to be chosen BY THE PEOPLE." Benjamin Rush echoed this emphasis on representative and populist politics when he wrote that, with those mechanisms in place, the Constitution was not in need of a Bill of Rights. "Without them," he explained to David Ramsay, "a volume of rights would avail nothing, and with them a declaration of rights is absurd and unnecessary." Rush believed that "the PEOPLE where their liberties are committed to an equal representation, and to a compound legislature (such as we observe in the new government) will always be the sovereigns of their rulers, and hold all their rights in their own hands." Rush claimed that those who called for a separate "bill of rights have not recovered from the habits they acquired under the monarchical government of Great Britain." Indeed, Rush's own experience with a culture that enabled

[41] *Independent Gazetteer*, October 27, 1787, chroniclingamerica.loc.gov.
[42] [Pelatiah Webster], "The Weakness of Brutus Exposed," November 8, 1787, in DHRC 14:71. (Emphasis in original.)

both a complex blend of ideas yet a common trust of representation allowed him to interpret the Constitution in a populist manner that some from other cultures could not; David Ramsay, whose experience as an adult in the South differed from that of Rush, could not share the same political assumptions, and thus disagreed with his assessment.[43]

The fight over the Constitution in Pennsylvania revolved around themes and issues that were crucial to that state's local political experience. The importance of popular politics, the representation of common people, the equality of law, and the potential for advancement marked the boundaries for discourse and debate. Federalists and anti-federalists alike agreed on the importance of these issues, and their disagreement came from their interpretation of how the Constitution fit those parameters. National issues were thus interpreted through local lenses. But even if local contexts shaped the contours of the debate, the results had much broader ramifications. Most obviously, the ratification and implementation of a vigorous federal government was the most tangible result, as the new political mechanisms reached far and wide. But there were other fruits that came as a result of this nationalist push, which ranged from more abstract embodiments like national voluntary institutions to more concrete realizations like Alexander Hamilton's plan for a national bank. This dialogue also established the groundwork upon which national parties arose the following decade: the insistence on shared principles that spanned across state borders proved to be a prerequisite for national cooperation and inter-state allegiances. It also paved the way for dissent, as these very same national organizations that were birthed during the period became flashpoints for political disagreements due to divergent interpretations of their scope and purpose.

This anxiety was found even at the moment of the Constitution's ratification. The frontispiece for the bound volume of the *Columbian Magazine* in 1788 featured an engraving by Philadelphian James Trenchard titled, "Temple of Liberty," which was accompanied by this poem:

> Behold! A Fabric now to FREEDOM rear'd,
> Approved by friends, and ev'n by Foes rever'd,
> Where JUSTICE, love, and PEACE but us ador'd

---

[43] *Independent Gazetteer*, November 10, 1787, LCP. (Emphasis in original.) *Columbian Herald*, April 19, 1788. David Ramsay to Benjamin Rush, November 10, 1787, in Robert L. Brunhouse, ed., "David Ramsay on the Ratification of the Constitution in South Carolina, 1787–1788," *Journal of Southern History* 9 (November 1943): 552.

IMAGE 1.3 James Trenchard, "Temple of Liberty," *The Columbian Magazine,* 1788, opp. P. 473. Engraving in Book. Rare Books and Special Collections Division, Library of Congress, www.loc.gov/exhibits/us.capitol/twnty4.jpg.

> Shall heal each Wrong, and keep ensheathed the Sword
> Approach then, Concord, fair Columbia's Son,
> And, Faithful Clio, write that "WE ARE ONE."

The image portrayed by this engraving and its prose was meant to capture the feeling of national unity inaugurated by the new Constitution. The government, Trenchard explained, was depicted as "A PLAIN BUT STATELY EDIFICE, in a durable style of architecture." It was built to last. Yet Trenchard also disrupted that very narrative. "Two of the columns are cracked," he wrote, "in allusion to the non-concurring states." The winged boy who is holding the Constitution in the engraving is specifically pointing to the cracks, as if to warn the present muse of history, Clio, who had mistakenly written that the American people "are one" (Image 1.3). The political body that was meant to embrace a united people was perhaps a superficial cover after all.[44]

Benjamin Rush was one Pennsylvanian who was grounded in his state's culture yet yearned to be a participant in and shaper of America's new republic. He therefore provides an important case study in the construction of nationalist politics at the local level during the 1780s. After his education in Edinburgh, Rush spent his life in Philadelphia as a noted physician, educator, university administrator, and political gadfly. Besides his voluminous correspondence, he produced a large corpus of writings on topics as diverse as philosophy, physiology, pedagogy, slavery, and politics. Identified as one of the leading residents of Philadelphia, he was also one of the most famous citizens of the United States. Most importantly, he consciously attempted to cultivate a nationalist idea that would capture his desired identity for the entire United States – he strongly believed that

---

CAPTION FOR IMAGE 1.3 (cont.)

In this image, the angel is attesting to the new "Fabric" dedicated to freedom encapsulated in the American nation. "Approach then, Concord, fair Columbia's Son," it urged. "And, faithful Clio, write that 'WE ARE ONE'." Published at the time of the Constitutional debates, the image was meant to symbolize American unity. Yet there was already a crack on the third-to-left column, which hinted at potential discord.

---

[44] James Trenchard, "Explanation of the Frontispiece," *Columbian Magazine* 2 (1788). See Slaughter, *State as a Work of Art*, 81–85.

the country would only meet its potential when it embraced a national character that united disparate states.

Yet he was far from representative, either of America in general or of Pennsylvanian in particular. That anxiety drove, in part, his appeal to a more cohesive culture. Further, he wasn't even representative of the federalist movement in which he took part. His vision of what a vigorous federal government personified often differed from those with whom he corresponded. It proves useful, then, to use him as a guide for these nationalist tensions, especially in comparison to someone like Noah Webster, a New Englander and fellow federalist who, though he supposedly shared the same political views, possessed a different ideological foundation based on a different cultural tradition. When Webster excitedly wrote to Rush in 1788 about "one new [project] in contemplation" – a national magazine – he wrote that it "pleases me, & probably please you, as it is <u>purely federal</u>." Yet the very term that Webster felt bound the two men of letters together, "federal," meant subtly – but importantly – different things.[45]

The debates surrounding the Constitutional Convention prompted both Rush and Webster to take part in a national discourse that shaped America's political future. Rush published several tracts during the 1780s – in fact, it was the most prolific period of his print career. Noah Webster was similarly productive, though most of his political views were found in one work, *Sketches of American Policy*, a 1785 pamphlet that, in his memory, was "the first public proposition" in favor of "the establishment of a National Constitution." He believed it was a direct influence on the Constitutional Convention. While he was overstating his credentials as America's first federalist, the sentiment captures how important he felt federalism was to the national discourse on politics. And though neither he nor Rush were strictly representative of the states in which they lived, they each incorporated cultural elements from their local context in constructing a sense of national belonging.[46]

Throughout his writings, and despite the lived reality, Benjamin Rush insisted that America was a nation for the free laborer. That Rush owned at least one slave when he posited this belief highlights the ideological divide of imaginative nationalism. He proclaimed that those who shared

---

[45] Noah Webster to Benjamin Rush, February 10, 1788, Benjamin Rush Collection, HSP. (Emphasis in original.) For background on Rush, see David Hawke, *Benjamin Rush: Revolutionary Gadfly* (Indianapolis, IN: Bobbs-Merril, 1971).

[46] *New York Herald*, July 20, 1796, chroniclingamerica.loc.gov.

his intellectual pursuits were expected to blend their physical and mental interests and be familiar with both books and farming equipment. This was not only because it would be impossible to make a living solely as a man of letters – though he did caution that "the United States as yet afford but little encouragement to the professors of most of the fine arts" – but because America held little interest for those who cannot take pleasure in the joys of common people. In his instructions to potential immigrants he warned, "Men of independent fortunes who can exist only in company, and who can converse only upon public amusements, should not think of settling in the United States." Those who claimed no "professional pursuits," he explained, "will often languish in America, from want of society." America's "scholars," if they could be described as such, "are generally men of business, and make their literary pursuits subservient to their interests." This was a breed of men cut apart from European elites.[47]

For Rush, the American character was inseparably connected to the American soil. "To the cultivators of the earth the United States opened the first asylum in the world," he remarked. Throughout his many publications, as well as private letters, he constructed the ideal of an "American" as someone who toiled with both mind and shovel, a laborer who accumulated modest wealth but maintained intellectual rigor. Such an understanding was rooted in the agrarian economy that surrounded him in the middle colonies. He urged immigrants to settle in Pennsylvania explicitly because the state possessed the land and opportunity required to help someone become an American citizen. Move to New England, he warned, and one may not find economic independence due to limited available land; move to the South, and one is exposed to a fragile economy that, because of its reliance upon slave labor, is prone to indolence. As long as the South continued to "tolerate negro slavery," it could never be an "agreeable retreat" for friends of liberty. America was uniquely special, but not all regions were created alike.[48]

While he emphasized the bounteous opportunities for all citizens throughout the nation, Rush's conception of American culture emphasized wealth inequality and the perpetuation of social class. Equality, a principle common in political and social writings in Massachusetts during the period, was notably absent in Rush's nationalist writings.

---

[47] Benjamin Rush, *Information to Europeans, Who are Disposed to Migrate to the United States. In a Letter from a Citizen of Pennsylvania, to his Friend in Great Britain* (Philadelphia: Carey & Stewart, 1790), 3–4.

[48] Rush, *Information*, 4, 14.

While he believed that all Americans were destined to achieve their own
success, he maintained the idea, shared with many others during the
period (particularly Thomas Jefferson and others in the South), of
a natural aristocracy in which individuals would organically fit into
different classes. His advice to prospective immigrants was not to expect
perfect equality, but to rather anticipate a natural economic "order"
based on one's skills. Those who demonstrated exceptional worth – likely
including himself – would establish themselves at the top of society. This
was also a general theme in his private memoirs: his ability to conquer the
many obstacles in his life afforded him certain privileges, which included
an education for his family that surpassed anything available to those in
the surrounding community. This debate over a growing capitalist institution was a central feature of Pennsylvania political culture during the
period and was a crucial aspect of how the region defined "democracy."[49]

In the North, Noah Webster encapsulated New England's egalitarian
rhetoric. For Webster, it was not the act of agriculture itself, or a natural
stratification of social order, that was crucial to the American character.
Instead, it was the equality implied by the nation's agrarian society.
"The great fundamental principle on which alone a free government can
be founded and by which alone the freedom of a nation can be rendered
permanent," Webster reasoned, "is an *equal distribution of property*."
While Rush's national vision was based on a class structure that, though it
allowed opportunity, still centered on the success of a few, Webster's
egalitarian nation collapsed boundaries and standardized variation.
"*A general and tolerably equal distribution of landed property is the
whole basis of national freedom*," he urged in his 1787 pamphlet defending the Constitution. "An equality of property, with a necessity of aliena-
tion, constantly operating to destroy combinations of powerful families, is
the very *soul of a republic*. As long as this continued," he further
explained, "the people will inevitably possess both *power* and *freedom*."
For Webster, the central dynamic of America's society depended on
a degree of equality, for it necessitated everyone to work for the same
level of success. Because of this emphasis on equal labor, then, the "radical
class" of Pennsylvanians who depended on the labor of others while

[49] Ibid., *Information*, 6–8. Benjamin Rush, "Travels Through Life: or, an Account of
Sundry Incidents and Events in the Life of Benjamin Rush born December 24 1745 Old
Style. Written for the Use of his Children," original drafts, APS; Parts 7 and 8, on his
religious and moral views, are especially acute with anxiety over his family's privilege
when compared to other Philadelphians. See also Shankman, *Crucible of American
Democracy*.

promoting their own philosophy led to the "hasty conduct" of the Pennsylvania legislature. Perhaps more importantly, the Southern practice of slavery was a gross violation of this national principle because it jeopardized the correct distribution of labor.[50]

Slavery was one thing both Rush and Webster could agree upon as a menace to America's character. But they still disagreed why that was the case. As early as the American Revolution, when Rush began to formulate what an American nation should look like, he argued that the youngest generation of slaves should be set free as an appropriate start for the young republic. "The plant of liberty is of so tender a Nature, that it cannot thrive long in the neighbourhood of slavery," he argued. "Remember the eyes of all Europe are fixed upon you, to preserve an asylum for freedom in this country, after the last pillars of it are fallen in every other quarter of the Globe." A decade after America's founding, Rush feared that slavery tore apart what was meant to hold America together: healthy familial and social relationships. Upon hearing a rumor in 1789 that Southern men were leaving their wives at a much higher rate than anywhere else in the country, he mused that slave culture led women to take a "small share … in the management of their families, in South Carolina," in turn rendering "them less necessary to the happiness of their husbands." If such were the case, it furnished "a new and strong argument against negro slavery." Slavery was harmful to society because it deadened the social passions of the slaveholders and lessened their sentiments. Put simply, it upended social and domestic order.[51]

Webster similarly believed that slavery was America's great "evil," but his opposition was primarily on economic grounds. "At present," he proclaimed in 1785, "it is the bane of industry and virtue." Slaves in the South "support luxury," Webster reasoned, and "vice and indolence more

---

[50] Noah Webster, *Sketches of American Policy.* (Hartford, CT: Hudson and Goodwin, 1785), 18. (Emphasis in original.) Noah Webster, *An Examination Into the Leading Principles of the Federal Constitution Proposed by the Late Convention Held at Philadelphia, with Answers to the Principle Objections that Have Been Raised Against the System* (Philadelphia: Prichard & Hall, 1787), 47 (emphasis in original); Webster's critiques of Pennsylvania are found in *An Examination*, 12, and *Sketches*, 22.

[51] [Benjamin Rush], *An Address to the Inhabitants of the British Settlements in America, upon Slave-Keeping. The Second Edition. To which are Added, Observations on a Pamphlet, Entitled, "Slavery not Forbidden by Scripture; or, A Defence of the West-India Planters." By a Pennsylvanian.* (Philadelphia: John Dunlap, 1773), 26. Benjamin Rush, "Commonplace Book, 1782–1792," entry for June 1789, Benjamin Rush Collection, APS. It should be noted that Rush's views on slavery were further complicated by the fact that he owned a slave himself between 1773 and 1793, and was never comfortable with the presence of free blacks in Philadelphia.

than all other causes. They may enrich their owners; but render them too often useless members of society." In Webster's conception of America, in which every citizen labored with their equal allotment, slavery's great threat was not the demise of morals, but the halting of industry – the heart of nationalism, and a key to the nation's identity. Race did not have as persuasive an argumentative point as agricultural labor. For Webster, to be American meant being industrious, and slavery was dangerous because it vitiated industriousness. The slave institution seemed as bad for white citizens as for their black property.[52]

But slavery was not the only moral issue at the heart of Rush's and Webster's nationalisms. Both figures relied on religious ideas when constructing ideas of political belonging. While Rush's Universalism pushed the boundaries of acceptable religion during the period, he still maintained that religion played a major role in American life. In a 1791 letter to Boston minister Jeremy Belknap, he warned that "the neglect of the Word of God and the Ordinances of the Christian Religion" was the cause for "a dissoluteness of morals" in the young nation. He forthrightly stated that his view of America, and his vision for America's future, was based on five assumptions:

    I. That Christianity is the most true and perfect religion, and that in proportion as mankind adopt its principles, and obey its precepts, they will be wise and happy.

    II. That a better knowledge of its religion is to be acquired by reading the Bible, than in any other way.

    III. That the Bible contains more knowledge necessary to man in his present state, than any other book in the world.

    IV. That knowledge is most durable, and religious instruction most useful, when imparted in early life.

    V. That the Bible, when not read in schools, is seldom read in any subsequent period of life.[53]

Rush's religious beliefs merged into his arguments for education. His vision of national education was universal – he felt that a systematic

---

[52] Webster, *Sketches*, 46.

[53] Benjamin Rush, *Defence of the Use of the Bible as a School-Book. In a Letter from the celebrated Doctor Rush of Philadelphia, to the Rev. J. Belknap, D.D. of Boston* (Concord, MA: George Hough, 1806), 9–10; Rush detailed his spiritual journey in Part 9 of his memoir: originally a mainstream Christian, he was influenced by the writings of John Richard Fletcher, and then converted to Universalism by Elhanan Winchester; Rush, "Travels Through Life."

education was especially required in Pennsylvania, since "our citizens are composed of the natives of so many different kingdoms in Europe" – and he felt the Bible was meant to serve as the standard for that education. All Americans, he argued, should be taught with the Bible, because it shared a standard base of morals. "The only means of establishing and perpetuating our republican forms of government," he argued, was "the universal education of our youth in the principles of christianity, by means of the Bible." The Bible, above all other texts, "favors that equality among mankind, that respect for just laws, and all those sober and frugal virtues, which constitute the soul of republicanism." Even if his own private beliefs did not match the religious mainstream, his commitment to a unified religious instruction permeated his nationalist vision. Indeed, biblical education represented the limits of Rush's comfort with diversity, because he did not appear comfortable with those who veered far away from the trodden path. "By producing one general, and uniform system of education," he explained, it "will render the mass of the people more homogeneous, and thereby fit them more easily for uniform and peacable government." Religion was required, but it had to be the correct form of religious guidance.[54]

This emphasis on Protestantism's dominance may seem odd for someone who was outside of the mainstream of Christianity. But his insistence on a religious tradition with which he was never fully comfortable captures an important element of Rush's nationalist vision: a pragmatic cooperation and desire for pluralism, albeit within certain parameters. Unlike the case made by the evangelical culture that would soon dominate American religion, Rush's conception of American Christianity was both vague and broad. In later, private ruminations, Rush explained his refusal to discuss his Universalism in public by saying that it would have alienated him from certain segments of society. Pragmatically, he felt that public discussions of eternal punishment, in which he did not believe, were helpful because they promoted good actions. In his words, it "restrained sinning." Even if the doctrines were not completely true, they provided the framework for proper citizenship.[55]

[54] Rush, *Defence*, 34. Benjamin Rush, *A Plan for the Establishment of Public Schools and the Diffusion of Knowledge in Pennsylvania; to which are Added Thoughts upon the Mode of Education, Proper in a Republic. Addressed to the Legislature and Citizens of the State* (Philadelphia: Thomas Dobson, 1786), 14.
[55] See his section on "Universalism," in his "Commonplace Book, 1792–1813," 322.

Rush was able to hold such a pragmatic religious framework in part because of the culture of religious difference present in Pennsylvania. Though settled as a Quaker colony, William Penn's "Holy Experiment" proved so successful at attracting immigrants from various nations and cultures that Quakers lost their majority in the state very early in the eighteenth century. And while Anglicanism maintained a strong presence in the state, Scottish and Irish immigration brought a large influx of Presbyterianism, and German settlers introduced Lutheran congregations along with smaller, and more radical, pietistic sects like the Moravians. Though some of these religious groups, particularly the German communities, refrained from becoming involved in mainstream Pennsylvania culture, the decades following the Revolution witnessed an increased mobilization that ensured a much more dynamic participation by the state's many religions and ethnicities. This set a standard for interreligious cooperation.[56]

In Pennsylvania, religion played a significant role as a unifying mechanism to which many different people could relate. But importantly, that success hinged on the state's refusal to institute a political test for doctrinal purity. That is, religion had principles, but not dogma. By cultivating an ecumenical support devoid of theological particulars, politicians could draw from a broader array of participants. The reality of numerous denominations in the state fighting for equal power forced a cultural framework that emphasized practice over belief. To the North, on the other hand, belief and practice went hand in hand. Noah Webster, himself a skeptic who was frustrated with his region's emphasis on correct doctrine during the 1780s and 1790s, complained that "every man in New-England is a theologian." Lived realities in the various states, therefore, introduced a divergence in providential narratives concerning religion's relationship to the nation, which often resulted in competing political theologies that had both ideological and practical implications.[57]

Rush's embrace of a broad yet unified body of Christian believers hints at his vision for society. His ideal Americans were social beings who

---

[56] For the early decline of Quaker dominance, see Gary B. Nash, *Quakers and Politics: Pennsylvania, 1681–1726* (Princeton, NJ: Princeton University Press, 1968).

[57] Webster, *Sketches*, 29. Webster's uncomfortable relationship with New England clergy is discussed in Joshua Kendall, *The Forgotten Founding Father: Noah Webster's Obsession and the Creation of an American Culture* (New York: Putnam, 2011), 264–266. For national covenants, see Nicholas Guyatt, *Providence and the Invention of the United States* (Cambridge: Cambridge University Press, 2007), 95–136, which has an especial focus on, and numerous examples from, New England.

understood themselves first and foremost in relation to their broader community despite religious, cultural, or ideological differences. Influenced by the social thought of Scottish philosophers like Frances Hutcheson, who consciously rejected the individualistic philosophies of people like Bernard Mandeville, Rush conceived of humans as sociable beings. In his memoirs, he recalled the strong "moral order" he experienced in Edinburgh during his studies. "This universal morality was not accidental," he reasoned. Rather, it was the effect of the "parochial instructions" of societal unity and the philosophical foundations of social necessity preached by city leaders. These local contexts and circumstances gave meaning to ideas, and guidance to individuals. The idea of a society working together, a principle central to works like Adam Smith's *Theory of Moral Sentiment*, buttressed Rush's later ideas of nationalism. An individual only achieved importance while in relation to a broader community.[58]

These views were largely reinforced by – or, perhaps, originated with – the Pennsylvanian culture that placed a premium on social participation. A culture founded as a heterogeneous society that included people from many different backgrounds, Rush's environment placed a premium on forfeiting one's interests on behalf of the community. Not only was society important, but it was meant to be large enough to embrace conflicting ideals and beliefs while still strong enough to forge a community based on shared allegiances. For Rush and other Pennsylvanians, this often meant cultivating a space in which local citizens could participate in as well as shape political and social structures. When Robert Woodruff, secretary to the British Loyalist claims official John Anstey on his tour through America shortly after the Revolution, visited Philadelphia in 1787, he noted that the city revolved around "volunteer societies" and "elected conventions." Groups like the Society of the Cincinnati, the American Philosophical Society, and many other social organizations, while perhaps maintaining a national membership, played a central role in Pennsylvania social life and shaped how citizens formed local and national allegiances.[59]

Rush's nationalism lacked both the homogeneity and exceptionalist strains more common in New England. This was largely because his

---

[58] Rush, "Travels Through Life," n.p.
[59] Robert Woodruff, "Travel Journal, December 17, 1785–May 1, 1788," manuscript, 58, APS. See also Albrecht Koschnik, *"Let a Common Interest Bind Us Together": Associations, Partisanship, and Culture in Philadelphia, 1775–1840* (Charlottesville: University of Virginia Press, 2007).

experience necessitated the acknowledgement of a broad range of cultures and ideas. Thomas Paine, who experienced the same Pennsylvanian culture as Rush, similarly wrote in 1790, "If there is a country in the world where concord, according to common calculation, would be least expected, it is America." Since the nation was made up "of people from different nations, accustomed to different forms and habits of government, speaking different languages, and more different in their modes of worship," Paine explained, "it would appear that the union of such a people was impracticable." At the time Rush was conceptualizing a framework for his new nation, two-fifths of the people who shared his state spoke German, a reality that most in the area had come to accept and incorporate into their imagined political body. In his letter advising potential immigrants, Rush spent several pages detailing all the different cultures brought to Pennsylvania from various countries, all of which added to the diversity of the region. "The variety of sects and nations, which compose the inhabitants of this state, has hitherto prevented our having any steady traits in our character," he confessed. But a result of "this variety" and "collision in opinions and interests" was that the state as a whole had been "greatly favoured [by] the progress of genius in every art and science." Diversity, in the end, was not a hindrance to national genius, but a foundation for virtue because it forced cooperation.[60]

Not every region had the same appreciation for diversity. In the states that composed New England, for instance, an emphasis on centralized authority, cultural submission, and even ethnic purity, influenced by the region's religious framework, led writers to decry deviation. Webster, perhaps more than any other individual in early America, desired a standardized national character – he was, after all, known for his project to install a unified dialect. "A national language is a national tie, and what country wants it more than America?" he asked in 1786. He was especially averse to the Southern states' refusal to adopt Northern cultural ideas. "Every prejudice, every dissocial passion is an enemy to a friendly intercourse and the fuel of discord," he exclaimed. "Nothing can be more illiberal than the prejudices of the Southern states against New-England manners," Webster bemoaned. "They deride our manners and by that derision betray the want of manners themselves." This problem had led to regional strife and national problems. One of Webster's primary

---

[60] Thomas Paine, "The Rights of Man, Part Second" in *The Complete Writings of Thomas Paine*, ed. Philip S. Foner, 2 vols. (New York: Citadel Press, 1969): 1:345–362, p. 360; Rush, *Information*, 12.

arguments for a national constitution in 1785 was that it would unify American culture. "Education will gradually eradicate [local prejudices], and a growing intercourse will harmonize the feelings and the views of all the citizens" he reasoned. Only the "removal of local prejudices" and "the annihilation of local interests" could solve the nation's ills. "We ought not to consider ourselves as inhabitants of a particular state only," Webster urged in the closing of his pamphlet, "but as *Americans*." He went on: "As the common subjects of a great empire[, we] cannot and ought not wholly to divest ourselves of provincial views and attachments; but we should subordinate them to the general interests of the continent." There was only one true vision of the American nation.[61]

This debate highlights a prime divergence between Rush and Webster. Based on the influence of his local context, Rush imagined a nation centered on compromise, collaboration, and a variegation of culture. This vision was rooted in his Pennsylvania context. Those in Massachusetts or, more broadly, New England, on the other hand, pointed to eventual conformity, consent, and a centralized authority. Webster's vision was therefore more centralized and homogenous. Both of these views had real political consequences, which included the government's role in dictating social order, the extent of federal sovereignty, and the nation's involvement with foreign countries. For instance, Webster warned, "we can have no union, no respectability, no national character, and what is more, no national justice, till the states resign to one *supreme head* the exclusive power of *legislating, judging and executing*, in all matters of general nature." This merging of societal critique with federal policy demonstrated the connection between the two in Webster's mind. To fulfill the necessity of cultural unification, Webster argued, the states must relinquish their individual sovereignties in favor of the broader nation. From this perspective, national deference took priority over provincial tradition.[62]

Faced with the prospect of a new nation, and plagued with the anxiety of creating a national culture, Rush and Webster, along with other Americans in the decade, appropriated their surrounding ideas, assumptions, and traditions, and projected an idea that was patterned after their own imagination. This meant different frameworks and definitions for a perceivably shared political discourse. For Rush, "federal" meant the

---

[61] Noah Webster to Timothy Pickering, May 25, 1786, in Harry Warfel, ed., *Letters of Noah Webster* (New York: Library Publishers, 1953), 52. Webster, *Sketches*, 44–45, 48.
[62] Webster, *An Examination*, 28. (Emphasis in original.)

confederation of disparate beliefs and ideas within an interconnected web that preserved the liberty of each expression. For Webster, it implied a cultural colonialism that spread from the government outward to all who were governed. In the same 1788 letter where Webster announced to Rush his "federal" project, he explained that "the best publications in Europe are conducted by societies of literary gentlemen" and cultivated a unified culture, primarily by providing "a mutual knowledge of the state of every part of America." Rush apparently demurred at the overall plan, because in his next letter Webster insisted the paper would not follow the "Philadelphia" model encapsulated by Rush's projects. Such a divergence in views concerning a magazine was indicative of their broader culturally conditioned paradigms concerning a nation.[63]

The decade following America's independence witnessed the first examples of citizens attempting to think federally, even before an institutional structure existed to validate those expressions. As John Tomlinson has rightly noted, the "'lived reality' of national identity" is found "in representations – not in direct communal solidarity." Yet these ideas had long-lasting ramifications as they culminated in federal and national institutions that outlived temporary debates. Ironically, these new institutions and ideas also set the stage for conflict due to their contested nature. Even the document that resulted from these cultural movements in 1787, which was designed to tether the various states together through a federal bond, was interpreted differently based on local traditions. This laid the foundation for later conflict as states became aware of what they interpreted to be constitutional misreadings and factional schism. This was a culture under transformation. The term "nation" was in the midst of a linguistic transition, as citizens in America and abroad reconceptualized what it meant to lend allegiance to a political body and what that allegiance had to do with cultural practice and the nature of society. Nationalism, then, was an imaginative, fraught, and local affair, despite its broader aspirations and appeals to the contrary.[64]

[63] Webster to Rush, February 10, 1788; Webster to Rush, February 24, 1788, Benjamin Rush Collection, HSP.
[64] John Tomlinson, *Cultural Imperialism: A Critical Introduction* (Baltimore, MD: ACLS Humanities, 1991), 83–84.

2

Local Preachers, Thanksgiving Sermons, and New England's National Covenant

As the principles and circumstances which dispose and constrain a people to assume a national capacity, and form a civil government, originate from God, and operate under the superintendency of his Providence, their national state and character are the effect of his appointment and agency, and he may be said to be their former and Creator.

–Levi Frisbie, 1795[1]

God having chosen them for his peculiar people, was pleased to raise them to distinguished eminence above other nations, in regard to privileges and benefits, both of a secular and religious nature; making them acquainted with his perfections, and instructing them in their duty, by special and extraordinary communications.

–Henry Cumings, 1797[2]

Religion framed how Anglo-Americans in the eighteenth century understood the world around them. One's relationship to God and God's relationship to a particular nation were key principles when conceiving a political body. In the premodern world, God was the one who organized communities around divinely appointed leaders, as the heads of state often coincided with the heads of church. Patriotism was therefore a religious rite. The American experiment, however, challenged this tradition on multiple fronts. First, the

---

[1] Levi Frisbie, *A Sermon Delivered February 19, 1795: The Day of Public Thanksgiving through the United States. Recommended by the President* (Newburyport, MA: Blunt and March, 1795), 10.

[2] Henry Cumings, *A Sermon Preached at Billerica, December 15, 1796, Being the Day Appointed by Authority, to be Observed Throughout the Commonwealth of Massachusetts, as a Day of Public Praise and Thanksgiving* (Boston: Thomas Fleet, 1797), 6.

diversity of religious belief and practice present in the newly united states upended basic expectations for homogeneous communities. And second, the federal Constitution formally abolished the establishment of religion at the national level. Yet conventional notions concerning religion's importance to governance remained. For many, religious ideas and practices still shaped their ideas of nation and union, even if those ideas diverged by region based on provincial customs and denominational dominance.

One particularly useful test case for process was national days of thanksgivings, in which local ministers appropriated presidential messages to fit parochial concerns. Congregationalist ministers in Massachusetts, a state that sought to perpetuate notions of ecclesiastical privilege and homogeneous theological compacts, were especially adept at molding national directives for their local flock. But spiritual authorities followed similar patterns elsewhere. And though their political theologies were steeped in America's new democratic experiment, they were simultaneously responding to similar religious anxieties present across the Atlantic world, where forms of radical dissent challenged basic beliefs regarding cultural unity. At a moment of transformation away from traditional models of denominational dominance, how could political order maintain some form of stability? This chapter details how American religionists in general, and Massachusetts Congregationalists in particular, constructed a sense of theological belonging that was rife with anxiety over state, regional, and national belonging.

Jeremy Belknap lived a mostly unremarkable life for much of his ministerial career. Born in Boston, educated at Harvard, and eventually appointed to a pulpit in Dover, New Hampshire, Belknap did not experience much that would differentiate himself from other New England ministers during the Revolutionary era. The only complaints from his parishioners were that he maintained a haughty attitude and delivered sermons so dull that he "scarcely" seemed "to even move his lips." Though Dover was a rural town of no more than 1,500 inhabitants, Belknap maintained an impressive correspondence with other ministers, politicians, and lettered men throughout the nation. And like his Puritan ancestors, he reached beyond his clerical role to embrace the profession of historian by writing the three-volume *History of New Hampshire* and the two-volume *American Biography*.[3]

[3] Louis L. Tucker, *Clio's Consort: Jeremy Belknap and the Founding of the Massachusetts Historical Society* (Charlottesville: University of Virginia Press, 2005), 12. Background for Belknap is from Tucker, *Clio's Consort*; George B. Kirsch, *Jeremy Belknap: A Biography*

While Belknap, like many Congregational ministers during the period, had no problem mixing nationalism with providentialism, his early writings recognized there was a careful balance to be kept between the two. Even if both religion and politics were important parts of his life, Belknap tried to keep church and state separate from each other in his two spheres of labor: on the one hand, Belknap wrote new sermons nearly every week – typically, several drafts of each sermon – that he carefully polished and preserved for his congregants and posterity; on the other hand, Belknap was intricately involved with the organization of both local and federal politics, and he maintained a voluminous correspondence with many of the figures that constructed America's governments during the 1780s. Yet neither written record, at least prior to 1786, ever mentioned the other – his sermons were devoid of political ideas, and his politics were devoid of religious rhetoric. Even his Fourth of July orations were empty of nationalism. His sermon on July 4, 1783, for instance, did not mention America, but rather focused on how "G[od] takes pleasure & delight in the *world* & its inhabitants for they are all conformed to him, partakers of his nature & image of his person." For the most part, Belknap wrote for a religious audience lacking national affiliation and a community of believers that could reside in any nation and any part of the world.[4]

But such an apolitical context for his sermons did not last. When the partisan factions of the early 1790s swept over the United States, Belknap's loyalty to the Federalist Party played a larger role in his thinking. His sermons decried radical democratic initiatives and, increasingly, foreign influences. Belknap's pulpit, like that of many other ministers during the period, became mobilized for political purposes. His 1797 thanksgiving sermon, for instance, addressed several timely social and political topics, such as a denouncement of France's atheism, a reminder of the "benevolent Providence" behind the American Constitution, as well as a defense of the national bank. As historians have demonstrated, this rhetorical strain was introduced in reaction to broader international factors, especially the French Revolution, that mobilized particular clergy in support of the Federalist Party.[5]

(New York: Arno Press, 1982); Russell M. Lawson, *The American Plutarch: Jeremy Belknap and the Historian's Dialogue with the Past* (Westport, CT: Praeger, 1998).

[4] Jeremy Belknap, sermon, July 4, 1783, 4, JBP. Jeremy Belknap, *The History of New Hampshire*, 3 vols. (Boston: Isaiah Thomas, 1784–1792).

[5] Jeremy Belknap, Thanksgiving Sermon, 1797, 1–4, JBP. See Gary B. Nash, "The American Clergy and the French Revolution," *William and Mary Quarterly* 22 (July 1965): 392–412; Rachel Hope Cleves, *The Reign of Terror in America: Visions of Violence*

There was another instigator for Belknap's transition toward a more
vocal political theology: his move from New Hampshire to Boston. He
assumed the pulpit of the city's Long Lane Church in 1787, which placed
him, for the first time since his studies at Harvard, in one of America's
most bustling cities. As a result, his local interactions with local politicians
and statesmen – including his founding of and participation in the
Massachusetts Historical Society in 1791 – began to influence his religious
duties, and his sermons began to include commentary on the ever-present
issues of the day. Even before the partisan battles between Federalists and
Jeffersonians, Belknap's religious discourse reflected his new locality by
trumpeting the provincial ideas and concerns that were then commonly
discussed in Boston. Local contexts cultivated particular expectations,
ideologies, and standards, which then reflected and reaffirmed provincial
ideas. Even Belknap, who had previously engaged in transnational discussions regarding religion, history, and politics, was both reliant on and
indicative of the immediate context in which he was placed.[6]

Even while rooted in his new context, Belknap and his fellow
Massachusetts ministers were still left to respond to a broader religious
climate that was in transition. The federal government had disestablished
religion, and while Massachusetts retained a privileged status for
Congregationalist churches for several more decades, the growth of competing religious sects, partisan discord, and even perceived deistic assaults
threatened to undermine the region's social stability. Events in the broader
Atlantic world appeared even more dire. Though Britain provided models
through which religion could supplement political rule, France's
Revolution shook common assumptions regarding ecclesiastical authority
in republican governments. The fear of France's "atheistic" influence
permeated Massachusetts sermons and hinted to religion's crucial role in
society. "The French nation," Belknap bellowed in 1792, is "subject to the
passions & prejudices of lawless rioters." Their "old God" is "dissolved
& their new one weak & imperfect." France's irreligion would only lead

---

from Anti-Jacobinism to Antislavery (New York: Cambridge University Press, 2009);
Matthew Rainbow Hale, "'Many Who Wandered in Darkness': The Contest over
American National Identity, 1795–1798," *Early American Studies* 1 (Spring 2003):
127–175.

[6] New Hampshire was the ninth state to ratify the Constitution, and it only did so after
a contentious debate that resulted in a long list of proposed amendments. In order to match
the climate, then, Belknap's sermons in the state read much like other sermons delivered in
New Hampshire. But once in Massachusetts, where his success and popularity were
connected to a new political climate and cultural rhetoric, his sermons matched others
that were being delivered in Boston.

them to anarchy. But what role *should* religion play in a new representative democracy? Like many of his contemporaries, Belknap struggled to imagine a united nation that could simultaneously be a chosen people.[7]

Despite the prevalence of religion in early America, historians still debate religion's role in American politics. The Revolution has been described as a "profoundly secular event," and ministers are typically depicted as responding to political developments. The new climate democratized religion, this narrative argues, and those denominations willing to adapt to a new environment gained dominance. Though a short challenge from Deism and skepticism was vanquished, ministers for the most part adopted the new civic constraints placed on ecclesiastical denominations. This is typically seen as the first step in America's path toward secularization, a separation between church and state was engrained into the nation's political culture.[8]

Yet this traditional narrative has been challenged of late. Even in a disestablished culture in which religion was pushed to the voluntarist sphere, denominations and ministers still played a crucial role in the formation of political ideals and practices. On the one hand, the emphasis on human potential and equality energized political mobilization and often fueled the developing Jeffersonian party. Simultaneously, conceptions of humanity's fallen nature allowed others to capitalize on the fear, distrust, and deception that followed political turnover, which resulted in Federalist control and partisan engagement. Just as the Revolution reoriented ideas of religious establishment following independence, so too did religious traditions shape civic engagement and citizenship belonging in the new nation. Even as they celebrated religious liberty through the separation of church and state, most imagined an unofficial alliance between the two as they worked toward the same goals. As one study on religious nationalism recently summarized, "the War of Independence posed rather than answered the question of American nationality."

---

[7] Jeremy Belknap, Thanksgiving Sermon, 1792, 18, JBP.
[8] Jon Butler, *Awash in a Sea of Faith: Christianizing the American People* (Cambridge: Harvard University Press, 1992), 195. See also Butler, "Coercion, Miracle, Reason," in *Religion in a Revolutionary Age*, ed. Ronald Hoffman and Peter J. Albert (Charlottesville: University Press of Virginia, 1994), 1–30, p. 19; Nathan Hatch, *The Democratization of American Christianity* (New Haven, CT: Yale University Press, 1989).

Religious ministers and activists were crucial to cultivating a lasting solution.[9]

There was a larger context for this phenomenon. To explore not only how political culture transformed religion but also how religion transformed political culture is to acknowledge that the Age of Revolution presented a number of competing models for civic theologies. As Linda Colley has demonstrated, religion provided the framework for British ideas of nationalism during the eighteenth century by piecing together the many disparate notions of patriotism and loyalty within their conception of providentialism. It would be expected, then, that Americans engendered something similar. Similarly, David Bell has argued that religion was at the center of French nationalistic thought before and during their revolution, as revolutionaries drew from both religious ideas concerning universal brotherhood as well as the ecclesiastical mobilization of the Catholic Church. Indeed, contrary to the previous literature on the Age of Democratic Revolutions that ignored religion and emphasized the secular nature of enlightenment thought, most scholars now agree that the political transformations that took place in the Atlantic world at the end of the eighteenth century were closely connected to a religious awakening that cultivated robust political theologies.[10]

For Americans in particular, the duties and obligations of citizenship were intimately tied to religious belief. Republican governance required a strident commitment to morals that many posited could only come from Christian teachings. The threat of deism – never a large numerical presence American society – presented an outsized peril in the minds of

---

[9] Sam Haselby, *The Origins of American Religious Nationalism* (New York: Oxford University Press, 2015), 1. See also Amanda Porterfield, *Conceived in Doubt: Religion and Politics in the New American Nation* (Chicago: University of Chicago Press, 2012); Spencer W. McBride, *Pulpit and Nation: Clergymen and the Politics of Revolutionary America* (Charlottesville: University of Virginia Press, 2017). For the merging of religion and republicanism, see Mark A. Noll, *America's God: From Jonathan Edwards to Abraham Lincoln* (New York: Oxford University Press, 2002). For general treatments of American religion during the period, see Butler, *Awash in a Sea of Faith*; Hatch, *Democratization of American Christianity*; Jonathan D. Sassi, *Republic of Righteousness: The Public Christianity of the Post-Revolutionary New England Clergy* (New York: Oxford University Press, 2008); Monica Najar, *Evangelizing the South: A Social History of Church and State in Early America* (New York: Oxford University Press, 2008); Jonathan Den Hartog, *Patriotism and Piety: Federalist Politics and Religious Struggle in the New American Nation* (Charlottesville: University of Virginia Press, 2015).

[10] Linda Colley, *Britons: Forging the Nation, 1707–1837*, rev. ed. (New Haven, CT: Yale University Press, 2009), 18, 54. David A. Bell, *The Cult of the Nation in France: Inventing Nationalism, 1680–1800* (Cambridge: Harvard University Press, 2001), 7–8.

ministers and politicians who feared that the shedding of traditional Christian values could only introduce anarchy. Rumors of skepticism and unbelief prompted alarm and retrenchment. The revolutionary age introduced as much cause for uncertainly as it did modes of governance. Even if clergymen lost intellectual authority in the wake of the Revolution, that did not depress the religiosity of their congregants. In response, many elites constructed a model of Christian common sense that underwrote much of their civic dialogue.[11]

However, it should not be taken for granted that the connections between civic and religious identities were inevitable. America's eventual blend of a religious nationalism was not the only model available. In France, nationalism was remarkably atheological prior to 1800. According to Bell, French citizens "increasingly defined themselves not as Catholics, or subjects, but as members of a *société, public, nation*, or *patrie* (and soon, *civilisation*) – forms of association that were not structured from without, by a God or a king, but arose from supposedly natural human qualities such as 'sociability' or 'patriotism.'" In conflicts with other nations, especially the English, the enemy was more often depicted as "barbaric" than as "heretical," a linguistic distinction that signified their lack of civilization, not a paucity of true belief. The subtle yet silent underpinning of their political theology was the Catholic commitment to universal humanity and the belief that all individuals were sinners in need of salvation – whether religious or secular. This would change during the French Revolution, of course, but in doing so, it introduced new possibilities as well. The resulting form of universal regeneration, for instance, eschewed the rhetoric of theological dogma at the center of a nationalist symbol. Yet that would not be the case in other revolutionary contexts, including in the example of the colonial revolution in Haiti.[12]

This is to be contrasted with the cultural heritage America received from Britain. There was a distinct link between God and government in Protestant England – and a particular God, at that. Religious universalism possessed much less capital, as the church was sponsored by the state and led by the crown rather than a foreign pope. When the leader of a religion overlapped with the leader of the empire, it was much easier to assume

---

[11] See Christopher Grasso, "Deist Monster: On Religious Common Sense in the Wake of the American Revolution," *Journal of American History* 95 (June 2008): 43–68.

[12] Bell, *The Cult of the Nation in France*, 47, 53, 84. For Haiti's religious context, see Terry Rey, *The Priest and the Prophetess: Abbé Ouvière, Romaine Rivière, and the Revolutionary Atlantic World* (New York: Oxford University Press, 2017).

that the two entities' interests aligned. But even here, neither Scotland or Ireland shared English's state-sponsored church within the British union. Ireland's religious allegiance pointed toward Rome, and Scotland's toward a Reformed Presbyterianism. These multifaceted tensions introduced a form of nationalism that collated disparate national bodies under the same king. So even the nationalist lineage inherited by Anglo-Americans was fraught with contested notions of ecclesiastical and secular alliance.[13]

America's resulting form of religious nationalism was in many ways both a response to these other traditions as well as a result of their parochial cultural climates. The varying degrees of disestablishment in particular states cultivated unique forms of patriotic imagination, as did the presence of competing denominations. Yet one anxiety transcended particular contexts: the urge to invoke a religious form of national belonging. The reciprocal relationship between local influence and national concerns produced a dialectic of appropriation and projection. For instance, while it is important to note that Jeremy Belknap's sermons represented how local culture shaped a minister's message, it is also important to recognize the reciprocal fact: that his weekly message played an important role in shaping those communities as well. For many Americans, including those in Belknap's congregations, it was from the pulpit that they learned their civic duties. To a significant extent, religious discourse shaped how American citizens understood their new nation. These messages they heard from the clergy also helped to shape their worldview in ways far more concrete than just the idea of God.[14]

Thanksgiving sermons provide an apt example of how the boundaries of local and national, religious and political were blended in the young republic. Starting with the Continental Congress during and immediately following the Revolution, and continued by George Washington and John Adams during their presidential terms, these were occasions in which the

---

[13] Carla Gardina Pestana, *Protestant Empire: Religion and the Making of the British Atlantic World* (Philadelphia: University of Pennsylvania Press, 2009), 33–99; Stewart J. Brown, *The National Churches of England, Ireland, and Scotland, 1801–1846* (New York: Oxford University Press, 2001).

[14] For the importance of sermons at the local level, especially in Belknap's region, see Harry S. Stout, *The New England Soul: Preaching and Religious Culture in Colonial New England* (New York: Oxford University Press, 1986); Stout "Rhetoric and Reality in the Early Republic: The Case of the Federalist Clergy," in *Religion and American Politics*, ed. Mark A. Noll (New York: Oxford University Press, 1990), 62–76.

federal government declared a Day of National Thanksgiving to be observed by all citizens. These festivities often included a published message from the president that was then delivered in public gatherings within local communities. "Whereas it is the duty of all Nations to acknowledge the Providence of Almighty God," George Washington declared in his first thanksgiving proclamation in 1789, "I do recommend and assign Thursday the 26th day of November next to be devoted by the People of these States to the service of that great and glorious Being, who is the beneficent Author of all the good that was, that is, or that will be." Americans were to be thankful "for the great degree of tranquility, union, and plenty, which we have since enjoyed." Celebrating this unity and peace, of course, was a political message in and of itself.[15]

The government's use of ministers and churches to disseminate political ideas was not new, especially within the Anglo-American context. The close relationship between the Church of England and the British crown enabled constant cross pollination in messages. State functions, including coronations, often took place in religious settings, reinforcing the intersectionality between the two spheres. This dynamic was replicated in other nations. Even following revolutions in France and Poland, the seat of political power in both contexts remained close to the altar, as secular pronouncements were still preached from the pulpit. Revolutionaries in France, though seemingly hostile to organized religion in general and the Catholic Church in particular, appropriated Catholic forms of instruction in their attempt to educate the masses. Yet in America, where there was supposedly no nationally established religion, it was a more precarious balance to affirm religious liberty but still utilize religious structures of power.[16]

---

[15] George Washington, "Thanksgiving Proclamation, October 3, 1789," *Papers of George Washington*, http://lcweb2.loc.gov/ammem/GW/gw4.jpg (accessed November 2012). Spencer McBride has argued that fast and thanksgiving sermons provided a tool for union during the Revolution. McBride, *Pulpit and Nation*, 11–37. David Waldstreicher argues that these sermons were primarily used as partisan tools as a way for clergy to regain authority in postrevolutionary America. Waldstreicher, *In the Midst of Perpetual Fetes: The Making of American Nationalism, 1776–1820* (Chapel Hill: University of North Carolina Press, 1997), 145–152. While both authors acknowledge the political tools of these events, they often understate the theological and intellectual underpinnings of these sermons. These were more than political platforms.

[16] Bell, *Cult of the Nation in France*, 7–10; Pestana, *Protestant Empire*; R.R. Palmer, *The Age of Democratic Revolution: A Political History of Europe and America, 1760–1800*, 2nd ed. (1959–1964; Princeton: Princeton University Press, 2014), 635–641.

There was a long intellectual genealogy for shaping national images within a Protestant framework. Most political thinkers believed that successful nations utilized state-sponsored religions which served as a purposeful tool in many fronts. In Britain, religion served as a melding force that streamlined the state's message and sacralized the nation's purpose. When the British Empire was originally conceived, Protestantism was seen as "the solvent of difference within the Three Kingdoms," an idea that became a staple within their nationalist thought – even if it was never fully realized. While religious diversity plagued the attempted conquest of cultural unity, many maintained that only under a shared notion of God could any sense of "Britishness" be accomplished. Even David Hume, a religious skeptic, believed that there was a universal human trait of fear that required religion to bring stability, order, and authority to a central government. Adam Smith similarly noted, "the clergy of every established church constitute a great incorporation," because as emissaries of the state they "can act in concert, and spirit, as much as if they were under the direction of one man." A collaborative religious identity, then, provided the tools through which Britishness was constructed: it allowed a providential chronology, divine authority, and sacralized common cause. Protestantism – and a shared Protestantism, at that – was central to British theories of nations during the Age of Revolutions.[17]

These ideas remained present in America following the Revolution. Far from a purely secular event, the War for Independence was understood by many citizens to be a religious revolt steeped in religiously infused conceptions of liberty. When constructing new state (and later, national) governments, religious principles were explicitly introduced into political policies. Most states required officeholders to be Protestant, affirm the reality of heaven and hell, and profess belief in the Trinity. John Adams, when writing the third article of Massachusetts's Declaration of Rights, argued that because "the happiness of a people and the good order and preservation of civil government essentially depend upon piety, religion,

[17] David Armitage, *The Ideological Origins of the British Empire* (Cambridge: Cambridge University Press, 2000), 61. Adam Smith, *An Inquiry into the Nature and Causes of the Wealth of Nations* (1776; Chicago: University of Chicago Press, 1976), 319. See also Leah Greenfield, *Nationalism: Five Roads to Modernity* (Cambridge: Harvard University Press), 51; Colley, *Britons*, 53–54. Hume's extended views on religion are found in *Dialogues Concerning Natural Religion*, 2nd ed. (London, 1779). For the role of religion in Hume's conception of government, see Timothy S. Yoder, *Hume on God: Irony, Deism, and Genuine Theism* (New York: Continuum, 2008), 135–136.

and morality," the legislature had the right to establish a state-funded religion "for the support and maintenance of public Protestant teachers of piety, religion, and morality in all cases where such provisions shall not be made voluntarily." Though the rise of evangelical sects soon challenged, and defeated, this notion of established churches, it was a potent belief at the heart of how many conceived a country's origin, purpose, and practice.[18]

Virginia proved to be the testing ground for a new mode of religious governance. Unorthodox elites like Thomas Jefferson and James Madison partnered with enthusiastic religious groups like the Baptists to confront the traditional form of religious toleration. Some leading figures, like Patrick Henry, echoed John Adams's defense of a loose form of religious establishment as necessary for social stability. Freedom of religious practice was assured, but structures of religious privilege should also be maintained. In response, anti-establishment proponents constructed arguments for a free marketplace for religious beliefs that matched the intellectual landscape of the new nation. Eventually the radical form of religious liberty won out, and its pattern was slowly replicated throughout the rest of the states. Yet more than disquieting Christian patriotism, the new religious libertarian climate heightened the anxiety over proving spiritual belonging.[19]

It is not a surprise, then, that the national government took advantage of these cultural tendencies in proclaiming National Days of Thanksgiving. Yet they were also dependent on immediate context and the personality of those in charge. George Washington's thanksgiving proclamations, published in 1789 and 1795, were very general in nature and focused on the perceived blessings bestowed by a benevolent God. Adams's thanksgiving proclamations of 1797 and 1798, by contrast, were much more partisan. Clergymen were free to interpret and enlarge upon these proclamations, and they often did so in ways that both revealed and retrenched local themes, tensions, and issues. Where the president was vague in both doctrinal matters and political application, the clergy were often explicit. Proclamations often invoked the generic "nature's God" of

---

[18] Constitution of the Commonwealth of Massachusetts, Part the First, Article Three, https://malegislature.gov/Laws/Constitution (accessed July 2014).

[19] See Frank Lambert, *The Founding Fathers and the Place of Religion in America* (Princeton: Princeton University Press, 2003), 207–287; John Ragosta, *Religious Freedom: Jefferson's Legacy, America's Creed* (Charlottesville: University of Virginia Press, 2013); Thomas E. Buckley, *Establishing Religious Freedom: Jefferson's Statute in Virginia* (Charlottesville: University of Virginia Press, 2014).

the Enlightenment, while most ministers made sure to clarify that it was the God of Protestant Christianity at America's helm. Proclamations were designed to bolster the president's current policies, yet ministers used them as vindication for their own political and religious views. And while the proclamations were designed to unify the disparate states, local appropriation often reinforced regional difference.

In general, clergymen recognized thanksgiving sermons as necessary for reminding citizens of their dependence on God. "Perhaps no other nation under heaven, at any period of time," preached John Murray in Boston, "hath had so much reason to praise the name of God with songs, and to magnify him with thanksgiving, as we have." The proclamation of such a religious message from the government was seen as a necessity for national unity – even in a disestablished nation. Understood as far from a mandatory practice of religious control, it was merely, according to Philadelphia minister George Duffield, a "summary survey of the contest wherein our country has been engaged, to excite gratitude to God, in your hearts and my own, for his great goodness bestowed upon us." Jeremy Belknap described the "practice" of thanksgiving sermons as "rational & useful, & it is our duty to obey the voice of our rulers, which in fact is the same thing with our own context; for our rulers would not call us to any duty witho[ut] knowing before hand if it was reasonable & practiceable." This merging of civic and religious duties revealed the assumption of religion's role within American nationalism, as patriotic duty merged with religious piety. Even if all citizens were free to practice their various religious faiths, this reasoning implied, the nation still owed an allegiance to God for that freedom.[20]

Providentialism was, of course, far from new, as it had been crucial to European conceptions of empire for centuries. One historian has noted that "Christian providentialism" was the "ideological taproot of British Imperialism." But more than serving as a symbol for Britain's evolving imperial ambitions, God's providential hand was identified as the cause for the nation's progress. From Oliver Cromwell in the seventeenth century to Edmund Burke in the eighteenth, a trenchant belief in divine involvement pervaded British political discourse and conceptions of

[20] John Murray, *The Substance of a Thanksgiving Sermon, Delivered at the Universal Meeting-House, in Boston, February 19, 1795* (Boston: John W. Folsom, 1795), 15. George Duffield, *A Sermon, Preached in the Third Presbyterian Church, in the City of Philadelphia, On Thursday, December 11, 1783* (Philadelphia: F. Bailey, 1783), iii. Jeremy Belknap, Thanksgiving Sermon, November 20, 1794, 2, JBP.

their empire. Even as Enlightenment ideas challenged principles of particular providence, broad perceptions of divine control remained intact.
Richard Price, who contested Britain's argument for divine right and
defended America's independence, still maintained that nations are
blessed only inasmuch as they followed principles of liberty that originate
with and are governed by God. In turn, Americans readily adapted these
ideas in their new political contexts following separation from Britain.
Thanksgiving sermons were one format to do so.[21]

Not every region, nor every denomination, embraced these patriotic
festivities with the same enthusiasm. Local ideas and practices, along with
theological and cultural traditions, either enabled or hindered the introduction of these religious and political rituals. In Massachusetts, where it was
common for ministers to play a predominant role in political affairs, and
where community and state functions often involved both religious rhetoric
and an ecclesiastical setting, thanksgiving sermons were easily embedded
into civic life. These national observances quickly became part of their
liturgical calendar. This was especially true with Congregationalists, as
they retained an established position within the state. When a Day of
Thanksgiving was declared, and a message was delivered to the local
community, it was assumed that the minister's sermon would then be
both delivered and published. Indeed, there were dozens of thanksgiving
sermons published by Congregationalist ministers following nearly every
designated day of thanksgiving, which made the genre an important and
common part of New England print culture. Further, the state of
Massachusetts continued its own regional tradition by declaring a state-
sponsored day of thanksgiving nearly every fall which, when coupled with
national celebrations, often made thanksgiving sermons a biannual event.[22]

[21] Richard Drayton, "Knowledge and Empire," in P.J. Marshall, ed., *The Oxford History of the British Empire, II: The Eighteenth Century* (New York: Oxford University Press, 1998), 231–252, p. 233. Richard Price, "Two Tracts on Civil Liberty, the War with America, and The Debts and Finances of the Kingdom" (1778), in *Price: Political Writings*, ed. D. O. Thomas (Cambridge: Cambridge University Press, 1991), 14–100, p. 15–17. For Price's political theology, see Benjamin E. Park, "Benjamin Franklin, Richard Price, and the Division of Sacred and Secular in the Age of Revolutions," in *Benjamin Franklin's Intellectual World*, ed. Paul Kerry and Matthew Holland (Madison, NJ: Farleigh Dickinson University Press, 2012), 119–135. For American and British providentialism in the seventeenth century, see Guyatt, *Providence and the Invention of the United States*, 11–93; Alexandra Walsham, *Providence in Early Modern England* (New York: Oxford University Press, 1999); Michael Winship, *Seers of God: Puritan Providentialism in the Restoration and Early Enlightenment* (Baltimore: Johns Hopkins University Press, 1996).
[22] By my count, no fewer than two dozen thanksgiving sermons were published following the National Days of Thanksgiving in 1789, 1795, 1798, and 1799.

Regions to the south were less given to the practice, as few denominations embraced the patriotic ritual as much as Congregationalists.
In Pennsylvania, while thanksgiving sermons were certainly present,
they were far from as common. Ministers gave sermons on the assigned
date in some years, but not in others. The reality of pluralism and the
contested space of competing religious groups rendered the sermons an
awkward fit for the state, as the few published texts mostly emphasized
the benefits of religious liberty and the importance of individual rights.
In South Carolina, by comparison, thanksgiving sermons seemed not to
play an important role at all, at least not until 1800, when they were
belatedly used in factional debates. South Carolinian newspapers merely
noted the appointed day and shared the president's message, but there
were few mentions of local gatherings and even fewer records of sermons
preached by local ministers. At the very least, thanksgiving sermons were
not part of Southern print culture and remained a mostly silent aspect of
their nationalist discourse.[23]

The Congregationalist ministers in Massachusetts, who often held
sympathies with the Federalist Party, thus provide a cogent case study in
the production of religious nationalisms during the 1790s. They were the
most earnest in exploring nationalist tendencies and the most adamant in
constructing a theological framework for political union. New England
Federalists were also more likely to have access to the press in the 1780s
and 1790s, which facilitated a larger corpus of their writing during the
period. In many cases, their notion of America was based on a covenant
theology that was deeply rooted in their religious worldview, and the
genre of thanksgiving sermons provided a dependable and authoritative
setting in which ministers could reaffirm a predominantly regional framework for understanding the nation. While thanksgiving sermons from

---

[23] Collections of sermons from prominent South Carolina ministers during the period lack
thanksgiving sermons. See, for example, Isaac Stockton Keith, *Sermons, Addresses, and
Letters: Selected from the Writings of the Late Rev. Isaac Stockton Keith, D.D. One of
the Ministers of the Independent or Congregational Church in Charleston, S.C.*
(Charleston, SC: S. Etheridge, Jr., 1816); Daniel Cobia, *Sermons by the Rev. Daniel
Cobia, A.M., Late Assistant Minister of St. Philip's Church, Charleston* (Charleston, SC:
John P. Beile, 1838); Edward Thomas, *Sermons by the Rev. Edward Thomas; Formerly
Rector of Trinity Church, Edisto Island, Late Rector of St. John's Parish, Berkley,
S. Carolina* (Charleston, SC: A. E. Miller, 1841); Robert Smith, *The American
Revolution and Righteous Community: Selected Sermons of Bishop Robert Smith*, ed.
Charles Willbanks (Columbia: University of South Carolina Press, 2007). James
Kershaw, the only minister I could find who delivered a thanksgiving sermon, was only
recorded doing so once: Kershaw Diary, February 19, 1795, James Kershaw Collection,
SCL.

Pennsylvania and South Carolina, not to mention sermons from non-Congregationalist ministers in Massachusetts, enable useful points of comparison, together they highlight the contrasting notions of nationalism, politics, and the presumed character that was meant to represent a unified country. So while these Congregationalists were far from representative of even the New England region, let alone American ministers as a whole, they provide a cogent example for how individuals used religion to shape a particularly political message.

In constructing these new political theologies, the terms that ministers employed were often in transition. Most importantly, Massachusetts's ministers intermingled notions of "state," "region," and "nation" in their nationalist rhetoric, which mirrored ideological transformations in the broader political climate. This linguistic ambiguity concerning geopolitical allegiance was indicative of the period. Even while there was an increase in nationalist sentiment, many in Massachusetts still thought of themselves as a "nation" with the other states of New England. Their sense of national allegiance was intertwined with the like-minded citizens of communities that shared their own customs and habits. The term "nation" remained an ambiguous word that could mean their local community, provincial region, or federal institution. These affinities often worked together, however. For example, in early 1787, a group of New England ministers came together to urge America to adopt a "federal head of the nation" in order to "preserve the faith of the nation inviolate." They hoped that "all states in the *Federal Union*, and all citizens of each *state*," would share the same "true political virtue, even *that patriotic benevolence* which shall cause all the members of the human body [to promote] the good of the whole body." They desired a "*Federal Head* of a *sovereign independent nation*" that would regenerate American society and unify the country. That this plea for a strong and energetic national government and culture came from a regional alliance highlights the tensions at play.[24]

Regional and national allegiances must not be understood as always in conflict. David Potter noted that the attachment of nationalism to the nation-state often "prevents the historian from seeing that in situations where nationalism and sectionalism are both at work, they are not

---

[24] *A Concert of Prayer Propounded to the Citizens of the United States* (Exeter, NH: s.n., 1787), 8–10. For New England's conflation of regionalism and sectionalism, see Perry Miller, *Errand into the Wilderness* (Cambridge, MA: Harvard University Press, 1956), 1–15; Sacvan Bercovitch, *The Rites of Assent: Transformations in the Symbolic Construction of America* (New York: Routledge, 1992).

necessarily polar or antithetical forces, even though circumstances may cause them to [confront] one another." Rather, in many instances, nationalism works best when it draws from sectional loyalty and capitalizes upon local allegiances. The regionalism in New England, moreover, was not replicated throughout the rest of the Union, especially in the South, for several more decades. As Michael O'Brien has noted, "it had been the hope of the American political experiment to achieve Union without centralization, and most antebellum Southerners understood the United States precisely as a collectivity of parts in which none, especially not the federal government, was dominant, but all were freely cooperative." It was only the "death of this political idea in the Civil War" that enabled them to embrace "region." Some states not only rejected the idea of a regional alliance, but held regional biases in contempt. William Maclay, a congressman from Philadelphia, complained that "the Eastern people seem to think that he made none but New England folks." There was enough jealousy to go around.[25]

This tension of regional and national interests was crucial for Massachusetts's ministers in the 1790s. Especially for those who possessed Federalist sentiments, it was a difficult balance to maintain the identities of the state, region, and nation at the same time. Such an imaginative construction required an eclectic framework for understanding allegiance and patriotism. The idea of a national covenant, then, served as a welding link that could preserve a regional identity, conceptualize a federal contract, and at the same time contemplate a path for the cultural regeneration and accountability. The irony was that in this construction of a national bond, their nationalist covenant theology planted the seeds for cultural disunion.

---

[25] David M. Potter, "The Historian's Use of Nationalism and Vice Versa," *American Historical Review* 67 (July 1962): 924–950, p. 931. Michael O'Brien, "Regions and Transnationalism," in O'Brien, *Placing the South* (Jackson: University Press of Mississippi, 2007), 3–9, p. 5. William MacLay, *Journal of William MacLay, United States Senator from Pennsylvania, 1789–1791*, ed. Edgar S. Maclay (New York: D. Appleton, 1890), 210. See also Kenneth M. Stampp, "The Concept of a Perpetual Union," in Stampp, *The Imperiled Union: Essays on the Background of the Civil War* (New York: Oxford University Press, 1980), 3–36; John M. Murrin, "A Roof Without Walls: The Dilemma of American National identity," in Richard Beeman et al., eds., *Beyond Confederation: Origins of the Constitution and American National Identity* (Chapel Hill: University of North Carolina Press, 1987): 333–348; Wilbur Zelinsky, *Nation into State: The Shifting Symbolic Foundations of American Nationalism* (Chapel Hill: University of North Carolina Press, 1989).

Massachusetts's Federalist ministers were not only earnest in the delivery of thanksgiving sermons, but they were often consistent in their message. Common among the dozens of sermons published each year was the belief in a national covenant that remained at the heart of their national identity, even within a national culture that increasingly emphasized individualism. When these Congregationalists rejected the idea of a divine sovereign king, they were forced to construct a new form of providentialism – that is, a novel way to trace their providential lineage. In lieu of a divine monarch, there was biblical covenant tradition: the Old Testament had established a pattern through which the House of Israel could receive blessings, and by following that model they could receive the same divine favors. That this idea pervaded British culture is seen in William Blake's famous poem, which was written a couple decades after American independence: "I will not cease from Mental Fight / Nor shall my Sword sleep in my hand: / Till we have built Jerusalem, / In England's green and pleasant land." This Israelite imagery was not confined to one side of the Atlantic.[26]

Covenant theology has long been identified as a central component of early New England thought. John Winthrop's 1630 "City upon a Hill" sermon – in which he told his company to "be knit together in this worke as one man," and that disunity and spiritual negligence would force God to "breake out in wrathe against us" – established a template for communal spirituality in the region for over a century. The concept has dominated Puritan historiography ever since. Yet historians have often argued that this worldview fell out of favor in the late eighteenth century. Perry Miller, for instance, argued that the practice of "revival" replaced the theology of "covenant" following the American Revolution because "it was no longer necessary to find space in their sermons for social theory." Many historians have since argued that the covenant theology of the Old Testament collapsed in the face of postrevolutionary America's dynamic religious marketplace. The individualism, populism, and democratic zeal in the early republic, it is believed, left little room for religion's social vision. "After the Revolution," wrote Michael Zuckerman, Americans "came to aspire to a character they had previously scorned, as free

---

[26] William Blake, "Jerusalem," *Blake: The Complete Poems*, ed. W. H. Stevenson, 2nd ed. (London: Pearson/Longman, 1989): 492. For the Bible's importance to American political thought during the period, see Eran Shalev, *American Zion: The Old Testament as a Political Text from the Revolution to the Civil War* (New Haven: Yale University Press, 2013).

individuals rather than as virtuous communards." Similarly, Gordon
Wood has argued that, "by concentrating on the saving of individual
souls, the competing denominations essentially abandoned their traditional institutional and churchly responsibilities to organize the world
here and now along godly lines." This was an age for a new American.[27]

But the rate of this dissolution, which was largely dependent on the
presence of religious diversity and growth of democratized denominations,
varied across the regions. In New England, tradition and circumstances
perpetuated the cultural power of both ministers and covenant theologies.
Even if disestablishment required that religious policing could not be done
through civil mechanisms, the expectation of societal piety remained.
Freedom of religion, they believed, established a context in which righteousness could be more easily discerned, as it was no longer coerced but
freely expressed. Indeed, New England's postrevolutionary covenant theology was rooted in the free expression of communal obedience, which could
only be achieved in a situation in which the state left religious authority to
ministers and individual members. That different geographic and cultural
contexts envisioned diverging connections between religion and society
offers important lessons for early cultivations of American nationalism,
for it struck at the heart of what "America" actually meant to various
believers. If Massachusetts's covenant theology and its emphasis on com-
munalism would have seemed foreign to those who inhabited the much
more pluralistic state of Pennsylvania, for instance, so too would the former's sense of nationalism that was based on such a worldview.[28]

[27] John Winthrop, "A Modell of Christian Charity," in *The Puritans: A Sourcebook of Their
Writings*, ed. Perry Miller and Thomas H. Johnson, 2 vols., rev. ed. (New York: Dover,
2001), 1:194–200, p. 198–199. Perry Miller, "From the Covenant to Revival," in *Religion in
American Life*, ed. James Ward Smith and A. Leland Jamison (Princeton, NJ: Princeton
University Press, 1961), 322–268, p. 333. Michael Zuckerman, "A Different Thermidor:
The Revolution Beyond the American Revolution," in *The Transformation of Early
American History: Society, Authority, and Ideology*, ed. James A. Henretta,
Michael Kammen, and Stanley N. Katz (New York: Knopf, 1991), 170–193, p. 185.
Gordon Wood, *The Radicalism of the American Revolution* (New York: Alfred A. Knopf,
1992), 333. See also Joyce A. Appleby, *Without Resolution: The Jeffersonian Tensions in
American Nationalism: An Inaugural Lecture Delivered Before the University of Oxford on
25 April 1991* (Oxford: Clarendon Press, 1992), 16; Stout, *New England Soul*, 312–331;
Donald Weber, *Rhetoric and History in Revolutionary New England* (New York: Oxford
University Press, 1988); Hatch, *Democratization of American Christianity*.

[28] For the transformation of ecclesiastical authority, see Christopher Grasso, *Speaking
Aristocracy: Transforming Public Discourse in Eighteenth-Century Connecticut* (Chapel
Hill: University of North Carolina Press, 1999). For the perpetuation of covenant theology's
importance in postrevolutionary New England, see Sassi, *Republic of Righteousness*.

Preachers were eager to explicate their theological nationalisms. John Leland, a native of New England who spent the 1780s in Virginia helping the state legislature secure religious freedom before returning to Massachusetts in 1791, was one of the local ministers who developed a provincial framework for an American covenant theology. (One of the reasons Leland left Virginia was because the state, in his mind, did not place enough importance on denominational identity and societal responsibility.) In his sermon *The Rights of Conscience Inalienable*, he drew from two sources that he believed worked hand in hand: John Locke and the Old Testament. From Locke, Leland learned the notion of "compact," which he termed the legal mechanism necessary to defend a community from the dangers of unrest and anarchy; from the Old Testament, he learned that the compact was a covenant based on the righteous principles given to the House of Israel. Even if he strongly opposed the establishment of religion, he still argued that "the basis of civil government" must still be founded upon the doctrines found in the Bible, as well as the pious principles "which the Almighty has erected in every human breast." This he termed "a *censor morum* over all [God's] actions." Leland's merging of a Lockean compact with a biblical covenant demonstrated the framework in which the language of liberty could still be invoked when perpetuating a particular religious identity. While a free market of religion was necessary for God's people to truly be proven, the principles upon which the nation would rise and fall depended on society's ability to follow the Bible's prescripts.[29]

This covenant theology was pervasive. David Tappan, a professor of theology at Harvard, referred to the nation's covenant as a "divine appointment" that connected America with "the ancient people of God," and acknowledged "the importance and utility of political and religious guides in a Christian state." Indeed, Tappan argued, "the public worship of the Deity, and stated instructions in religion and morality, appear as necessary and beneficial to the state, as they are to the souls of individuals." This analogy of state to individual underscores the powerful metaphor of a covenant – just as the salvation of individual worshippers depended on their ability to follow God's dictates, so did the success of a nation depend on its citizens' capacity to do likewise. This was a theology of the state.[30]

---

[29] John Leland, "The Rights of Conscience Inalienable," in *Political Sermons of the American Founding Era: 1730–1805*, ed. Ellis Sandoz, 2 vols. (Indianapolis, IN: Liberty Fund, 1992), 2:1071–1101, p. 1081–1083.

[30] David Tappan, *A Sermon for the Day of General Election* (Portsmouth, NH: John Melcher, 1792), 6, 12.

These tensions were on full display in the region's thanksgiving sermons. Predominant within this covenant theology was the role of providence in distilling a nation with a particular character. Thomas
Brockway, for instance, urged his audience to remember that it was
God "that holds the balance of national power in his own hands."
Joseph Willard, in his address that same year, noted that "God is the
first cause, and without him nothing can be brought to pass." Levi
Frisbie, minister at Ipswich, proclaimed, "God is said to make or create
a people," which is accomplished "by the agency and direction of his
providence." If the covenant is kept, Frisbie reasoned, "they are formed
into a nation, united by the bonds of civil society, and placed under the
influence of civil government." Through this process, even if secular laws
and non-ecclesiastical leaders are in control of the nation, God remained
the author of the "United States," just as he had "created the nation of
Israel." Frisbie further explained the broader parameters of America's
covenant with God:

Therefore as the principles and circumstances which dispose and constrain
a people to assume a national capacity, and form a civil government,
originate from God, and operate under the superintendency of his Providence,
their national state and character are the effect of his appointment and agency,
and he may be said to be their former and Creator – And if their government
and civil institutions are wise and righteous, and if the officers and magistrates
who are to administer this government, to form and execute its laws and
regulations, are wise, just and faithful in the discharge of their duty, then they
are dignified and warranted by the sanction of the divine authority and
approbation.[31]

An acute sense of particular providence – the belief that God was in
charge of the intricate details of life and events – saturated these ministers' sense of nationalism. This both reaffirmed the country's chosen
status and also validated its notion of religion's importance within the
new republic. Everything that happened to America through the first few
decades of the nation, reasoned Hinsdale minister Bunker Gay, happened for a reason: "God is aiming to train us up, by various mercies
and judgments, well adapted to the end," he taught. And that end, he
explained, was to cultivate a godly "character" best equipped to meet

---

[31] Thomas Brockway, *America Saved, or Divine Glory Displayed, in the Late War with
Great-Britain. A Thanksgiving Sermon* (Hartford, CT: Hudson and Goodwin, 1783), 6.
Joseph Willard, *A Thanksgiving Sermon Delivered at Boston, December 11, 1783, to the
Religious Society in Brattle Street* (Boston: T. and J. Fleet, 1784), 19. Frisbie, *Sermon
Delivered February 19, 1795*, 9–10.

Christ's heavenly kingdom. America was a chosen nation because America had chosen God.[32]

The ministers' emphasis on providential control was easily appropriated from the religious realm to political practice, as it drew from a still powerful strain of Calvinism that was eroding elsewhere in America. If God was in control of the nation's progression, then he was also the author of the government system that had been implemented. What Americans should truly be thankful for, preached Cambridge pastor Thaddeus Fiske, was how God had established "the excellent fabric of our present Federal Constitution" from the "ruins of the old confederation." This document, among many things, "establishes among us *liberty with order*" – the latter statement being a Federalist catchphrase during the period. These ministers not only sacralized political concepts – typically the Federalist notions of control, the triumph of an energetic federal government, and the importance of a centralized union – but also politicized their religious position. By reaffirming the notion of the American nation being a blend of religious and federal control, they solidified a character of the American people that was intimately conjoined to religious belief – particularly, *their* religious belief.[33]

Connected to their notion of providentialism was the importance of humility about one's talent, frugality in temporal matters, and skepticism toward emotion. Since the nation's prosperity depended on God's will, not the individual's own strength, it was crucial to remember their depraved and dependent status. As part of their reaffirmation of humanity's lowly position and communal responsibility, ministers used their sermons as a warning voice against the expanding individualist, capitalist, and egotistical culture of early America – the very culture some historians have argued dominated the religious sphere. Ward Cotton warned, "afflictions are sometimes sent upon us to wean our affections from the world, & its enjoyment & to disengage us from our undue attachment to them." Cotton feared that the growing commercial market, the increase in speculation, and the emphasis on costly apparel would threaten the nation's social stability: "When we place our affections so strongly on

[32] Bunker Gay, *To Sing of Mercy and Judgment: Recommended and Exemplified in a Discourse, Delivered on a Day of Publick Thanksgiving* (Greenfield, MA: Thomas Dickman, 1793), 9.

[33] Thaddeus Fiske, *Thanksgiving and Prayer for Public Rulers, Recommended in a Discourse, Delivered at the Second Parish in Cambridge, February 19, 1795, Being the Day of National Thanksgiving in the United States* (Boston, 1795), 3. (Emphasis in original.)

the things of the world, as to neglect religion and eternity, they are oftentimes reward from us, to teach us [our] vanity." For Cotton and many others in Massachusetts, the growing economy posed as many problems as it conferred blessings. This skepticism toward materialism stands out when compared to the ministers in Pennsylvania and South Carolina who, for the most part, embraced what they saw as the "industriousness" of the young republic.[34]

In response to political turmoil as well as the growing democratic sects in their midst, these Massachusetts ministers also emphasized the fallibility of human emotions. Without the "necessary and effectual restraints" of government and religion, warned Fiske, "the passions of men, gaining an ascendant influence over reason and the rules of morality, would spread universal anarchy, ruin and misery over the world." It was necessary to couple religion with government because "without the principles and rules of religion and morality, a republican government would soon fall into ruin. Godliness alone," he further reasoned, "can prevent the arrogance of prosperity, or the wanton abuse of liberty, and give proper subjection, order and tranquility, to the great body of a free people." The "passions" of humankind must be checked in order to maintain stability. A fear of humanity's depraved character, though rarely explicitly mentioned, undergirded much of their cultural "safeguards." "We ought to be influenced by principles more than passion, and by sentiments of religion," explained Boston preacher John Eliot, "as much as by the emotions of humanity." Amanda Porterfield has noted how religions took advantage of political distrust during the period. "Religious institutions," she wrote, "grew as much to manage" human depravity "as to relieve it." Religion was necessary to curb humankind's foibles.[35]

Yet it would be a mistake to overemphasize their rhetoric of depravity at the expense of the community's potential. Indeed, the intended

---

[34] Ward Cotton, "On Sympathy," October 2, 1795, insert between pages 8–9, Ward Cotton Papers, Houghton Library, Harvard University, Cambridge, MA. See also his Thanksgiving sermon, "On Time," November 1794, in the same collection. For industriousness being praised in religious rhetoric, see Butler, *Awash in a Sea of Faith*, 164–174. As Mark Peterson has demonstrated, however, this anti-commercialist rhetoric in New England was often tempered by a tepid embrace of the market system: Peterson, *The Price of Redemption: The Spiritual Economy of Puritan New England* (Palo Alto, CA: Stanford University Press, 1999).

[35] Fiske, *Thanksgiving and Prayer for Public Rulers*, 3, 16. John Eliot, *A Sermon, Delivered on the Day of Annual Thanksgiving* (Boston: Samuel Hall, 1794), 5. Porterfield, *Conceived in Doubt*, 2. See also Samuel Austin, *A Sermon, Delivered at Worcester, on the Day of Public Thanksgiving* (Worcester, MA: Leonard Worcester, 1797), 17.

sanctification and uplift of God's providence was one of the elements that separated Massachusetts from other states. The Puritan tradition in New England emphasized an ideal of communities progressing forward together toward a more "godly" society and egalitarian community. Their rhetoric concerning human depravity, the necessity of humility, and the importance of community did not overcome their keen notion of a postmillennial perfectionism – a belief that, through Christ, His commandments, and communal responsibility, humankind could reach a higher state. While it was not the belief of individual mobility later trumpeted in the Jacksonian period, or even the industriousness then present in the middle colonies, this discourse did portray, if subtly, the potential for the improvement of one's status. "America is a poor man's country," declared Joseph Dana. "Here the children of the poor are instructed at the public expense" in order for them to eventually enjoy the higher blessing and advancement that "belongs to him." America, within this framework, was both debased when considered without the grace of God, but it was also intimately perfectible with divine aid, a place where individuals could obtain a higher station and better life. If citizens lived up to their side of the divine covenant, they were promised blessings and improvement.[36]

This is to be contrasted with the providentialism then being preached by elites in places like South Carolina. While Charleston Episcopal minister Arthur Buist agreed that the "doctrine of Particular Providence" was the driving principle of religion, his providentialism reaffirmed the status quo rather than pointing to a future moment of perfection. One must accept "afflictions, trials, and stations" as part of particular providence, he taught. Rather than seeking to improve one's status, it is better to accept that one's current position was designed "under the guidance of our Heavenly Father, who careth for us." James Malcomson similarly argued that, as it was "our duty as ministers of the gospel, to warn you against corruption," he was authorized to "exhort you to beware of moral, and political corruption." Specifically, Malcomson exhorted his congregants to "suppress *ambition*, to beware of *faction*, and to live

---

[36] Joseph Dana, *A Sermon, Delivered February 19, 1795, Being a Day of General Thanksgiving, Throughout the United States of America* (Newburyport, MA: Blunt and March, 1795), 8–9. The foundation for this reformist impulse is outlined in David D. Hall, *A Reforming People: Puritanism and the Transformation of Public Life in New England* (New York: Alfred A. Knopf, 2011). See also David Walker Howe, *Making the American Self: Jonathan Edwards to Abraham Lincoln*, 2nd ed. (New York: Oxford University Press, 2009).

peaceably with all men." This streak of conservatism was one of the main elements that retarded the growth of evangelical sects in the region. Just as certain religious groups were being "democratized" in order to flourish in the new republic, conservative figures in deep Southern regions often rejected those developments as threatening American order.[37]

In South Carolina, social stability was seen as both the goal for religious observance and the heart of their theological nationalism. Even evangelical ministers argued that religion, according to one preacher, ought to teach congregants to be "satisfied with the station, tho' humble, in which heaven hath affixed him." The poor and enslaved are not to envy "the rich and the great" nor be "anxious for change." It would be naïve to think that various individuals' positions in life were left to "blind *chance*," Baptist minister Henry Holcombe explained, because "God's providence is universal and particular." As part of a divine plan, God *"effects* the good which exists, *permits* the evil, and *restrains* the rest." Even the "most minute" elements of society "have an astonishing influence on a long series of interesting dispensations," and thus *"all things* were made the subject of divine determination." Another Baptist minister, Richard Furman, argued that Americans must "learn sincere and humble resignation to the sovereign pleasure of Almighty God" in every "afflicting dispensation of his providence," regardless of how troubling or complicated. Citizens must know their place in society.[38]

Religion served an important role in the state, though that role was primarily to reaffirm social order and solidify cultural cohesion. William Hollinshead noted that the "advantage of public worship" is to remind the individual of their place and role in their community. "Religion is the first bond of the social compact," he believed, "the only tie of union among mankind, which can preserve that harmony, good order, and

---

[37] Arthur Buist, *A Sermon, Delivered in the First Presbyterian Church, on Thursday, Nov. 7, 1798, Being the Day of Thanksgiving, Humiliation & Prayer* (Charleston, SC: Wm. Riley, 1798), 18. James Malcomson, *A Sermon, Preached on the 14th of July, 1794, Being the Anniversary of the French Revolution* (Charleston, SC: Harrison and Bowen, 1795), 34. For religion as source of social complacency, see Najar, *Evangelizing the South*.

[38] Thomas Reese, *An Essay on the Influence of Religion, in Civil Society* (Charleston, SC: Markland and M'Iver, 1788), 67. Henry Holcombe, *A Sermon, Containing a Brief Illustration and Defence of the Doctrines Commonly Called Calvinistic* (Charleston, SC: Markland and McIver, 1793), 8. (Emphasis in original.) Richard Furman, *Humble Submission, The Duty of a Bereaved Nation; A Sermon, Occasioned by the Death of His Excellency General George Washington* (Charleston, SC: W. P. Young, 1800), 20. See also Henry Holcombe, *A Discourse on the Sovereignty of the Deity* (Charleston, SC: Markland and McIver, 1793).

decorum, which are essential to the common good." The "common good," in many instances, implied a staid social order that prevented change and tumult. Presbyterian Isaac Stockton Keith explicated this mix of theological predestination and social crystallization:

As our times are thus in the Lord's hands; as all our affairs, our interests, our comforts, our trials, personal and relative; as, in a word, all the circumstances of our lives, and of our deaths, are under his direction, and subject to his disposal, are ordered and arranged according to the unerring dictates of his infinite wisdom, and the immutable determinations of his holy will; it must surely be our indispensable duty, with attentive minds, to observe, and, with adoring hearts to acknowledge, the hand of God, in all the events which take place around us; and especially in all the occurrences, which have a more immediate relation to ourselves, and to those with whom we are most intimately associated, and in whom we are most deeply interested.[39]

Keith would elsewhere make the connection between religious predestination and social cohesion more explicit in a sermon on the importance of "trusting in God." "The observations which have been offered, on *the nature of a genuine and proper trust in God*," he reasoned, "will, at the same time, admit of an easy and useful application to *the state of the community*, in which the affairs of individuals, are, as it were, blended and formed into one common interest." He blasted his "fellow citizens" who failed to support the federal, state, and local authorities, and argued that "*the whole American people* must be penetrated" by a sense of providentialism about the nation, and that an "instantaneous, patriotic impulse" should drive both political and religious thought. Simon Francis Gallagher, a Catholic priest in Charleston, similarly stated that God "forges chains" throughout society that were designed to keep America stable and righteous. Israel of old, Gallagher warned, faltered once people

---

[39] William Hollinshead, *On the Advantages of Public Worship: A Sermon* (Charleston, SC: Markland and McIver, 1794), 8, 12–13. Isaac Stockton Keith, *The Providence of God, Ordering and Conducting the Affairs of Men* (Charleston, SC: W. P. Young, 1806), 23. See also Keith, *National Affliction, and National Consolation! A Sermon, on the Death of General George Washington* (Charleston, SC: W.P. Young, 1800), 24–25. Elsewhere, Hollinshead argued that one could only access God's grace through the embrace of their predetermined social position. See Hollinshead, *All Fulness Dwelling in Christ: A Sermon* (Charleston, SC: Markland and McIver, 1787). Nicholas Guyatt has argued that, after the seventeenth century, "many Britons and Americans came to regard personal providentialism as superstitious and backward even as they continued to believe that God directed the fates of nations." Guyatt, *Providence and the Invention of the United States, 1607–1876*, 5. Yet for many in South Carolina, personal and national providentialism remained closely intertwined into the nineteenth century.

became impatient and ungrateful for their status and role within society, and worked to dissolve the social chains that held their nation firm.[40]

Much of this message could be easily translated into political meanings, especially in the decade following the Constitution's ratification. Richard Furman believed that Christianity was "calculated to promote all the true interests of men, and admirably adapted to advance the *happiness of society*." That goal, he further explicated, "corresponds with the constitution, and present state of human nature." However, the direct equivalency of religion to America's federal document highlights the blurred boundaries in Furman's political theology. Thinking federally, Furman stated, "we see the humble followers of Christ 'flowing,' as it were, together from different churches, and distant parts of the country." The goal of religion, as with politics, then, was to "keep the unity of the spirit in the bond of peace." The dangers in this pursuit arose from "our own corruptions, jarring passions, mistakes respecting interest and duty, and, in general, from our imperfection in the present state of things." The devil's opposition to America's peaceful union was found in the presence of controversy and contention. On the other hand, peaceful submission and humble duty would ensure the nation's survival.[41]

This was an idea embedded in their culture. A decade later, a South Carolinian traveling through the northern states complained that religions in the region "unhinged [citizens] from those industrious habits & that honest course of life which they had previously been attached," and "consequently seek to destroy that harmony in the community without which there can be no safety, no happiness & no protection for property." Religion, in short, was meant to maintain social cohesion and stymie communal unrest, and it failed when it allowed or encouraged citizens to question and challenge their social status. Keith argued that "a willing subjection to the authority of God," as well as their "state leaders," would

---

[40] Isaac Stockton Keith, *Trust in God: Explained and Recommended, in a Sermon, Preached, with Some Special Reference to the State of the Public Mind, in the Prospect of War* (Charleston, SC: W. P. Young, 1807), 15, 17. (Emphasis in original.) Simon Francis Gallagher, *A Sermon Preached on the Ninth Day of May, 1798, Observed as a Day of Fasting and Prayer, to Implore the Divine Aid and Protection in Favor of the United States* (Charleston, SC: W. P. Harrison, 1798), 8.

[41] Richard Furman, *Unity and Peace: A Sermon. Preached at the High Hills of Santee, November 4, 1793* (Charleston, SC: Markland, 1794), 3, 4, 18. (Emphasis in original.) For the importance of religion to social and civil society in the South during this period, see Najar, *Evangelizing the South*; Rachel N. Klein, *Unification of a Slave State: The Rise of the Planter Class in the South Carolina Backcountry, 1760–1808* (Chapel Hill: University of North Carolina Press, 1990), 272–286.

bring "the highest stage of national prosperity," even if many were left in their providential "stations" in life. It is necessary for the "common welfare," he reasoned, that some remain complacent fulfilling the "social duties" expected in their "respective spheres."[42]

Indeed, one of the growing rifts between the South and the North was how they understood religion's role in reforming society: whereas Massachusetts's particular providentialism led many there to strive to improve their moral and ethical issues, South Carolina's version drove some merely to freeze their society in time and resist reform and change. This fissure in providentialism signaled a deeper cultural discontinuity between the states that would widen in coming decades, as they represented differing visions of what the nation really entailed. These were more than just doctrinal disagreements. They were evidence of diverging trajectories for understanding America.[43]

In the wake of the French Revolution, Samuel Spring was more optimistic about his community than he was his nation. When he delivered his thanksgiving sermon in February 1798 to his Newburyport, Massachusetts, congregation, he identified three primary blessings for which America should be grateful: being spared "from the fatal plague" that moved through the middle colonies, not being infected with the insurrectionist spirit that instigated the Whiskey Rebellion in western Pennsylvania, and avoiding the influence of the "French atheists" who were behind the chaos then spreading across the Atlantic. "No year, since the American revolution," he declared, "had been so deeply marked with mercies and judgments." The quasi-war with France in the previous few years had taken its toll, and Spring believed that the extent of France's nefarious plots was only now being discovered. They "have undertaken to

---

[42] "Letters of an American Traveller, Containing a Brief Sketch of the Most Remarkable Places in Various Parts of the United States & the Canadas, with Some Account of the Character & Manners of the People, Written During an Excursion in the year 1810," manuscript, SCHL, 8. Isaac Keith, *The Friendly Influence of Religion and Virtue on the Prosperity of a Nation, a Sermon, Preached to the Independent or Congregational Church, in Charleston, South Carolina, June 14, 1789* (Charleston: Markland and McIver, 1789), 5, 9–10.

[43] Christine Leigh Heyrman has noted that established churches opposed religious movements that "undermined the stability and unity of southern communities by challenging the hierarchies of class and slavery that properly kept people apart, while preaching against the customary pleasures that occasionally brought people together." Heyrman, *Southern Cross: The Beginnings of the Bible Belt* (New York: Alfred A. Knopf, 1997), 15. See also Klein, *Unification of a Slave State*, 271–282.

manage our elections, and to direct our cabinet," he proclaimed, and had attempted to "trample upon the United States." All in all, "the French are the most deceitful, persidious, avaricious, cruel and murderous monsters in the world." Even from the pulpit on a patriotic and religious holiday, Spring hardly minced words.[44]

In the Age of Revolutions, individuals on both sides of the Atlantic were forced to reconsider the relationship between religion, society, and government. And while many historians have argued that an increasing number of people began to view politics through a purely secular prism, religion continued to hold sway with many. Rousseau, for instance, looked to Moses as the premier example for turning a "national body" into "a political Body" that lived together with stability and peace. Contemporary governments based on secular constitutions were feeble, he argued, while Moses's was stable. Indeed, Rousseau's primary critique of "modern nations" is that there are "many lawmakers among them but not a single lawgiver." In his *Social Contact*, the French philosopher insisted on the necessity of "a purely civil profession of faith" that, though steering clear of particular dogmas, helped instill "sentiments of sociability" shared by the entire nation. Similarly, in Germany, Friedrich Schlegel argued for a symbiotic relationship between religion and politics: "Politics (as the art and science of the community of all human development) is for the periphery what religion is for the centre." If the two are incongruous, the entire system falls apart. Far from becoming inconsequential, religion only became more crucial to political discourse as nations were recognized as social constructions and expected to evolve in order to match society.[45]

This became an even more potent topic during the debates surrounding the French Revolution, especially in the Anglo-American world. In Britain, Edmund Burke accused the French of tossing out their federally established religion that had served as a stabilizing feature of government.

---

[44] Samuel Spring, *Thanksgiving Sermon, Preached November 29, 1798* (Newburyport, MA: Desire, 1798), 16, 19, 21, 22.

[45] Jean-Jacques Rousseau, "Considerations on the Government of Poland and on its Projected Reformation" (1772), in *The Social Contact and Other Later Political Writings*, ed. and trans. Victor Gourevitch (Cambridge: Cambridge University Press, 1997), 177–260, p. 180. Rousseau, "The Social Contact" (1762), in *The Social Compact and Other Later Political Writings*, 39–152, p. 150. Friedrich Schlegel, "Philosophical Fragments" (1797–1801), in Frederick C. Beiser, ed. and trans., *The Early Political Writings of the German Romantics* (Cambridge: Cambridge University Press, 1996), 159–168, p. 165. See also John Robertson, *The Case for the Enlightenment: Scotland and Naples, 1680–1760* (Cambridge: Cambridge University Press, 2005), 31–32.

"The spirit of nobility and religion" cultivated by a state-sponsored ecclesiastical structure, Burke argued, kept nations grounded in social, moral, and religious principles that were crucial for the country to survive. In response, Mary Wollstonecraft argued that a deluded devotion to state religion, rather than natural religious sentiments, was at the heart of this mistaken political theology. Religion is "the cultivation of the understanding and refinement of the affections," she believed, and should naturally percolate from the citizen body rather than be forced upon them by the state. Indeed, Wollstonecraft reasoned, Burke's argument would "undermine" both the state *and* religion. Even more radically, Thomas Paine, writing during the French Terror, argued for the abolishment of organized religion within a democratic society altogether because they "terrify and enslave mankind and monopolize power and profit." These were merely three expressions, strung across a very dynamic spectrum, within a vigorous debate that had begun to change the course of religion's role in society.[46]

Despite taking place across the Atlantic Ocean, the French Revolution had a disproportionate impact on America's political and religious culture. The nation's reaction to the Reign of Terror, which took place at the very moment America's two competing parties were taking shape, caused many citizens to reassess their support of France's revolt. Previously, there had been general enthusiasm for their sister nation's cause, but France's quick spiral into violence led many Americans, especially those associated with the Federalist Party, to cut cultural ties and denounce the French nation's recent and radical developments. This conflict proved a crucial moment in American politics, as it forced significant developments in the nation's concept of exceptionalism, justification for violence, and understanding of democracy. And given that religion was always at the center of their discussions concerning France, it also both shifted and validated competing theologies of national belonging.[47]

---

[46] Edmund Burke, "Reflections on the Revolution in France" (1790), in *Revolutionary Writings*, ed. Iain Hampsher-Monk (Cambridge: Cambridge University Press, 2014), 1–250, p. 81. Mary Wollstonecraft, "A Vindication of the Rights of Men" (1790), in *A Vindication of the Rights of Men with A Vindication of the Rights of Women*, ed. Sylvana Tomaselli (Cambridge: Cambridge University Press, 1994), 1–64, p. 40, 50. Thomas Paine, "The Age of Reason, Part I" (1794), in *Political Writings*, ed. Bruce Kuklick (Cambridge: Cambridge University Press, 2000), 265–318, p. 268. See Marilyn Butler, ed., *Burke, Paine, Godwin, and the Revolution Controversy* (Cambridge: Cambridge University Press, 1984).

[47] See, especially, Cleves, *Reign of Terror in America*; Hale, "Many Who Wandered in Darkness"; Hale, "On Their Tiptoes."

Much of America's anti-French rhetoric was inherited from the British tradition. Religious prejudice formed an integral element of Anglo-American nationalist discourse in a way that permeated their politics, and Catholic France was often identified as an oppressive "other" against which they posited their own notions of liberty. Linda Colley noted that "a vast superstructure of prejudice throughout eighteenth-century Britain" was directed against the Catholic and the French. But not all of America reacted the same way to France's downfall, or with the same fervor. For New England, the biggest threat presented by France was what they interpreted to be a rejection of religion's role in society and the rupture between church and state. Samuel Spring's reference to "French atheists" in his Thanksgiving sermon was indicative of the challenge many Massachusetts ministers sensed in regard to their own political theology. Just a year earlier, Henry Cumings had warned that "whoever, upon the plea of conscience, endeavours to abolish religion ... is a dangerous member of society, and unfit to be trusted with any offices of honour and emolument." Clearly threatened by the potential of a secular revolt, and likely buttressed by a newly present, if never very strong, threat from deism in the last decade of the eighteenth century, it was important to reaffirm the close relationship between religion and politics. Even if disestablishment implied the separation between ecclesiastical leadership and the government, there was a renewed commitment to conjoin religion and society.[48]

Many feared that the French Revolution was part of a global threat toward belief in general. Atheism, deism, and other ideologies that displaced orthodox faith seemed on the rise across the Atlantic. Nobody represented that threat more than Thomas Paine. "It is necessary to be bold," Paine explained to fellow skeptic Elihu Palmer, because while "some people can be reasoned into sense ... others must be shocked into it." In the introduction to *Age of Reason*, his popular and controversial pamphlet that attacked organized religion, he admitted his excitement over "the exceeding probability that a revolution in the system of government would be followed by a revolution in the system of religion." The "circumstance that has now taken place in France," he believed, would finally inaugurate a global transformation that would overturn priestcraft. Joel Barlow, a diplomat, politician, and businessman from

---

[48] Colley, *Britons*, 36. Cumings, *A Sermon Preached at Billerica, December 15, 1796*, 15. For Christianity's response to the thread of deism, see Grasso, "Deist Monster." See also Bell, *Cult of the Nation in France*, 44–49.

Massachusetts who helped published Paine's *Age of Reason* and penned one of the few American defenses of the controversial tract, posited that Christian belief was incompatible with America's rational age. Progress depended on a nation's ability to "banish [revealed religion] as much as possible from society," he wrote in a biting treatise that was never published. Tellingly, Barlow's history of humanity and predictions for its future were distinctly wedded to its attachment to other nations and cosmopolitan cultures. The entirety of Western civilization depended on a move toward universal rationalism. America could only thrive if it embraced a transnational brotherhood with other democratic societies, especially revolutionary France, and broke the shackles of organized religion.[49]

The reaction to Paine's message, and the transatlantic threat it represented, was swift and vociferous. At least 100 rebuttals to *Age of Reason* were published over the next decade, and most denounced the global skepticism that challenged religious authority. Jeremy Belknap dismissed the work as "a species of vulgar infidelity, founded partly in pedantry, partly in debauchery and partly in ill manners, [that] is insinuating itself into the minds of the thoughtless." The American republic was to be built on something much more stable. As another respondent to Paine wrote, Christianity was "the most perfect standard of duty erected," designed to "engage man to an endless progression in virtue" within the civic sphere. John Adams's reaction to *Age of Reason* was both similar and succinct: "The Christian religion is, above all the religions that ever prevailed or existed in ancient or modern times, the religion of wisdom, virtue, equity and humanity, let the Blackguard Paine say what he will." The response to Paine exhibited a matrix including Christian orthodoxy, political conservatism, and nascent exceptionalism. As Americans established new foundations for a national character, radicals like Paine and transatlantic counterpoints like France were cast aside.[50]

---

[49] Thomas Paine to Elihu Palmer, quoted in David Moncure Conway, *The Life of Thomas Paine: With a History of his Literary, Political, and Religious Career in America, France, and England* (New York: G. P. Putnam's Sons, 1893), 2:298. Paine, "Age of Reason: Part 1," 267–268. Joel Barlow, "Notes on the History of Religion and Atheism," Notebook 1796–97, 11, 17, in Barlow Papers, Series One, Houghton Library, Harvard University, Cambridge, MA.

[50] Jeremy Belknap, *Dissertation on the Character, Death & Resurrection of Jesus Christ, and the Evidence of his Gospel; With Remarks on Some Sentiments Advanced in a Book Intitled "The Age of Reason"* (Boston: Apollo Press, 1795), 8. Donald Fraser, *A Collection of Select Biography ... To Which are Prefixed Two Letters to Thomas Paine, Containing Some Important Queries and Remarks Relative to the Probable*

More broadly, clergy defended the role of Christian belief as a crucial stabilizing force for the nation. A Christian defense transcended the mere squabbles with Paine. The stakes were much higher. Specifically, once again drawing from the theology of human depravity, religion was presented as necessary to control passion and curtail anarchy. "Religion is the only safeguard of a free people," explained Boston minister Thaddeus Fiske, "and they who disregard its principles, or manifest a disposition or conduct that tends to lessen a veneration for the deity, are essentially unqualified to beat the head of government." Religion, though technically not afforded an official place within the nation's government, was still part of the nation's identity, and thus needed to be taken into consideration when controlling people and policies. "That men destitute of religion, or the fear of God," he concluded, "are unfit to lead and govern the important affairs of nations, [and] we have a recent and unhappy example in the late rulers of France, in her revolution." America, due to its religious commitment, was a nation apart.[51]

This mindset framed how many saw the transatlantic debate. Thomas Baldwin, pastor of the Second Baptist Church in Boston, was quick to suggest how America could avoid France's state. "As a nation we form a particular character," he counseled, "in distinction from that of individuals." The nation thus had a choice between "the amiable features of virtue and religion" and the "base picture of vice and infidelity." There was no moderating option. Even though Baldwin did not share the same covenant theology as his Congregationalist neighbors, he replicated their cultural framework for America as a chosen nation destined for true believers. In order to be a "Christian" nation, which Baldwin believed was necessary for survival, Americans must, among other things, "acknowledge the eternal God to be the Creator, Preserver, and upholder

Tendency of his Age of Reason (New-York: for the author, 1798), 10–11. John Adams, Diary, July 26, 1796, in *The Works of John Adams*, ed. Charles Francis Adams (Boston: Charles Little and James Brown, 1841): 3:421. For bibliographies of these responses, see Edward H. Davidson and William J. Scheick, *Paine, Scripture, and Authority: The Age of Reason as Religious and Political Idea* (Bethlehem, PA: Lehigh University Press, 1994), 108–116; Michael L. Lasser, "In Response to *The Age of Reason*, 1794–1799," *Bulletin of Bibliography* 25 (1967): 41–43; Gayle Trusdel Pendleton, "Thirty Additional Titles Relating to *The Age of Reason*," *British Studies Monitor* 10 (1980): 36–45. See also H. T. Dickinson, "Thomas Paine and his American Critics," *Enlightenment and Dissent* 27 (2011): 174–185; Seth Cotlar, *Tom Paine's America: The Rise and Fall of Transatlantic Radicalism in the Early Republic* (Charlottesville: University of Virginia Press, 2011).

[51] Fiske, *Thanksgiving and Prayer for Public Rulers*, 16.

of all things," acknowledge that "the system of truth contained in the Bible to be *his word*," and "acknowledge [God] as our rightful Sovereign, and live in subjection of his laws." Throughout his thanksgiving sermon, Baldwin consistently interweaved the "sovereignty" of the United States with the "sovereignty" of God's kingdom. He used the terms interchangeably in a way that embodied the integrated framework of religion and politics that drove his bold claims: America was meant to be a godly country.[52]

The ministerial engagement with partisan politics remained a common feature of many sermons in Massachusetts, especially on days of thanksgiving. Such was to be expected with the culture's blurred ecclesiastical and civic boundaries. Unlike in other states, explicit politics and policies were a frequent occurrence in New England sermons. Thomas Barnard, pastor of the North Church in Salem, merely repeated a common refrain when he declared it was "through the benediction of our Almighty Guardian in Heaven" that "THE FEDERAL AND STATE GOVERNMENTS HAVE ACTED IN ACCORD" in establishing constitutional principles and alleviating concerns over sovereignty. To Barnard, it was as much his duty to educate his congregants on the benefits of Federalism as it was to remind them of the grace of God.[53]

This anxiety was expressed through different means south of New England, especially where religious establishment was more tenuous. For Ashbel Green, a minister in the famed Second Presbyterian Church in Philadelphia, for example, there should be a wall between religion and politics. "To commend or to censure the systems of Party politicians" and "party politics," he reasoned, "is far beneath the object for which I should appear in this desk, or you assembled in this house." Indeed, Green was one of many ministers in the middle colonies who expressed angst over a relationship between church and state that they considered to be too close. A tradition of pluralism had influenced how those in Pennsylvania managed the two malleable spheres, and citizens in the region remained cautious over how to emphasize liberty while not trampling on the rights of any minority. Lacking the majority status of Federalist and

---

[52] Thomas Baldwin, *A Sermon, Delivered February 19, 1795: Being the Day of Public Thanksgiving Throughout the United States* (Boston: Manning & Loring, 1795), 7–8. (Emphasis in original.)

[53] Thomas Barnard, *A Sermon, Delivered on the Day of Annual Thanksgiving, December 15, 1796* (Salem, MA: Cushing, 1796), 8. (Emphasis in original.)

Congregationalist ministers in New England, religionists in Pennsylvania had to be more ecumenical.[54]

The principle of disestablishment, rather than the dogmas of providentialism, dominated Pennsylvanian thanksgiving rhetoric. "Religious liberty," Philadelphian George Duffield declared in his 1783 Thanksgiving sermon, "is a foundation principle in the constitutions of the respective states, distinguishing America from every nation in Europe." Our greatest blessing in the nation is "our religious privileges," Ashbel Green agreed a decade later. "These ought to stand foremost in every enumeration of the divine favours because they are the greatest of all." Indeed, for most thanksgiving sermons given in Pennsylvania during the 1790s, the most common invocation was gratefulness for this liberty of religious expression and freedom of conscience: it was the very venue for religious experimentation, not merely the results of piety and dogma, which buttressed America's religious identity in the region.[55]

For many in Pennsylvania, the spirit of religious liberty trumped the emphasis on religious influence, even if the two were never fully separate. Congressman, and later governor, William Findlay, when writing a manuscript history of his state's development, argued that "what contributed more to the rapid population and prosperity of that comparatively new colony than anything else was the equal protection afforded to all religious sects who lived peaceably." Importantly, it was not the principles, let alone a biblical covenant, that grounded his nationalist construction, but the energy, enthusiasm, and voluntarism of disestablishment that had created an industrious environment in which citizens could make choices and reap their rewards. It had sadly been part of the national, as well as regional, history, Findlay explained, that "the authority of Religious meetings aided the execution of the laws," because it most often turned out to be the case that "when they got possession of political power, they exceeded the bounds of equity in order to retain it." This led many Pennsylvanians to exercise that power in a way that "paid more respect to their own particular opinions, than they did to the obligations for the moral and political, to provide for the equal and efficient protection of their fellow citizens." Even within America, Pennsylvania seemed unique.[56]

---

[54] Ashbel Green, *A Sermon, Delivered in the Second Presbyterian Church in the City of Philadelphia, on the 19th of February, 1795, Being the Day of General Thanksgiving Throughout the United States* (Philadelphia: John Fenno, 1795), 20.

[55] Duffield, *Sermon*, 16. Green, *Sermon*, 21.

[56] William Findlay, "An Account of Pennsylvania Written by the Honorable William Findlay in 1812 to William Plumer," manuscript, William Findlay Collection, HSP.

It was the energetic, nearly capitalistic, spirit of religious liberty, this line of reasoning implied, that brought America's true democratic success, not the expectation of particular creeds or principles. When Elhanan Winchester, who was a pastor at the Baptist Church in Philadelphia from 1780 through 1787 before he turned to Universalism, framed America's history, he identified the Revolution as a war against the British ministry and its establishment, not just the government. In his estimation, the Revolution – and thus, the American republic – was all about the principle of religious freedom. Indeed, this reputation for religious equality had already spread across the Atlantic: English dissenting minister Richard Price described Pennsylvania as "one of the happiest countries under heaven" because "all sects of Christians have been always perfectly on a level, the legislature taking no part with any one sect against others, but protecting all equally as far as they are peaceable." Even Thomas Jefferson felt similarly. "Their harmony is unparalleled," he wrote shortly after the Revolution, "and can be ascribed to nothing but their unbounded tolerance." This was a key component to the middle colonies' sense of identity, which they then transposed in their conceptions of America in general. Indeed, it was an especially acute interplay between a regional and national sense of self.[57]

This had become a common understanding in the region. Even William White, a popular Philadelphia minister who scoffed at those who claimed a strong connection "between civil government and religion" was unnecessary – a belief he claimed earned him the titles "infidel" and "fanatic" in the City of Brotherly Love – maintained that the best role for religion was to teach general principles, not particular policies. "Religion is the proper principle of all duty," he reasoned, but this did not necessitate a direct involvement with party politics. The "Christian Society," even if it took its place within a larger political body, was based on different rules and only worked best when it was freed from the shackles of both state intervention as well as intervention in the state's business. His Episcopalian background allowed him to embrace a civil religion that was more ecumenical than dogmatic. "However high the claims of this spiritual community," he declared in 1786 at the opening of the Episcopal Church in America, "they are not such as interfere with the rights of

---

[57] Elhanan Winchester, *A Century Sermon on the Glorious Revolution* (London: J. Johnson, 1788), 7–8. Price, "Two Tracts," 18. Thomas Jefferson, "Notes on the State of Virginia" (1787), in *The Portable Thomas Jefferson*, ed. Merrill D. Peterson (New York: Penguin Books, 1977), 23–232, p. 212.

sovereignty, or with the duties of citizens and subjects." Religion was meant to influence American citizens, of course, but that method of persuasion, outside of New England at least, remained separate and distinct from the state that gave it liberty.[58]

Yet Federalist ministers in New England freely invoked the power, potential, and specifically the reach of the federal government, especially after the rise of partisan politics. Massachusetts residents were to be thankful, Boston minister John Murray invoked, for the fact that "our government is not monarchical, is not aristocratical, it is not democratical; but it is infinitely preferable to all, *It is Federal.*" He claimed that "our Federal Constitution being a collection of constitutions, is on earth, what the galaxy, or Milky Way, is in the heavens, where the combining lustre of the stars form one glorious splendour, which, instead of diminishing the light of any particular luminary, adds to the transcendent brightness of the whole." David Osgood similarly argued in his 1795 thanksgiving sermon that "our federal government is the greatest, the chief, and, in fact, the basis of the whole. Its form and constitution are by wise men universally admired." Further, "the wisdom, integrity, ability and success of its administration have commanded the respect and applause of the world." In looking back on the nation's history, Osgood was outspoken in reinforcing the federalist narrative of American government:

> Previous to the adoption of this most excellent form of government – under the old confederation, these states presented to the world a many-headed monster, frightful and alarming to all the lovers of peace and good order ... The federal government was no sooner organized, than it speedily rescued us from this eminently hazardous situation. It gave fresh vigor to each of the state governments; awed into submission the factions through all the states; restored the course of justice, and thereby established peace and good order among the citizens at large.

This peaceful union was tested, Osgood continued, by the nefarious French Minister Edmond-Charles Genêt and the "tumult and confusion" caused by a factious party "ill affected toward the federal government." Because the uproar took an especially strong hold in the "western counties in

---

[58] William White, *A Sermon on the Reciprocal Influence of Civil Policy and Religious Duty. Delivered in Christ Church, in the City of Philadelphia, on Thursday, the 19th of February, 1795, Being a Day of General Thanksgiving* (Philadelphia: Ormrod & Conrad, 1795), 9, 20. William White, *A Sermon, Delivered in Christ-Church, On the 21st Day of June, 1786, at the Opening of the Convention of the Protestant Episcopal Church, in the States of New-york, New-Jersey, Pennsylvania, Delaware, Maryland, Virginia, and South-Carolina* (Philadelphia: Hall and Sellers, 1786), 5.

Pennsylvania," there was a "rise in rebellion" in that region. These usurpations were a threat to the nation's union and peace, Osgood warned.[59]

Such was the tenor of most thanksgiving sermons in Massachusetts delivered by Congregationalist ministers. In many cases, especially following the French Revolution, the local pulpit became a place that reinforced and validated provincial political messages. And in doing so, they transformed a national ritual meant to unify disparate regions into an event that perpetuated regional division. Massachusetts's citizens did not need to subscribe to partisan newspapers in order to encounter political attacks or factional accusations. Ministers cultivated ideas of the nation, and of the people that inhabited it, as much as those who were elected as politicians. And the resulting conceptions of nationality depended as much on the local religious framework as it did on national principles.

The lasting implications of these confrontations were seen in the birth and mobilization of similarly-minded groups. In the wake of these debates, and in the face of growing Jeffersonian opposition, the Congregationalist and Presbyterian Churches, who had previously been historical rivals, agreed to the 1801 Plan of Union, which was meant to further harness their cultural aims. This ecumenical decision between two Calvinist organizations was built on a mix of frontier missionary necessities and ideological commonalities. It also set the stage for similar coalitions that were more overtly political. Indeed, the Federalist Party, especially in New England, was birthed out of these same religious concerns and structured in ways that reflected spiritual practices. At the moment of the Federalist coalition, for instance, Timothy Dwight explained how "Rational Freedom cannot be preserved without the aid of Christianity." Moreover, the Calvinist belief in a divine covenant and providentialist path enabled an institutional outlook that promoted public morality and social cohesion – elements that were central to the growing Federalist Party. Thus John Adams, while serving as president in 1797, could express his concern that Americans continue to maintain "a rational spirit of civil and religious liberty, and a calm but stead determination to support our sovereignty, as well as our moral and religious principles." This was a theology of governance.[60]

---

[59] Murray, *Substance of a Thanksgiving Sermon*, 18. (Emphasis in original.) David Osgood, *A Sermon Delivered on the Day of Annual Thanksgiving, November 20, 1794* (Boston: Samuel Hall, 1794), 16–18.

[60] Timothy Dwight, *The Nature, and Danger, of Infidel Philosophy, Exhibited in Two Discourses, Addressed to the Candidates for the Baccalaureate, in Yale College, by the*

Even after the party's demise a few decades later, there remained a spirit of consent and cultural structure that stemmed from these Congregationalist visions of a national compact. As their political institution faltered, new voluntary associations that sought to prolong their political and cultural messages were raised in its place. In an age of nation-building, many New Englanders, especially those of a Federalist persuasion, translated these ideals into actions and organizations. These were far from abstract and academic discussions. Rather, they were crucial moments in the beginnings of America's political tradition.

A thanksgiving sermon delivered by Samuel Kendal, minister of the Congregational Church in Weston, Massachusetts, in 1795 serves as a potent example of how all these elements – New England covenant, the region's pious patriotism, and Massachusetts's constructed nationalism in the wake of the French Revolution – were intertwined. The year in which the sermon was given was an eventful one: news of France's Reign of Terror was received by an earnest American audience, the Whiskey Rebellion was quelled by the federal government in western Pennsylvania, and there was a growing rift between two developing political parties. Focusing on how one Congregationalist minister in Massachusetts responded to this tumultuous moment in the Age of Revolutions illuminates the local appropriation of broader themes.

In January of 1795, George Washington declared "Thursday, the nineteenth day of February next, as a Day of Public Thanksgiving and Prayer." He encouraged local communities to "meet together, and render their sincere and hearty thanks to the Great Ruler of nations." He explicitly referenced the "calamities which afflict so many other nations" in order to highlight "the present condition of the United States" – something he attributed to "the Divine Benificence towards us." But more than general pious sentiments, the proclamation possessed an important, if subtle, political message: besides using Federalist buzzwords like the need to "establish liberty with order," it identified "the suppression of

Rev. Timothy Dwight, D.D. President of Yale College; September 9th, 1797 (New Haven, CT: George Bunce, 1798), 11. John Adams, "Speech to Both Houses of Congress," November 23, 1797, in *The Works of John Adams, Second President of the United States*, ed. Charles Francis Adams, 10 vols. (Boston: Little, Brown, 1850–56), 9:121–126, p. 121–122. See Den Hartog, *Patriotism and Piety*. For the role of religion in the rise of the Jeffersonian Republican Party, see Porterfield, *Conceived in Doubt*, 147–175. For the growth of these ecumenical missionary institutions and their impact on nationalist imaginations, see Haselby, *Origins of American Religious Nationalism*.

the late insurrection" and the nation's ability to avoid "foreign war" – key principles of Washington's administration and main tenets of his political platform – as proof of America's providential blessings. By couching his ideas and achievements in religious rhetoric and recommending local congregations to do the same, Washington enlisted ministers to reaffirm his policies to their congregations. The president aimed to frame how citizens understood their country and his presidency through grounding his Federalist agenda in providential terms.[61]

One of the many clergymen in Massachusetts who responded to Washington's request to deliver a thanksgiving sermon on February 19 was Samuel Kendal. Born in 1753, Kendal had fought in the Revolutionary War, was educated at Harvard, and was appointed to Weston's pulpit by his thirtieth birthday in 1783. Though he later played a role in the state's reaction to the War of 1812, he had done little to differentiate himself from other Congregational ministers by 1795. Indeed, he is most useful in this context explicitly because he was representative of, rather than dissented from, most of the ideas and practices of postrevolutionary New England ministers. His thanksgiving sermons were no different.[62]

Kendal prefaced the published version of his sermon by explaining the relationship between a federal religious message and the nation's commitment to religious liberty. Washington's declaration was given "not by *command*, or *appointment*," but "in compliance with the pious *recommendation* of our FEDERAL HEAD." The former description was fitted for the religious despotism America had rejected, and the latter was "a language more congenial with our notion of liberty." The goal of this event was not to force belief upon constituents, but "to unite the hearts and voices of the millions in FEDERATED AMERICA to render a *voluntary* tribute of praise and gratitude to ALMIGHTY GOD, for his goodness to us as a people." That Kendal felt it necessary to defend the proclamation in the first place revealed his anxiety over the blurred boundaries of church and state. His vision of America, like that of his Massachusetts contemporaries, embraced a limited notion of religious toleration, but also maintained the necessity for the people to establish a "proper" religion. He acknowledged the necessity of grounding the

[61] George Washington, *By the President of the United States of America, A Proclamation* (Philadelphia: Broadside, 1795).
[62] Background for Kendal comes from George A. Robinson, *A Biographical Sketch of Rev. Samuel Kendal, D.D.* (Boston: George Ellis, 1897).

religious message within the "language" of liberty, which is what required Washington's proclamation to be read as a mere "pious recommenda-tion," but he insisted that the religious message itself was crucial to the nation's prosperity. This was a transition and awkward phase for repub-lican rhetoric.[63]

Kendal began his sermon with a quotation from scripture, something Washington never did in his proclamations. Though Washington's lan-guage remained broad enough to fit into various religious traditions – he used titles like "Great Ruler of Nations" in the place of "God" – Kendal, like most of Massachusetts's ministers, made sure to tie the deity of America to the deity of the Bible. Kendal opened with a verse from Psalm 15: "Happy is that people that is in such a case; yea, happy is that people whose God is the Lord." He then explained that the same princi-ples of righteousness that governed David's people in ancient Israel still governed Washington's people in the United States. This was a simple and common extension of New England's biblical typology, in which Calvinist ministers equated their civilization with the blessed House of Israel in the Old Testament. This covenant implied that, even if the state could not enforce particular religious dogmas, the nation's survival depended on its righteous observance of divine laws. Kendal's decision to address the fact that some of his congregants were disappointed that Washington had not explicitly mentioned the Bible or Jesus Christ, which was assumed to be a "deficiency in the proclamation," demonstrated that some people were less willing to fully embrace Washington's ceremonial and abstract deist language. Political theology was a fraught practice.[64]

Kendal's sermon did not limit itself to general biblical principles and an implied connection between a Protestant covenant and national prosper-ity. It also made explicit references to political policies and nationalist agendas. He denounced those who wished to introduce the "spirit of France" into America because "we cannot justify the rashness of parties and factions" that were designed to shake the nation's stability. He echoed the Federalist mantra that "liberty without order in the body politic" is a great "solecism," and that "anarchy" was "as destructive to true rational liberty, as the most absolute despotism ever known." He reminded his listeners that "previously to the adoption of the federal constitution," order and liberty were in a "precarious" state, and that

[63] Samuel Kendal, *A Sermon, Delivered on the Day of National Thanksgiving, February 19, 1795* (Boston: Samuel Hall, 1795), 5. (Emphasis in original.)

[64] Kendal, *A Sermon*, 6–7, 9.

the recent "rashness of parties and factions" fighting against the federal government portended a similar circumstance. There "cannot exist any reason, or cause," he warned, "which will justify the rising of a part of the people" against the government and its leaders. "May anarchy never rear its hydra-head in the United America," Kendal closed. The minister's message was clear.[65]

That Kendal's thanksgiving sermon was in part a discourse on the depravity of humankind and the providence of God as well as a vindication of the Federalist agenda demonstrated the blurred boundaries of nationalist rhetoric in postrevolutionary Massachusetts. "Prudent and patriotic ministers and members of the legislative body," Kendal explained, were to work "in perfect union with the President ... in the preservation of peace and order." The New England notion of national authority depicted shared responsibility by those in federal offices and those in religious pulpits. Due to the Congregational Church's strong hold within the region, at least until the end of the century, the British tradition of pious patriotism and religious observance inherited by America continued to infuse New England political rhetoric.[66]

These interweaving influences succeeded in cultivating a providential framework through which many citizens of Massachusetts understood themselves, their government, and their new nation. The theology of humanity's fallen state both buttressed and expanded the Federalist idea of unstable citizens who required the control of an energetic government. Federalist ministers and their congregants could easily embrace the idea of a fallible populace in need of federal oversight because it matched their conception of a sinful flock in need of a sovereign shepherd. Their idea of what the American nation – both the government and the governed – really meant was thus deeply rooted in a political theology common in their religious community. Comparing this idea to that of regions further south exposes deep fissures within a broader nation that contained competing forms of both nationalism and religion.

Subtle, if significant, divergences in political theologies were not the only elements that caused divisions, however. Ministers in Massachusetts and New England also explicitly laid the groundwork for later national disunion. In constructing a national ideal based on a biblical covenant, Congregationalists were forced to consider how other regions fit into

---

[65] Ibid., 13, 17, 18, 26, 30.   [66] Ibid., 16–17.

that covenant. Even within two decades following independence, New England had already developed a distinct regional and religious identity, and people within that region – as well as the rest of the nation – were well aware of that fact. So how could they establish a national covenant that was not shared with the rest of the nation? This was accomplished through a number of ways: by positing their desired covenant as prescriptive rather than descriptive, by acknowledging that religious freedom had highlighted problems that other states had not yet solved, and by presenting their own region as a precedent for the correct balance of freedom, control, and religion.[67]

First, these Congregationalist ministers were willing to designate other states as unfortunate examples of the consequences of broken covenants. Massachusetts's clergymen frequently discussed regional issues and declared divine blessings and chastisements on various states. They highlighted, for instance, the fact that New England did not suffer major casualties when other states dealt with plagues or other issues. David Osgood pointed out how "the West-India Islands, and some of the southern states," suffered "an unusual mortality," and that citizens of Massachusetts should acknowledge that "others from whom this blessing [of health] is withdrawn, [and] it ought to excite our gratitude afresh, that to *us* it is still continued." Eliphalet Gillet, pastor of the South Church in Hallowell, noted that while "generally speaking, throughout the [Massachusetts] Commonwealth, the voice of health has been heard within our dwellings," one only need to turn an "eye for a moment to the state of Newyork [sic]" or "Philadelphia" to see what happens when "there is not a loud call for gratitude to heaven." Francis Gardner, Congregationalist pastor in Leominster, noted how "contagious, mortal diseases have prevailed in some parts of the land," but that "we have in good degree enjoyed the blessing of health" due to their reverence toward God. New England was a chosen people, but the same couldn't be said of other regions.[68]

But more than the mere connection between religious deviancy and divine retributions, ministers in Massachusetts anxiously denounced the political "fanaticisms" they felt were rampant in other states. John

---

[67] See, for example, Baldwin, *Sermon, Delivered February 19, 1795*, 16–18; Cumings, *Sermon Preached at Billerica, December 15, 1796*, 27–28.

[68] Osgood, *A Sermon Delivered on the Day of Annual Thanksgiving*, 12. Eliphalet Gillett, *A Sermon Preached at Hallowell, On the Day of the Anniversary Thanksgiving* (Hallowell, MA: Wait and Baker, 1795), 9–10. Francis Gardner, *A Sermon, Delivered on the Day of Annual Thanksgiving* (Leominster, MA: Charles Prentiss, 1796), 16–17.

Andrews blasted the "insidious exertions of strangers, inimical to our peace" that threatened the nation's stability in "sister states." Thomas Baldwin similarly denounced the "unhappy insurrection" that resulted from Pennsylvania's radical culture, and hoped for "the strengthening and cementing of the union" through more federalist politics. In many cases, events like the Whiskey Rebellion served as evidence for the fact that other regions were failing to follow the proud example of Massachusetts's stable political culture. This seemed to reaffirm the New England region's prominent place within the hierarchy of the new nation.[69]

That those in Massachusetts, perhaps more than any other state, were conscious of their own provincial identity and blessings, and often depicted their state as separate to and distinct from the rest of American culture, is key to how they understood their relationship within an evolving nation. Even while they declared that America would only succeed through its ability to keep a biblical covenant with God, they were also willing – perhaps anxious – to cut off other regions and states that did not meet that standard. This in turn made their covenant one between God and the like-minded New England states – a "regional" nation, rather than the "federal" nation. The United States, in this construction, could be dissolved if necessary. Therefore, even as the ministers declared national unity and cohesion, their rhetoric and theology provided a release mechanism through which they could sever themselves from those that failed to follow the covenant's expectations. Nationalism had become an implicitly fractured concept within Massachusetts's political theology within a decade after the Constitutional Convention. On the one hand, this allowed New England the ideological foundation upon which to present itself as a model for the rest of the nation to follow – the necessary savior of the country. On the other, it provided an escape clause for Massachusetts to possibly sever ties with deviant states.[70]

Many of these themes were, of course, present at various times in both Pennsylvania and South Carolina during the period, but rarely with as much frequency and fervency as in Federalist Massachusetts among

---

[69] John Andrews, *Sermon, Delivered February 19, 1795, Being a Day of Public Thanksgiving, Throughout the United States of America* (Newburyport, MA: Blunt & March, 1795), 19. Baldwin, *A Sermon, Delivered February 19, 1795,* 17.

[70] The early creation of an identity with regional and national tensions is ably explored in Stephanie Kermes, *Creating an American Identity: New England, 1789–1825* (New York: Palgrave Macmillan, 2008).

Congregationalist ministers. Rather, each state had their own major themes that cropped up repeatedly in their sermons, which in turn cultivated unique communities of discourse that framed political theologies. Further, there was also diversity within each state, especially when comparing more urban areas to backcountry communities, as well as between denominations. In Boston, for instance, Baptist ministers offered a much different outlook on American political culture, with some being forthright in their arguments for abolition. "As we desire and enjoy LIBERTY and FREEDOM ourselves, we will not forget our brethren, who are in captivity and slavery," preached Thomas Baldwin. "We will not only pray for them," Baldwin continued, "but whenever we shall be called upon by proper authority, we will cheerfully subscribe for their redemption, and restore them again to the embraces of their friends, and the blessings of freedom." Some in Massachusetts grew tired of the Congregationalist rhetoric, as one 1795 newspaper complained the ministers appeared more as "party managers rather than spiritual teachers." Yet these complaints only reaffirmed the prominence of the Congregationalist message and nationalist vision.[71]

These broad and, at times, abstract principles significantly influenced on how particular individuals constructed ideas about their own nation. These ministers helped cultivate the framework in which their congregants could interpret their world and the events taking place within it. They also laid the groundwork for broader affiliation and political allegiance. And in so doing, they perpetuated regional ideas and parochial concerns already present before the Constitution. In an Age of Revolutions in which everything seemed in transition, religion provided the tools through which to construct a consistent allegiance. Understanding this process – this "practice" of nationalism – is crucial to reconstructing the provincial mindsets of early Americans. Even when they attempted to cultivate a broader sense of nationhood, religious communities often created nations after their own likeness and image.

---

[71] Baldwin, *A Sermon, Delivered February 19, 1795*, 22. Newspaper quoted in Haselby, *Origins of American Religious Nationalism*, 77.

PART II

IMAGINING DISUNION

George Washington could already see the growing political factions by the end of his presidency in 1796. Aided by Alexander Hamilton, he hoped to address these ills in his farewell address. "In contemplating the causes which may disturb our union," he declared, the greatest problem appeared to be geographic and ideological discord. He warned about "designing men" who "may endeavor to excite a belief that there is a real difference of local interests and views." Washington hoped the nation would recognize that the Union was held together by shared values and priorities. Only a few decades later, however, another Southerner, John C. Calhoun, scoffed at the hope for a unified American culture. There were such distinct interests, he argued in his "Disquisition on Government," that a numerical majority of Northern voters proved to be tyrants over Southern planters. He argued that the government should be comprised in a way to represent "interests as well as numbers," where representatives not of states but rather of "interests" (like slaveholders) had the power to overrule conflicting policies. Not only were America's interests divided, but they were often directly competing.[1]

How did people grow apart so quickly? The following three chapters explore how citizens in three states – Massachusetts, Pennsylvania, and South Carolina – conceived new forms of political belonging as the perceived national unity of the founding period gave way to ideological strife and, eventually, military conflict. If positing a novel form of cultural union was an imaginative enterprise, so too was conceiving political disunion.

---

[1] George Washington, "Farewell Address," September 17, 1796, Library of Congress, LOC, www.loc.gov/resource/mgw2.024/?sp=229 (accessed February 2017). John C. Calhoun, "A Disquisition on Government," vol. 1 of *The Works of John C. Calhoun*, 6 vols. Richard K. Crallé, ed. (New York: D. Appleton and Company, 1854–1857), 28–29.

3

(Re)Constructing State, Nation, and Empire in the Second War with Great Britain

It depends more upon Massachusetts than any state in the Union to save us from civil war, and, in the event, a despotic government.

Manasseh Cutler, 1802[1]

Another state has acquired the epithet of the cradle of the revolution, but may it not be said of this, that she nursed it with the fabled tenderness of that bird, which furnishes an emblem of eternal love? Promptly she stood forth the first, to constitute that body which organized opposition, and e'er the general voice had called into action the eloquent pen of a Jefferson, Carolina was forever free.

–William Johnson, 1812[2]

Whenever it shall appear that these causes are radical and permanent, a separation by equitable arrangement, will be preferable to an alliance by constraint, among nominal friends, but real enemies, inflamed by mutual hatred and jealousies, and invited by intestine divisions, contempt, and aggression from abroad.

–Proceedings of the Hartford Convention, 1815[3]

---

[1] Manasseh Cutler to Ephraim Cutler, March 14, 1802, in *Life, Journals and Correspondence of Rev. Manasseh Cutler, LL.D.*, ed. William Parker Cutler and Julia Perkins Cutler, 2 vols. (Cincinnati, OH: James Clarke, 1888), 2:98.

[2] William Johnson, *An Oration, Delivered in St. Philip's Church; Before the Inhabitants of Charleston, South-Carolina, On Saturday the Fourth of July, 1812, In Commemoration of American Independence; by Appointment of the '76 Association, and Published at the Request of that Society* (Charleston, SC: W. P. Young, 1813), 17.

[3] *Public Documents, Containing Proceedings of the Hartford Convention of Delegates; Report of the Commissioners, While at Washington; Letters from Massachusetts Members in Congress* (Boston: Published by Order of the Senate, 1815), 15.

War had the potential to transform both a nation's boundaries as well as priorities. In the 1770s, war with Britain created thirteen united states and forged a nationalist identity that, while reconstructed and realigned in the following decade, held firm as part of American public discourse. Less than a half-century later, Americans again faced an armed conflict with the United Kingdom as well as a possible turning point in political union. Prodded both by the direction of America's political tradition as well as the complications imposed by the crisis with England, citizens in Massachusetts, along with several other New England states, came to question the physical and ideological limits of America's federal body. They feared that the United States might no longer properly represent their interests. Could an expanding nation outgrow its governing purpose?

Americans were not the only people in the Atlantic world pressured to reconsider geographic and cultural borders in the face of military conflict. Across the ocean, the Napoleonic wars forced Europeans in a host of nations to similarly address issues of allegiance. This chapter engages the various strands of nationalism that developed during the first decade of the nineteenth century by once again focusing on Federalist ministers and politicians in Massachusetts, and it examines how those tensions came to the forefront during the War of 1812. These debates only make sense within the broader Atlantic context of war and patriotism during the same period, especially the awakening of German nationalism and the evolutions of ethnic and civic forms of patriotism. The flowering of American patriotism that followed America's second battle for independence is well known – "the people," Albert Gallatin wrote in 1815, were now "more American; they feel and act more as a nation; and I hope that the permanency of the Union is thereby better secured" – but such a political and cultural unification was never inevitable, let alone undisputed. The war tested both the boundaries and purposes of the American empire and, as a result, introduced new patterns of balancing state and federal interests.[4]

––––––––––––

The first decade of the nineteenth century proved to be a disappointment for many elite politicians in Massachusetts. The diminishing power of the Federalist Party, the rising Republican dominance, and the perception of an increasing threat to religious and social cohesion – all of these impulses

––––––––––––

[4] Albert Gallatin to Matthew Lyon, May 7, 1816, in *The Writings of Albert Gallatin*, ed. Henry Adams, 3 vols. (Philadelphia: J. B. Lippincott, 1879), 1:700.

combined to make many worry for the nation's future. In part due to his declared commitment to restore America's potential and reverse its cultural demise, Abijah Bigelow, a lawyer born in England and educated at Dartmouth, was elected to the Massachusetts House of Representatives in 1807 and the United States Congress in 1810. Bigelow was only one of many Federalists whose simultaneous disappointment with American politics and commitment to the American union led to a tumultuous debate over the state's role within the nation. For these individuals, even if the nationalist flame had dimmed, it was not too late for it to be reignited.

In an oration delivered on the Fourth of July, 1809, Bigelow used the ceremonial occasion to identify the primary cause of the nation's ills. "Of the various dangers to which Republics are explored," he warned his audience, "none threaten their existence more than foreign influence and particularities on the one hand, and internal factions and division on the other." He explained that the first threat was destined "to produce dangerous and fatal alliances," and the second to "beguile the people to withdraw their confidence from their wisest and best citizens, and bestow it upon Demagogues, who do not deserve it." These interconnected threats, according to Bigelow, had already taken root within American culture, as citizens "felt this fatal effect." Indeed, Bigelow feared that the rotten disease of the French Revolution had "spread desolation and waste wherever [the ideas of radical democracy] go, [and] has already had a most astonishing influence upon the politics, the sentiments and the morals of the American people." Akin to the "plagues of Egypt," these demoralizing principles had "swarmed in all parts of the United States." The nation was under siege.[5]

Yet Bigelow was not quite ready to give up on the young republic. "I trust in God," he declared, that "there is yet a spirit in the American people, which when properly directed, will secure us from danger." He believed a valiant effort would enable "reason [to] prevail over faction," halt Americans' "hatred [of] England [before] plung[ing] us into a war," and cease the "fatal alliance with France," which was, after all, the root of all these problems. Bigelow was far from alone with these concerns. Harrison Gray Otis, another Massachusetts state congressman, similarly wrote that, though "the government of this country is unquestionably intimidated though not corrupted by France," and that "the mass of people are infected with strong prejudices against Britain," there still

[5] Abijah Bigelow, Fourth of July Oration, 1809, 5, 6, 10, Abijah Bigelow Papers, AAS.

remained "the most intelligent and respectable men in the country [that] are not however of this description." Those with a correct understanding of how the nation and the broader economy worked, he reasoned, "tremble for the prosperity and fate of Britain, and consider her justly as the Bulwark of the liberties of this country and mankind." While Bigelow and Gray both believed an undue influence of French radicalism had destabilized the American nation, they still held that a restoration of true Anglo-American priorities could reform the republic before it was too late.[6]

There is a seemingly puzzling thread in Bigelow's and Otis's remarks. That these Massachusetts politicians, only three decades after the United States had gained its independence from the British crown, and amidst another escalating conflict with England, invoked a connection to British patriotism in their own construction of America's future hints at the contested practice of nationalism in the years leading up to the War of 1812. The events and circumstances that preceded the conflict with Great Britain forced many to reconsider the nature of and commitment to an American national ideal, and the results of the war once again both reaffirmed and revised those impulses throughout the country. Every state was forced to question the importance and nature of union during this period, but the anxiety was especially acute in Massachusetts, where politicians actively sought to reaffirm and develop a state identity that was alternatively specified as unique to Massachusetts, New England, and America in general. These competing and overlapping allegiances were both muted and emphasized at alternating points, and could serve as either unifying or divisive depending on the occasion and context. Indeed, public and private discussion concerning the conflict only deepened the divisions of national interests while at the same time bolstering unionist discourse among the various states.

One of the reasons for this regional angst was a growing national disagreement concerning America's geographic focus. While many in Massachusetts, especially those of the Federalist persuasion, continued to look east toward Europe, and especially Britain, for a future of Atlantic collaboration, many others increasingly looked west for further expansion. As president, Thomas Jefferson oversaw a radical extension of American land that represented a tangible realignment of American interests. After the addition of the Louisiana Territory, which doubled the nation's property, Jefferson explained, "by enlarging the empire of liberty, we multiply it's auxiliaries, & provide new sources of renovation."

---

[6] Ibid., 11–12. Harrison Gray Otis to Henry Gray Otis, Jr., April 30, 1811, HGOP.

America, if it was to thrive, must pay attention to "the interests of my Western brethren," because that was the country's future. Many citizens followed the clarion call for settlement. Within four decades of the ratification of the Constitution, the West grew to contain more residents than the original thirteen colonies had at the moment of the nation's founding. Kentucky and Tennessee alone came to hold more people than New England. Not only did this change the literal shape of America's boundaries, but the admission of new states shifted the balance of national interests.[7]

Not all were happy with this development, especially those in Massachusetts. Fisher Ames, for instance, complained in the wake of the Louisiana acquisition that America's eagerness to settle westward was akin to rushing "like a comet into infinite space." The zeal, though commendable, had a price. "In our wild career, we may jostle some other world out of its orbit, but we shall, in every event, quench the light of our own." Ames feared that the admission of more states meant a dilution of New England's power, which implied a concomitant shift with America's character. Another Massachusetts politician, the congressional delegate Stephen Higginson, believed that Jefferson and "the Virginia faction have certainly formed a deliberate plan to govern and depress New England; and this eagerness to extend our territory and create new States is an essential part of it." Whereas Jefferson and the hundreds of thousands of Americans who supported expansion saw this "renovation" as crucial for America's national claims, others interpreted it as a threat to what they envisioned their nation to comprise.[8]

These debates over America's parameters played a big role in the coming of the War of 1812, especially given that some of the primary, albeit often silent, reasons for the conflict was further westward and northern expansion. The acquisition of Canada and the undisputed sovereignty of western lands were strong temptations for American politicians who viewed the nation as an evolving empire. Yet these same concerns

---

[7] Thomas Jefferson to Benjamin Chambers, December 28, 1805, *National Archives: Founders Online*, http://founders.archives.gov/documents/Jefferson/99-01-02-2910 (accessed February 2015). See also Peter S. Onuf, *Jefferson's Empire: The Language of American Nationhood* (Charlottesville: University of Virginia Press, 2000).

[8] Fisher Ames to Christopher Gore, October 3, 1803, in *Works of Fisher Ames, With a Selection from his Speeches and Correspondence* (Boston: Little, Brown and Company, 1854), 324. Stephen Higginson to Thomas Pickering, November 22, 1803, in "Letters of Stephen Higginson, 1783–1804," in *American Historical Association Annual Report* 1 (1896): 837. See also Sam Haselby, *The Origins of American Religious Nationalism* (Oxford University Press, 2015), esp. 1–3.

were points of consternation for those who felt that America was losing its original intention and changing its foundational balance of interests. Massachusetts angst over the War of 1812 is best understood when their anguish over real and possible geographic expansion is placed alongside their economic and trade concerns with England. They were pulled in two different directions. Not only did they possess prolonged sympathies with the British Empire that were not present in the rest of the nation, but they also had poignant fears concerning the American empire that was then being shaped.[9]

Though conflict with Britain was far from new, this was a new age of battle for the Western world. The Napoleonic Wars introduced a new perspective with which Europeans understood international conflict. What had previously been perpetual wars that primarily involved kings and militias and only occasionally disrupted society, the cultural, social, and intellectual developments of the eighteenth century, especially the 1790s, now made war a new and terrible entity. Military strategist Carl von Clauswitz declared in 1812, "it is not [now] the king who wages war on the king, not an army against another army, but a people against another people." Elsewhere during the same period, von Clauswitz famously stated that war was the "continuation of political intercourse, carried on with other means." War was now a cultural moment, not merely a military engagement. An aged Edmund Burke noticed this shift in 1796 and described it as "an armed doctrine" that incorporated physical, moral, and even spiritual sensibilities. To go to war in the early nineteenth century implied recognition of broad cultural implications that transcended the battlefield. Just as Americans geared up for another British conflict, Johann Gottlieb Fichte delivered a series of lectures, later compiled as *Addresses to the German Nation*, which asked similar questions concerning cultural nationalism. Fichte, like many other German authors during the decade, came to view the period as a "war of liberation" that regenerated German culture and birthed a new era of romantic nationalism. War can just as easily tear apart national cohesion and political allegiance as it can strengthen it.[10]

[9] For northern and westward expansion at the center of the War of 1812, see Alan Taylor, *The Civil War of 1812: American Citizens, British Subjects, Irish Rebels, and Indian Allies* (New York: Alfred A. Knopf, 2010).

[10] Carl von Clauswitz, quoted in David A. Bell, *The First Total War: Napoleon's Europe and the Birth of Warfare as We Know It* (Boston: Houghton Mifflin Company, 2007), 10. Edmund Burke, *Two Letters Addressed to a Member of the Present Parliament, on the Proposal for Peace with the Regicide Directory of France* (London: F. and C. Rivington,

Set against this backdrop, America's second conflict with Britain and the perpetual battle with nationalist identities takes on a new hue. Much had changed in the three decades since Americans declared independence. Politicians were not just defining their nation in contrast to the British Empire, but they were left to define the nature of America's empire as well. In an age of radical geographical expansion and frequent statehood admission, this was a crucial debate. It was within this context that many individuals in Massachusetts began to question whether they belonged to the Union at all. In an Atlantic world where national allegiances were becoming much more crucial to a society's identity, Federalists in Massachusetts explored options of realignment and reconceptualization. Ironically, their responses to this national and transnational conflict laid the foundation for America's states' rights philosophy, which emphasized the importance of regional interests over national stability. These ideas would remain fallow for the time being, especially in the wake of the war's ending, but they set the stage for later nationalist conflict.

After John Adams lost to Thomas Jefferson in 1800, Massachusetts feared that a new political order had overcome the nation. A Virginian once again held the presidency, and Jefferson, and later Madison, lacked the Federalist sympathies that had made Washington amenable to New Englanders. As a result, many despaired over their state's fallen status. "We are parties in name to a confederacy," claimed one Bostonian pamphlet, "over which we have no influence, nor control, nor effective voice in the national councils, and the wishes and the policy of New England are only known as they furnish themes for the invective and irony of those who rule the nation." Some smelled a conspiracy. "The Virginia faction have certainly formed a deliberate plan to govern & depress New England," hypothesized Stephen Higginson. But whether it was the deliberate machinations of a small number of Virginians or the unexpected realities of the party system, politicians in Massachusetts were worried they were becoming increasingly insignificant. By 1810, one senator came to fear that "it is written in the volume of fate, that a President is never again to come from New England." Massachusetts, previously seen as the cradle of liberty and the flame that ignited the

1796), 22–23. See Bell, *The First Total War*, 9–13, for a general overview of this transformation.

Revolution, was now at the mercy of other states that did not share the same cultural outlook on America's future or even a similar understanding of American culture itself.[11]

Many of these Federalists were on the defensive not only because of political divisions within the broader nation, but also because of cultural disharmony within the state of Massachusetts itself. Though Federalists remained in power for much of the first decade of the nineteenth century, Democratic-Republicans made inroads and eventually achieved high political offices. Elbridge Gerry became the state's first non-Federalist governor in 1810, and in 1811 Joseph Bradley Varnum became its first senator from the Democratic-Republican Party. Thus, the state's, let alone the region's, political and cultural identities were never as harmonious as Federalists voices liked to depict. If they could not dominate their own state, how could they shape the broader nation? This imbedded an anxiety to conceptualize a unified society in the face of competing political visions.

Yet even as their political power appeared to diminish, a commitment to cultural superiority remained central to the Federalist Party's nationalist rhetoric. If Massachusetts's influence was on the decline, it was not due to a lack of either ability or earnestness. Fisher Ames argued that "of all colonies that ever were founded," Massachusetts remained "the largest, the most assimilated, and to use the modern jargon, *nationalized*, the most respectable and prosperous, the most truly interesting to America and to humanity, more unlike and more superior to other people, (the English excepted,) than the old Roman race to their neighbours and competitors." The fact that Ames compared Massachusetts, and not America, to England is indicative of how nationalist language retained a local framework for many. Indeed, his use of "nationalized" as a descriptor for the state's culture reveals how porous local and federal identities remained during the period. This linguistic dexterity embodied the cultural tensions at work.[12]

[11] *A Defence of the Legislature of Massachusetts, or the Rights of New England Vindicated* (Boston: Reperatory Office, 1804), 4. Stephen Higginson to Thomas Pickering, November 22, 1803, Thomas Pickering Papers, MHS. James Loyd to Harrison Gray Otis, HGOP. See also Thomas Dwight to Jedidiah Morse, December 19, 1800, Joel Warren Norcross Papers, MHS. For the political transformation that followed the "Jeffersonian Revolution" in 1800, see James Horn, Jan Ellen Lewis, and Peter S. Onuf, eds., *The Revolution of 1800: Democracy, Race, and the New Republic* (Charlottesville: University of Virginia Press, 2002).

[12] Fisher Ames, *The Works of Fisher Ames*, ed. Seth Ames, 2 vols. (Boston: Little, Brown and Company, 1854), 2:134. (Emphasis added.)

If Massachusetts's residents were forced to look outside their own state borders, they rarely looked beyond the general region of New England. One Boston resident wrote, "the God of nature, in his infinite goodness, has made the people of New England to excel every other people that ever existed in the world." Similarly, George Washington Stanley, in an address that was meant to celebrate America's independence, noted that "inhabitants of new England" were, first and foremost, dedicated to being "in principle New-Englandmen." Perhaps based in angst over their frustrated national ambitions, these politicians blended Massachusetts and New England identities in a way that cultivated a strong regional allegiance. Not only did those in the state continue to invoke the term "national" when describing their local affairs – though the adjective was becoming more frequently used in relation to the United States – citizens of the state retained the belief that their particular nationalist culture superseded those of other states.[13]

There was an ethnic component to these nationalist imaginations, especially in the face of increased immigration. This emphasis on ethnicity may seem out of place within America's typical pluralist – though still European-American – discourse. Scholars have argued that the ethnic basis for nationalist language found in most European nations never really appeared in the United States. Yet just as America's tension with Britain increased, many in Massachusetts and other New England states loudly reaffirmed the purity of their English heredity. Part of this was political angst toward the South. But it was also rooted in a perceived cultural discontinuity with the entire nation. Alden Bradford, later Secretary of the Commonwealth, claimed in 1805 that the state's ancestors were "of a totally different character" than the mixed heritage found in other regions. When Jedediah Morse wrote his history of New England, he explained that the region's population descended from people who were "almost universally of English descent," a virtue absent in other parts of America. Similarly, minister William Cunningham Jr. proclaimed to his congregation, "our progenitors were choice scions from the best English stock. They were not plucked up and thrown upon these wilds to live or die, as the convicts at Botany-Bay and other parts of New Holland." Nor, he more directly explained, "did their natural wants force them here for

---

[13] *Columbian Centinel*, February 2, 1814, MHS. George Washington Stanley, *An Oration, Delivered at Wallingford, August 8th, 1805: In Commemoration of the Independence of the United States* (New Haven, CT: Sidney Press, 1805), 11.

substance, like the wild *Irish* and sour *Germans* in *Pennsylvania.*" Ethnic homogeneity was central to the Massachusetts imagination.[14]

Ethnic nationalism was far from new. Indeed, the idea that nationality was based more on a common ancestry than a civic allegiance predominated European thought prior to the late eighteenth century. And ironically, it was the very type of national consciousness that many American nationalists rejected during the founding period. Yet it claimed strong cultural capital among Federalists in Massachusetts during the decade preceding the War of 1812. For many, it was a way to stave off political opposition from heterogeneous Southern communities. More importantly, however, it was a way to theoretically breach nationalist allegiance by reinterpreting what a "nation" meant in the first place. This appeal to ethnic nationalism through a mythic past of social homogeneity was bred from anxiety over whether they shared the same political interests upon which the American union was perceivably built. It provided the intellectual tools with which to construct a competing vision that validated their culture in opposition to Virginian resistance.[15]

Those in Massachusetts were not alone in hearkening to a mythic ethnic past in response to political turmoil. Indeed, the Age of Revolutions witnessed a number of communities seeking a nationalist identity that was centered on a narrow interpretation of ethnicity within a broader context of political heterogeneity. Though the common understanding of democratic reform during the period privileged civic over ethnic alliance, such a triumph was far from unanimous. Understanding these competing models makes sense of the cultural currents from which Americans drew. Across the Atlantic in the previous two centuries, for instance, many Germans, spread across forty-one separate territories in Prussia, Austria, and various bodies of the Confederation of Rhine,

---

[14] Alden Bradford, *A Sermon Delivered at Plymouth, December 2, 1804, on the Anniversary of the Landing of Our Fathers in December, 1620* (Boston: Gilbert and Dean, 1804), 7. Jedediah Morse, *The American Universal Geography, Or, A View of the Present State of All Empires, Kingdoms, States, and Republics in the Known World, and of the United States in Particular* (Boston: Isaiah Thomas, 1802), 310. William Cunningham, Jr., *An Oration, Pronounced at Fitchburg, July 4, 1803* (Leominster, MA: Adams & Wilder, 1803), 5. (Emphasis in original.)

[15] See John A. Armstrong, *Nations Before Nationalism* (Chapel Hill: University of North Carolina Press, 1982); Anthony D. Smith, *The Ethnic Origins of Nations* (New York: Blackwell, 1986). Historians have often argued that nationalism during this time was either "ethnic" or "civic." However, as can be seen in the American context, both conceptions of nationalism could be present at the same time, and they worked together in an uneasy yet dynamic manner.

inaugurated the birth of a new cultural nationalism that was meant to unite a disparate people. Though loosely connected, at least in theory, to the Holy Roman Empire of the German Nation, political allegiances were in flux even as Napoleon attempted to conquer the entire continent. In response to this political realignment, there were many German authors who sought to form a cultural identity that would unite a divided and beleaguered people. One novelist noted in the midst of the early crisis, "I see Saxon, Bavarian, Württemberg, and Hamburg patriots," but "German patriots, who love the entire *Reich* as their fatherland ... Where are they?" Confronted with political instability and the threat of war, many Germans looked to an ethnic foundation to save them from potential oblivion.[16]

It was at this moment that Germans began to imagine something resembling a "German nation." In doing so, they provided examples of cultural nationalism for a new political order. Whereas nationality had previously been connected to the broader, if disparate, empire or, more often, the local municipalities, authors like Johann Gottfried Herder argued that the nation was actually comprised of individuals who shared an ethnic and cultural tradition. In part a response to France's broadening civic nationalism, Germans cultivated a sense of *Volksnation* that encompassed all its people, no matter their distinct feudal or state institutions. These ideological underpinnings allowed the very concept of a German nation to be possible to someone like Fichte, whose famous *Speeches to a German Nation* were delivered when there was no such thing as a German political body. The Age of Revolutions did not mark the end of ethnic belonging as a primary source for nationhood.[17]

German nationalism was not a direct source for those considering the limits of American political union in Massachusetts, but the example proves worthwhile for two reasons. First, it demonstrates the liminality of ethnic and cultural identities in the Age of Revolutions. A new democratic culture seemed to shed previous social order based on lineage, but the chaotic results left some to consider the potential negative ramifications. In this light, Alden Bradford's seemingly quixotic statements

---

[16] Christoph Martin Wieland, quoted in Gregory Moore, "Introduction," in *Fichte: Addresses to the German Nation*, ed. and trans. Gregory Moore (Cambridge: Cambridge University Press, 2008), xi–xxxvi, p. xiv.

[17] Joachim Whaley, "Reich, Nation, Volk: Early Modern Perspectives," *Modern Language Review* 101: 442–455; David Martyn, "Borrowed Fatherland: Nationalism and the Language Purism in Fichte's *Addresses to the German Nation*," *Germanic Review* 72 (1997): 303–315.

concerning his fellow Massachusetts citizens' genetic makeup does not seem as ill fitted for the day. Second, it provides a potent example of how others drew from these cultural depositories in order to react to difficult political realities. The Germans, similar to those in Massachusetts, faced a grim political future in the first decade of the nineteenth century in which they believed their rights and interests were not being accounted for, and were therefore forced to construct reasons for their situation and meaning for their struggle. In New England, they could blame it on the inordinate power of Southern states, as Jedediah Morse did in his geopolitical narrative of American history. Fichte's *Characteristics of the Present Age*, written in Germany around the same time, similarly depicted a historical framework in which Germans were punished for not following the correct cultural blueprint. Both turned to romantic notions of ethnic belonging to address national problems.[18]

But Americans in Massachusetts were not quite ready to make the same radical pronouncements as Fichte and other German romantics. They were, at that point, unwilling to cut the cord to America's union. Even as many feared a diminished status for their state and some radicals, like Timothy Pickering, began to experiment with ideas of separation, most retained a firm connection to the idea of union and demonstrated mixed, yet concurrent, allegiances to state and nation. Massachusetts was destined, they believed, to be the redeemer state in a fallen nation, and their glory was to be found *through* the American system, not *outside* of it. "It depends more upon Massachusetts than any other state in the Union," wrote Manasseh Cutler, "to save us from civil war, and, in the event, a despotic government." Similarly, Fisher Ames, when he considered the direction state politics should take, claimed, "if the Federal party [in Massachusetts] can save itself it will save the country." The reformation of the state's political structure, they believed, was the only solution to a country that had lost its way.[19]

This was a powerful idea for many. Only by remaining firmly attached to the nation, as Joseph Buckingham explained, could the state legislature "rescue our country from destruction." This nationalist structure envisioned by these Massachusetts Federalists depended on the preservation

[18] For Fichte's historical narrative, see M. H. Abrams, *Natural Supernaturalism: Tradition and Revolution in Romantic Literature* (New York: Oxford University Press, 1971), 217–219.
[19] Cutler to Ephraim Cutler, March 14, 1802, in *Life, Journals and Correspondence of Rev. Manasseh Cutler*, 2:98. Fisher Ames to Roger Wolcott, December 2, 1802, Roger Wolcott Papers, Connecticut Historical Society.

and triumph of their particular brand of politics, which they argued was based upon a proper understanding of the Constitution. "If the nation is to be saved," Buckingham explained, "we think this great result can only be produced by the operation of all the talents, all the resources, all the energy, and all the virtues of Massachusetts." As the state's economy grew increasingly grim due to Madison's embargoes, their rhetoric became increasingly earnest. "The preservation of the sacred fire of liberty," proclaimed an 1812 election circular, "and the destiny of the republican model of government are deeply, and perhaps *finally* staked, on the question now to be decided by the Electors of Massachusetts." The state's emphasis on their importance to federal politics blended their parochial concerns with nationalist expression.[20]

The messianic language of these political arguments highlighted the risk of their project. Redeeming the nation required a regeneration of its cultural politics. This, again, was a common theme in the Age of Revolutions. In France, for instance, national regeneration often took religiously rhetorical forms like "revival," "restoration," or even "resurrection." Fichte's *Letters to a German Nation* took on a distinct messianic tone, as he declared that "saving" a sense of German nationalist unity would in turn "save" the world. "If you sink," Fichte told his audience, "all humanity sinks with you." This was a concept that transcended nations and denominations, though each of those contexts appropriated it in different ways. It also emphasized the transformative nature still believed to exist through religious belief within democratic institutions. Federalists in Massachusetts, in response to internal and external conflicts, were addressing a broader Atlantic problem of representation and national belonging.[21]

But they faced what seemed an insurmountable problem at home. America, especially after 1800, seemed to be moving in a fundamentally different direction than what those in Massachusetts original desired. The nation was far from the homogenous culture they believed was necessary for a national compact. After John Adams left the White House, they were

---

[20] Joseph Buckingham, *The Ordeal: A Critical Journal of Politicks and Literature*, February 18, 1809. Nicholas Tillinghast et al. to Oliver Harvey, November 7, 1812, Broadside Collection, LOC. (Emphasis in original.) See also Otis et al. to Timothy Bigelow, February 9, 1810, Miscellaneous Collection, MHS; Ames, *Works* 2:131; *Centinel*, March 2, 1805, MHS; *The Patriotick Proceedings of the Legislature of Massachusetts, During their Session from January 26 to March 4, 1809* (Boston: J. Cushing, 1809): 99.

[21] Bell, *Cult of the Nation in France*, 75. Fichte, *Letters to the German Nation*, 155.

faced with the prospect of diametrically opposed and competing regional cultures, which they decried as the "new system" in political pamphlets. Southern control and westward expansion dominated federal concerns. At times, this anxiety led to an increase in their ethnic rhetoric and their belief in cultural superiority; at other moments, it forced them to consider how they could work through the political system with states that did not share the same views. But in most cases, they cast their own parochial activities as necessary to reform and regenerate the broader country, an action that was to be accomplished through both example and influence. That they sought to reform the nation through their own machinations is obvious, but within those machinations, they were left to deal with national concerns that stemmed from cultural discontinuity.

The distinctness of these Federalists' message is clear through a comparison to their American contemporaries. Elsewhere in the nation there was an increase in nationalist cultural rhetoric and calls for a united front that embraced divergent cultures. Jeffersonians based their discourse on an assumption that theirs was the voice of the nation with a heterogeneous society yet homogenous body politic. One Charleston resident, after acknowledging that there were rocky moments between the state and the nation, pleaded, "Now that the tree of liberty has become strong, towering and luxuriant, let us forget the storms that beat upon its youthful branches, and almost shook it from its base." America had survived its turbulent years, and thus a firm devotion to the Union was now necessary. Once all the states were more firmly united, "the cultivation of taste and science, and the dissemination of truth and reason" would spring from a shared national character. Even as New England questioned its position in the Union, Southern states reaffirmed their commitment.[22]

Western settlement intensified these issues. Ever since their colonization, eastern citizens worried that these western societies lacked the cultural connection to bind them to the federal union. As far back as

---

[22] Hext McCall, *An Oration, Delivered in St. Michael's Church, Before the Inhabitants of Charleston, South-Carolina, on the Fourth of July, 1810. In Commemoration of American Independence. By Appointment of the American Revolution Society, and Published at the Request of that Society, and also of the South-Carolina State Society of Cincinnati* (Charleston, SC: W. P. Young, 1810), 4, 16–17. For the increase in nationalist rhetoric, especially in the South, see Alan Taylor, "Dual Nationalisms: Legacies of the War of 1812," in *What So Proudly We Hailed: Essays on the Contemporary Meaning of the War of 1812*, ed. Pietro S. Nivola and Peter J. Kastor (Washington, DC: Brookings Institution Press, 2012), 67–96.

1755, Benjamin Franklin worried that the new communities in "the great country back of the Appalachian mountains" would make them different "from our people, confined to the country between the sea and the mountains." These fears continued during the constitutional debates, as John Jay "fear[ed] that Western Country will one day give us trouble" because "govern[ing] them will not be easy." Thomas Jefferson similarly worried that Westerners might wish to "declare themselves a separate people." Cultivating a sense of American nationalism west of the Appalachian Mountains was far from determined. Yet with the growth of the Jeffersonians came a distinct democratic impulse in northwestern states. Congressmen like Jonathan Jennings in Indiana and Jeremiah Morrow in Ohio tethered the northwestern frontier to a Jeffersonian image of America as a workingman's nation, often in contrast to both the slaveholding South and the Federalist Northeast. For conservatives in New England, then, the western settlement's development reinforced their sense of isolation in the broader republic. They were now surrounding on all sides by people who held a different conception of America.[23]

The growing conflict with Britain over trade, and the increasing lust for more land and federal expansion, threatened to test these strains of nationalist and sectionalist thought. For Massachusetts, the embargoes declared by the federal government in retaliation for Britain's impressment practices crippled its economy, and the addition of more states promised to damage the already-delicate position of the state within the country. For Southern states like South Carolina, the conflict promised a chance to prove their nationalist project – a loose connection of states tied together more through national pride than a centralized government – could withstand an international crisis, and that the acquisition of more land provided the opportunity to expand the nation's interconnected economy and growing empire. A second war with Britain enabled citizens from all states to measure the nation's growth and progress since the Revolution, as well as reconsider the purpose and goals for their developing republic.[24]

[23] Benjamin Franklin, "A Plan for Settling Two Western Colonies" (1755), in *The Papers of Benjamin Franklin: Digital Edition*, http://franklinpapers.org/ (accessed January 2015). John Jay to Jefferson, April 24, 1787, in Julian P. Boyd et al., eds., *Papers of Thomas Jefferson* (Princeton: Princeton University Press, 1955–), 11:313–314. Jefferson to Madison, January 30, 1787, in *The Portable Thomas Jefferson*, 417. See Haselby, *The Origins of American Religious Nationalism*; Wood, *Empire of Liberty*, 357–365.

[24] As Nicole Eustace has argued, the war can be considered "a cultural event as much as a military one"; its importance was found in pamphlets and broadsides as much as

War with Britain came at a time when cultural fracturing was becoming increasingly evident. In 1808, the British spy John Henry described America as an unstable "coalition of heterogenous interests, opinions and prejudices." In his estimation, they were "seventeen states and *no hoop* will make a barrel that can last long." Many observers had long assumed this loose "coalition," yet the extending print culture and expanding geography of the Union brought the issues to the forefront. The conflict, then, enabled Americans to experiment with shaping popular opinion. A society at war was a society that could contest arguments and shift interests. While the battle originated over naval rights and land disputes, it quickly became a venue through which America's tenuous patriotism, latterly stressed by sectional factions, was tested and reconsidered. If the conflict is best understood as a civil war, then the domestic disputes are as crucial as the international ramifications.[25]

Indeed, the War of 1812 was a serious test for America's fragile, and fractured, nationalist imagination. Some saw the war as a sequel to the Revolution and a chance for citizens to prove their patriotic allegiance. James Madison, in his declaration of war, framed support for the military cause in nationalist terms: "I do moreover exhort al [sic] the good people of the United States, as they love their country," he exclaimed, "and they value the precious heritage derived from the virtue and valour of their fathers." They should support the government "in preserving order, in promoting concord, in maintaining the authority and the efficacy of the laws, and in supporting and invigorating all the measures which may be adopted by the Constituted Authorities, for obtaining a speedy, a just, and an honourable peace." An anonymous essayist in Baltimore concurred and stated that war was "the parent of noble feelings and the touchstone, in republics, of real talents and worth," and that another battle with Britain would instill the "heart with hope and confidence" and return the country to "the scene of American glory in arms." The renewed war

---

battlefields and warships. Eustace, *1812: War and the Passions of Patriotism* (Philadelphia: University of Pennsylvania Press, 2012), x.

[25] John Henry to Herman Witsius Ryland, November 16, 1807, and June 5, 1808, in *The Political Adventures of John Henry: The Record of an International Imbroglio*, ed. E. A. Cruikshank (Toronto: Macmillan, 1936), 9, 33. (Emphasis in original.) Taylor, *The Civil War of 1812*. While Taylor's use of the term "civil war" mostly refers to the borderland disputes with Canada, the conflict between political parties and American sections loomed large within his framework. For an argument that print culture began to further expose the cultural divides in America during this period, see Trish Loughrin, *The Republic in Print: Print Culture in the Age of U.S. Nation Building, 1770–1870* (New York: Columbia University Press, 2009), 303–440.

with the British tyrants "will purify the political atmosphere, and break down the entrenchments by which chicanery fortifies itself in undue prerogatives." Through patriotism forged by conflict, many believed, American nationalism would be reaffirmed and the citizens "may rival the immortal men of 1776." Yet that result was far from assured.[26]

———————

Celebrations of America's independence were always highly contested and politicized activities in the early republic. Patriotic rituals were occasions on which citizens could experience, protest, and reaffirm national and political meanings. This was especially the case during moments of cultural ferment, as conceptions of what "American" meant were challenged and patriotic events were subverted in order to present dissenting and competing ideals. By "celebrating" America, participants prescribed nationalist ideas onto their surrounding culture, and these prescriptions were often based more in anxiety than reality. As a result, celebrations of the "Glorious Fourth" became poignant moments for citizens throughout the nation to express forms of national belonging. They therefore offer an important insight into how nationalism was constructed, practiced, and expanded at the local level. This was especially true during the War of 1812, as these rites afforded many in Massachusetts the opportunity to demonstrate disapproval of the country's current trajectory. These wartime orations, intended to spread across the state through an energetic print culture, are crucial texts for understanding how various individuals appropriated cultural and traditional ideas when confronted with a national message they neither recognized nor supported.[27]

A central issue for many in Massachusetts was the task of differentiating the nation's founding war, to which they held allegiance, and the conflict then taking place, from which they dissented. Benjamin Nichols, in an oration delivered in Salem, emphasized the distinctions between the two battles. Unlike 1776, where the purpose was clear and justified, he explained, "the cause *so* alleged by our Government for the *present* war" was much more in doubt. Nichols believed that "the British claim [for] the right of impressing their seamen from our merchant vessels" was not as

[26] James Madison, "By the President of the United States of America, a Proclamation," June 19, 1812, in *War Declared Against Great Britain, with an Exposition of Its Motives* (Washington, DC: s.n., 1812): 27. *Niles' Weekley Register*, December 7, 1811, LOC.

[27] Waldstreicher, *In the Midst of Perpetual Fetes*, 3; see also Len Travers, *Celebrating the Fourth: Independence Day and the Rites of Nationalism in the Early Republic* (Amherst: University of Massachusetts Press, 1997).

convincing as "unlimited taxation" had been. Indeed, Nichols suspected that "the question of impressments has been grossly misrepresented," especially once Britain promised to revoke the practice on the eve of the battle. The true cause for the war therefore remained vague. There was simply no comparison between the conflicts. The War of 1776 was based in the character of liberty and patriotic pride, he explained, while the War of 1812 was based in greed and Anglophobia.[28]

Yet Nichols was anxious to prove his commitment to national pride even as he questioned federal authority. Speaking as if for the entire region, he proclaimed, "let it not be said, that because the people of New-England oppose the present war, they are destitute of patriotism, or influenced by British partiality." Rather, he explained, "in a war of necessity, we should rush forward to meet the enemy, with as much ardour, at least, as the nabobs of Virginia or the backwoodsmen of Kentucky." The fracturing taking place between states over national priorities was not due to New England jealousy, but to a federal government that both overlooked the interests of a particular region and counteracted those interests to a dangerous extent. "Our government," Nichols pronounced, "appear[s] determined to drive the people of New-England, and particularly of Massachusetts, to a state of desperation." Indeed, even while reassuring his state's commitment to nationalist ideals, Nichols warned of a scenario in which the national union could be severed:

Notwithstanding all the injuries inflicted upon us by our national rulers, we will still yield them the deference to which they are entitled by the Constitution. We will yet labour to preserve the Union, and endeavour to believe, that we are still to be protected as members of the confederacy. But if the period should ever arrive, when the conclusion is *forced* upon us, that it is the settled purpose of our rulers to distress and impoverish us, to trample upon our rights, and to be our tyrants instead of our protectors, we shall not only be at liberty, but it will be our duty to *protect* ourselves, and to withdraw all connexion from men, who, while they are pretending to be legislating for our good, are riveting upon us the chains of slavery. Let us preserve over our rulers a constant and watchful jealousy; for this is our birthright, and our only security against oppression. Our fathers fought for independence, and obtained it. Let it never be said, that they fought only for themselves; that they reared up sons unworthy of their sires, and transmitted their privileges to men who were willing to be slaves.[29]

[28] Benjamin Nichols, *An Oration, Delivered on the Fifth of July, 1813, in the North Church in Salem, in Commemoration of American Independence* (Salem, MA: Joshua Cushing, 1813), 7. (Emphasis in original.)
[29] Nichols, *An Oration*, 12, 21, 23–24. (Emphasis in original.)

Several things in Nichols's warning embody the growing tensions of nationalist discord promulgated by New England Federalists and deserve close attention. First was his use of the word "confederacy," which was a rare term for New Englanders to use at the time. Following the Constitutional Convention, most citizens in the Northeastern states eschewed the characterization of the nation because it represented, in their opinion, a sectional mindset that did not acknowledge the power and prominence of the federal authority. "Confederacy," for many, was a term used by individuals who argued for state sovereignty, most especially participants in the Democratic-Republican Societies – a point that New Englanders often made when contesting Southern politics. That Nichols used the word here in his strongly worded warning to the federal government signified a mindset that emphasized states' rights within a loose federal umbrella. He then reaffirmed the confederal idea by outlining the negative outcomes posited if federal actions were "*forced*" upon individual states. By depicting the federal government as "tyrants" who trampled upon states' rights and placed upon them "the chains of slavery," Nichols showed a willingness to differentiate his own state from the broader federal union. The actions of "America" in this hypothetical framework were not associated with all of the states within its boundaries, and these could justify serious repercussions.

Some went further in placing ideological wedges between states. Congressman Abijah Bigelow, writing to his wife from Washington, DC, mocked how Southerners invoked "the Spirit of Seventy Six" when they discussed the need to repulse Britain and extend the American empire. Such a comparison, Bigelow felt, was blasphemous. He complained that the "southern" and "western" people, who he described as "most zealous for war," were ignorant of the true principles upon which the nation was built: patience, peace, and a republic small enough to maintain cultural continuity. Those outside of New England failed to understand what a virtuous citizenry entailed and were therefore not "interested in representing the sentiments of the people," but were rather only interested in listening to those whose views were "in accordance with their own." He especially blamed "the people of Georgia & South Carolina" who were "aggrandizing [sic] themselves by speculations &c." These Southern states hoped to "rise upon the ruins of the country," Bigelow hypothesized, primarily through an attempt to "enrage the people of New England against the British, and make the war popular." The conspiratorial fear of Southern dominion encapsulated Massachusetts Federalists' antagonistic approach to the rest of the Union.[30]

The context for Bigelow's accusations mattered. The Fourth of July was an opportune time for him to contrast Southerners with "the noble spirit of our Fathers, who had the wisdom to declare, and the fortitude to maintain their independence." For Bigelow, these founding principles were the hallmarks of America's nationalist spirit, and were a far cry from the conquering lust that made the country "weak, spiritless, and inefficient," and prone to "idle debate" and military overreach. In 1776, "the strength, the talents and best blood of the country were in favour of the war," but now the most righteous citizens were "against it." Clearly, Massachusetts was a better embodiment of America's ideals, even if those ideals were now under siege. Indeed, Bigelow was convinced that James Madison and his fellow Southerners "hate the federalists of the eastern States quite as bad as they do the British, and would crush them to the dust if they dared." That hatred was rooted in envy of Massachusetts's "superior industry," "prosperity," and "strength," and these conspiratorial actions were "determined to bring us to a level with them." Southern and Western states not only ignored America's true nationalist principles, but they were set to erase them from the republic through a conspiratorial plan to lessen their congressional representation.[31]

While Bigelow's conspiracy was far-fetched, he was correct that Western states were indeed much more likely to back the conflict with Britain. The congressional vote to go to war relied upon near-unanimous support from the Western states of Ohio, Kentucky, and Tennessee. "Let war therefore be forthwith proclaimed against England," declared Henry Clay, the earnest Kentucky senator. The conflict, Clay explained, "involve[s] no local interest," as the New Englanders demurred, because the aims of the conflict affect "deeply the best interests, of the whole American people." In the Great Lakes area, Americans were anxious to push off native settlement and claim more land for white colonization. Republican journalists insisted that the conflict with Britain would reaffirm the region's centrality within the expanding American empire. William Hull, selected by Madison to be the brigadier general of the Army of the Northwest, raised enough troops from Ohio and Michigan to march on what was eventually an ill-fated mission to secure Canada.

---

[30] Bigelow to Hannah Bigelow, April 8, June 12, June 14, and June 26, 1812, Bigelow Papers, AAS.
[31] Bigelow to Hannah Bigelow, July 4, and July 21, 1812, Bigelow Papers, AAS.

More successfully, Andrew Jackson mustered enough support in the southwestern states to colonize native lands and push Indians, who Jackson believed sided with the British, further west, thus bolstering national hope in an otherwise frustrating war. These efforts were not matched in New England, where the military was never able to raise enough support to even launch an attack in order to claim Canadian land. To Westerners, this was evidence that their commitment to the nation was stronger than those in the Northeast.[32]

War Hawks in the South were even more vehement in their denunciation of New Englanders and their parochial vision of America. Citizens in South Carolina, especially, used the occasion to bolster their patriotic credentials. As tensions escalated over Jefferson's embargo in 1807, minister Isaac Keith argued that "the feelings [of] *the whole American people* must be penetrated" by national duties. He condemned all "fellow citizens" who placed local concerns over federal interests. Such a stance, he argued, would bring *"national dishonour."* Support for Jefferson was so loud that John Rutledge, an outnumbered Federalist in Charleston, complained that the South Carolinians who supported the measures "know nothing of & care nothing for commerce," but rather followed blindly the national interests forced upon them by Washington in an attempt to prove their patriotic loyalties. Most South Carolinians rallied behind the cause when it began in 1812. On June 12 of that year, "an uncommonly numerous and respectable meeting of the citizens of Charleston took place" and discussed the "perilous and alarming situation of the country." While they agreed that the nation's principles largely relied upon peace, "the repeated aggressions and hostile conduct of the belligerents" of Britain justified "an immediate declaration of war." They announced their approval of the "wise and energetic measures supported by our members and adopted by congress." Importantly, however, they based their support for the war on "the patriotism of [American] citizens." Declaring war on Britain was not just to secure naval rights or new territory, but also for "the maintenance of national honor" and "the preservation of its dignity." They believed it was imperative to follow Madison into a second battle for independence with Britain. It was an act steeped in nationalist pride.[33]

---

[32] Henry Clay, newspaper editorial, April 14, 1812, in James Hopkin, ed., *The Papers of Henry Clay*, 11 vols. (Lexington: University Press of Kentucky, 1959–1992), 1:645, 647. See Taylor, *Civil War of 1812*, 157–173.

[33] Isaac Stockton Keith, *Trust in God: Explained and Recommended, in a Sermon, Preached, with Some Special Reference to the State of the Public Mind, in the Prospect of War* (Charleston, SC: W. P. Young, 1807), 16–17, 28. (Emphasis in original.)

South Carolinians were conscious of Northern angst over the war and responded in kind. William Johnson, in his Fourth of July oration in 1812, directly challenged Massachusetts's lack of patriotism and questioned the state's claim to a nationalist heritage. While the state "has acquired the epithet of the cradle of the revolution," it must be asked if "she nursed it with the fabled tenderness of that bird, which furnishes an emblem of eternal love?" The unfortunate answer was "no," as it had been neglected by the North and saved by the South when "called into action [by] the eloquent pen of a Jefferson" and supported by "Carolina." Now that national interests were in proper hands, the country was finally "forever free." The South, now the true "cradle of liberty," knew it was not in the nation's best interests to prioritize regional over national concerns, and it was to Massachusetts's shame that the state had forgotten this patriotic principle. Indeed, the only challenge to America's greatness was "a want of unanimity – a narrow minded distrust of the rulers of our choice," a fault most recently demonstrated in lack of support for the war. By removing the nationalist crown from Massachusetts and placing it upon the head of South Carolina, Johnson reorganized the geographic center for America's imagined heritage. On the next year's Fourth of July, another speaker declared that "our mother tongue has no fit name" for those who opposed the war. The nation, another South Carolinian explained, was based in unity and sacrificed interests. He acknowledged that "statesmen may differ upon the policy of a war," but that "once proclaimed," unity was the only option. Allegiance during war was the hallmark of nationalism.[34]

Indeed, Massachusetts's reluctance toward the war caused many onlookers to question the state's commitment to Union. One South Carolina newspaper criticized the state by publishing a satiric advertisement that called out its governor, Caleb Strong: "*A Federal Governor wanted. –* Five hundred dollars reward will be given to any good citizen who will give information of a man fit for a Federal Governor for

John Rutledge to Harrison Gray Otis, July 27, 1806, HGOP. *Resolution of the Citizens of Charleston, Approbatory to the Measures of Government* (Washington, DC: Roger C. Weightman, 1812), 2–4.

[34] Johnson, *An Oration, Delivered in St. Philip's Church*, 8, 17. J. S. Richardson, *An Oration, Delivered in St. Michael's Church, Before the Inhabitants of Charleston, South-Carolina, On Monday the Fifth of July, 1813, (The Fourth Being Sunday), In Commemoration of American Independence; by Appointment of The '76 Association, and Published at the Request of that Society* (Charleston, SC: W. P. Young, 1813), 13, 17.

Massachusetts the ensuing year. He must be devoted to England, and in all his Speeches proclaim them the '*Bulwark of Our Religion*'." Highlighting Massachusetts's connection to Britain and questioning the sincerity of their religious rhetoric, the anonymous author depicted the state as a treasonous and hypocritical region that lacked patriotic zeal. They were, in an important sense, un-American. A failure to support the nation at war nullified any claim to nationalist belonging.[35]

Religion would once again play a central role in these debates. Though Massachusetts's ministers developed and cultivated a political theology that justified insurgency and war only four decades prior, the War of 1812 prompted many to reverse those trends and instead preach a national compact that emphasized peace and stability. While the sincerity of their rhetoric can be questioned, the persuasiveness of their message signified their ability to utilize a cultural and nationalist strain that claimed deep roots in the state. Biblical texts, local traditions, and cultural assumptions all served as raw materials that were appropriated for political ends, and they were reconstructed to package nationalist ideas. Those who did not support the war crafted a nationalist platform that was steeped in their covenant tradition and denounced what they believed to be an unjust war. The conflict with Britain, they believed, was antithetical to their national values.

A pacifist theology that eschewed bloodshed and proclaimed peace was a powerful tool for confronting an administration they believed dedicated to war. Elijah Parish, a Congregationalist minister in Byfield, likened America's demise to the moment when the early Christian church had "become so wicked, as to be no longer a *true* church and therefore, represented by a beast or the horn of a beast." The declension narrative of America's prowess was akin to the declension narrative of Protestantism: the rejection of an original, divine compact led to the embrace of worldly powers at the expense of one's soul. Parish argued that the very nature of the war went against the character of the region.

------

[35] Reprinted in *Massachusetts Manual: Or Political and Historical Register, For the Political Year, from June 1814, to June 1815* (Boston: Charles Callender, 1814), 63. The phrase "Bulwark of Our Religion" was one that Strong used in his dissenting rhetoric concerning the war, and it highlighted his unease with America's direction by promoting peace and Anglophilia as crucial to national character; the term, in turn, became a common point of critique; for one Massachusetts broadside that criticized Strong for the term, see *The Bulwarks of Religion* (Boston: Coverly, 1812).

"If I understand the character of New-England," he explained, this "wanton mischief is not compatible with your views, your temper, your invincible determinations." To support war would be to "change the radical traits of your character, [and] you must cease to be New-England men." This argument enabled Parish not to relinquish his revolutionary heritage, but rather repackage it into a "just" war based on true, defensive elements, rather than the "unjust" and oppressive conflict in 1812. Indeed, if the audience has "some of your father's blood yet in your veins," then they must "protest against the war." Parish argued that America's transition into a warlike nation was akin to the Catholic Church's transition from Christ's followers to a Pope's empire. America was at a crossroads:

A new era of American history now commences. Soon shall we be established as Mount Zion, or thrust down to ruin. The circumstance and characters of distant generations will be formed by measures now adopted. When they come to the present page of our miserable story, future historians will pause, for fear, that the truth should seem the effusion of falsehood or delirium and prevent the sale of their work. To write in a sober history, that a nation with more than a thousand miles of sea coast, adorned with a rich border of affluent towns and cities, without any commanding fort, or army, or navy, or any adequate defence, and with uncounted millions on the ocean, or in the hands of the foe, did in 1812, declare an offensive war against the most powerful nation on the globe, will bid defiance to all belief.

Parish argued that, by pushing ahead in an "unjust" war which would break the national covenant and betray the national character, Americans would initiate a collapse of civilization not unlike that experienced by the Roman Empire. The fall would be so great, in fact, that future historians would be unable to fathom its demise. This was, of course, all due to a breach in the national vision.[36]

Much of this was in reaction to the nation's recent imperial trajectory. The United States, to those who rejected the war, was not meant to be an aggressive empire. Governor Caleb Strong warned that overexpansion would bring "severe calamities" to the republic and that conquests triggered "rash counsels and extravagant measures." When citizens "acquired the title of conquerors," he reasoned, "they have invariably and speedily lost their form of government." Because it made citizens look aggressively outward, Samuel Worcester argued that war incited "all the bad passions of our nature." Such a shift in national character would

---

[36] Elijah Parish, *A Protest Against the War: A Discourse Delivered at Byfield, Fast Day, July 23, 1812* (Newburyport, MA: E. W. Allen, 1812), 5, 13, 17, 20–21. (Emphasis in original.)

"shake not only the pillars, but the very foundation of the Republick." Minister John Lathrop agreed, and he denounced the radical passion that drove the war by pleading that God "would humble the pride and subdue the lusts and passions of men, from whence wars proceed." These were all characteristics that were foreign to the Protestant nation many envisioned. Rather, America was meant to be based on the cool, reasoned principles of Christian forbearance and stability, which never sought vengeance where not required. To break that spirit would be to enrage God and ensure destruction.[37]

War was both a symbol of and the instigator for a fallen nation. As Brown Emerson explained, imperial battles were "at once the cause and the effect of great corruption in the principles and manners of the people." Many ministers feared that the war was a sign that America had reached a point of no return. William Ellery Channing stated that the increased "civil commotion" should be viewed as "the worst of national ills," because it led to social problems like "defrauding the government" and the "lawless pleasure of immoral pursuits." The covenant that was so crucial to Congregationalist political theology appeared to be hanging by a thread, and social tumult was evidence that it would not hold much longer. America could only survive through a pious tradition of peace and righteousness. An aggressive attack on England – the nation, of course, that New England states continued to present as their ethnic and political forbearer – severed the divine protection it needed. "A nation has reason for fear," Channing explained in 1814 as the war ravaged on, "in proportion to its guilt; and a virtuous nation, sensible of its dependence on God, and disposed to respect his laws, is assured of his protection." By breaking this covenant, the American government put its citizens at risk.[38]

---

[37] Strong to the Massachusetts Assembly, May 28, 1813, in *Public Documents, of the Legislature of Massachusetts: Containing the Speech of His Excellency Governor Strong, with the Answer of the Senate and House of Representatives* (Boston: Russell and Cutler, 1813), 13. Samuel Worcester, *Calamity, Danger, and Hope, a Sermon, Preached at the Tabernacle in Salem, July 23, 1812, the Day of the Public Fast in Massachusetts, on Account of the War with Great-Britain* (Salem, MA: Joshua Cushing, 1812), 9. John Lathrop, *The Present War Unexpected, Unnecessary, and Ruinous, Two Discourses Delivered in Boston* (Boston: J. W. Burditt, 1812), 18–19.

[38] Brown Emerson, *The Causes and Effects of War: A Sermon, Delivered in Salem, August 20, 1812, the Day of National Humiliation and Prayer* (Salem, MA: Joshua Cushing, 1812), 11–12. William Ellery Channing, *A Sermon, Delivered at Boston, July 23, 1812* (Boston: Greenough and Stebbins, 1812), 10–13. William Ellery Channing, *A Sermon, Delivered at Boston, July 4, 1814* (Boston, 1814), 7–8.

The threat was clear to these ministers that the United States had lost its righteous legacy. John Smith, speaking to his congregation in Haverville, Massachusetts, cautioned, "we cannot use the language of our fathers, and the pious friends of our country, in their appeals to heaven, [as they had] at the commencement of the revolutionary war." This was a false equivalency that struck at the heart of what the ministers believed the American nation really implied. While the founding fathers had indeed "appeal[ed] to Heaven" and "cried to God" for success on the battlefield, their prayers were in line with the principles of a national covenant founded upon peace and liberty. The Revolution was merely a way to preserve those crucial ideals. In contrast, the current war with Britain "[came] from the lusts and vicious principles and habits of ungodly men," and as a result "it tend[ed] directly to increase the same lusts, principles, and habits." The present conflict was rooted in a thirst for power and desire for blood. These were not the principles and habits of an American people but were rather foreign imports from other nations and cultures. Indeed, it was the French who were guilty of "combining ... the wildest passions with the most deliberate perfidy." America was following a dangerous precedent.[39]

Blaming France had become a common tradition in New England – as it had been in Old England – but it once again highlights the Atlantic dimension of their nationalism. These threats to national unity were not only dangerous in content, but they were foreign in origin. International entanglements were to be expected, but only on the correct basis of shared interests and principles. If America lost its beneficial relationship with Britain, then it would not be long before "our country should be filled with Frenchmen of all denominations." Instead of "the pure religion of the Gospel," explained Reuben Holcomb, America would be "polluted with all the corruptions of popery, and heathenism united, and the ministers of the meek and lowly Saviour, be driven into exile, or fall a sacrifice to Gallic insolence and madness." The United States was falling apart because it had become transfixed with the Napoleonic spirit, which had originated with "the antichrist, that denieth the Father and the Son." The War of 1812 betrayed everything for which the nation was supposed to stand and signified a decline toward worldly heresy.[40]

[39] John Smith, *An Apology for the Friends of Peace* (Haverhill, MA: W. B. & H. G. Allen, 1812), 3–4, 11, 13, 18.
[40] Reuben Holcomb, *A Discourse in Two Parts Delivered at Sterling, Massachusetts, Thursday, July 23, 1812* (Boston: I. Sturtevant, 1812), 18.

There was a hemispheric, as well as an Atlantic, context for this anxiety. Everything seemed in transition on the entire American continent. Just as America entered its second war for independence, Spanish Americans were entering into their first. The Latin American revolutions that transformed the continent during this same period highlighted the broader contours of the cultural transformation. Caitlin Fitz noted that the "simmering convergence of conflicts imbued many in the United States with a growing sense of inter-American solidarity" – at least for those in favor of war, anyway. While calls for patriotic sympathy pervaded many American festivals during the War of 1812, New England Federalists were much more reserved. The war hawks and republicans outnumbered and overshadowed New Englanders' petitions for peace and stability. They were not only becoming isolated within the American nation, but they seemed like a minority within the American continent. Lines were being redrawn and allegiances recast across the entire Atlantic. The total war of the Napoleonic Era left few cultures on solid ground, and some worried the world was changing too fast, believing that parts of the old world deserved retention.[41]

These were definitions and characteristics for which Federalist ministers in Massachusetts felt the need to fight. This was a cultural as much as a political crisis. Throughout the middle and Southern states, as Nicole Eustace has argued, nationalists during this period shifted the "emphasis from fathers to lovers," both heterosexual and homosocial, in constructing a horizontal basis for citizenship, and passions were understood to be a crucial part to the American character. Ideas of love, imagination, and passion were depicted as the driving forces for civilization. These ideas fed into the modern notions of civic nationalism. When James Madison declared a day of fasting shortly after the war began, he asked God to "animate their patriotism" through the "passions" of liberty – elements that were, implicitly, crucial characteristics of the patriotic citizen. What was at stake was a conflict between competing views of America's character, God's role in instilling that character, and the contrasting opinions over the role and nature of passion in the republic. For many Federalists in Massachusetts, however, these principles risked the societal stability that was necessary to maintain the Union. David Osgood denounced the increasing number of people who were "liable to corrupt prejudices and passions," because they

---

[41] Caitlin Fitz, *Our Sister Republics: The United States in an Age of American Revolutions* (New York: Liveright, 2016), 40. See also Caitlin Fitz, "The Hemispheric Dimensions of Early U.S. Nationalism: The War of 1812, Its Aftermath, and Spanish American Independence," *Journal of American History* 102, no. 2 (September 2015): 356–379.

had become "caught and entangled in the toils of Bonaparte, that rival of Satan himself in guile and mischief." Even the Massachusetts Federal Court declared that "the real cause of the war" could only be traced "to a violent passion for conquest." Not all in America were enthusiastic about geographic expansion and imperial growth. To many, such trends and passions cut against the foundations of the nation's identity. Nationalism had to be built on something much more stable.[42]

While it is impossible to gauge the depth of these ideas throughout the state outside of politicians, it is possible to track the success of the message when it came to winning elections. And indeed, this trenchant Federalist discourse became increasingly convincing to the Massachusetts public as the war progressed. Caleb Strong, five years after losing his position as governor to the Republican swell in 1807, was convinced to return from retirement and make another run for the same office. He was elected based on his anti-war rhetoric and his adamant defense of a strong regionalist identity. Barnstable County, a seaport community that was previously a stronghold for Republicans, proves an apt example. In 1810, Republican Elbridge Gerry received 62 percent of the votes in the county, and in 1812 he still garnered 57 percent. Yet by 1813, Strong had seized control of popular support and won the county with 62 percent – a margin of victory that would continue the next year as well. This trend was seen in most state-level elections in 1812 and 1814, with the latter elections finally placing enough Federalists in the state congress to move forward toward a convention designated to consider drastic actions. While there were several reasons that led to Federalists pushing back against the Republican groundswell of the first decade of the nineteenth century, their embrace of a strident ethnic nationalism and distrust for a stronger centralized government controlled by non-New England states was part of their central message that returned them to state power.[43]

Developments in the war soon turned in their favor. When, in 1814, the British invaded New England in the spring and infiltrated Washington, DC, and burned the White House later in that fall, moderates in Massachusetts reached a tipping point. The moderates now wondered if their connection to the nation justified even tepid support for the

[42] Eustace, *War and the Passions of Patriotism*, 28–29, 35. David Osgood, *A Solemn Protest Against the Late Declaration of War* (Cambridge, MA: Hilliard and Metcalf, 1812), 9. Quoted in Eustace, *War and the Passions of Patriotism*, 69.
[43] These voting statistics come from *A New Nation Votes: American Election Returns, 1787–1825*, elections.lib.tufts.edu (accessed March 2015). My thanks to Andrew Robertson for helping me digest this material and its relevance for this project.

government. The Federalists who desired radical action finally gained enough popular support and called for a convention in Hartford to address these issues. Harrison Otis Gray declared to the state legislature that, as the administration's actions "relied upon the passions and sufferings," it was time to correct them with measured and balanced negotiation. The government had displayed a "disloyalty to its interests," and the state was left to make amends. A Massachusetts committee circulated a letter to other New England states that called for an occasion "to procure such amendments to be effected in the national constitution as may secure to them equal advantage." While there may be national resistance due to "jealousy and fear," these changes were necessary to preserve American principles and restore balance to a fractured nation. And unlike a decade earlier, Otis, Strong, and the other proponents of this sectionalist identity now had enough votes to support their measures.[44]

There was broad support for these actions. In response to the motion, counties throughout Massachusetts delivered their own written memorials in a show of support. These documents provided an important thermometer for tracing popular support for this nationalist ideal. For instance, the citizens of New Bedford argued, "the time has arrived in which it is incumbent on the people of this state, to prepare themselves for the great duty, of protecting, by their own vigour, their unalienable rights." Hatfield residents similarly believed that the present administration and war assured "the certain destruction of our moral virtues, the basis of our republican institutions." And Brookfield authors declared they "will not be slaves" to Southern states, nor "submit to be the willing Dupes of wanton Oppression, foreign or domestic." Many saw these calls for radical action as the state finally rallying to preserve the nation. And while other New England states participated, it was Massachusetts's politicians who led the cause. It finally seemed time for the state to fulfill its role as savior and redeemer of the nation.[45]

---

[44] Harrison Gray Otis, "Report to the Commonwealth of Massachusetts," delivered in the Senate October 12, 1814, HGOP. "Resolution of the Massachusetts General Court Authorizing the Invitation to Other New England States to the Hartford Convention," October 17, 1814, HGOP.

[45] *Centinel*, January 26, February 6, February 13, 1814, AAS. James Banner has argued that the convention was "almost entirely a Massachusetts affair whose antecedents were to be found at least as far back as the decade before Jefferson's election," and that such an action had precedents in the state. Banner, *To the Hartford Convention: The Federalists and the Origins of Party Politics in Massachusetts, 1789–1815* (New York: Alfred A. Knopf, 1970), ix, 294–306.

One of the most striking aspects of the Hartford Convention's resolutions was their moderation. After several years of angst in Massachusetts and New England, especially after British troops had invaded the region and rumors of secret communications with the king proliferated, many expected Federalists to secede from the Union and rejoin the British Empire. Radical voices like those of Thomas Pickering, who loudly and relentlessly denounced the importance of Massachusetts's attachment to the America and emphasized the benefits of separation, coupled with Governor Caleb Strong's threatening rhetoric, seemed to impel schism at a moment of American weakness. Yet for many other Federalists, both in New England and elsewhere, the convention represented the last hope of saving the nation. New York politician Gouverneur Morris wrote that he "looked with anxious interest at the Proceedings of your state and, recognising the apathy of others, felt, as an American, some little Self Respect when I perceived a glimmering from the lamp of public spirit in Massachusetts," he concluded. "How bright in 1775!" Hopes were similarly high in Boston. "It lies with the [Hartford] Convention," wrote Joseph Lyman in late 1814, "as God's Instrument to save our country in this hour of her greatest distress and peril." It was to be a momentous occasion.[46]

But due to the moderating forces within the convention, most notably Harrison Gray Otis, the resolutions were remarkably conciliatory. The convention's proposals were indeed critical of Madison's administration and forthright in recommending suggestions, yet they were couched in a pacifying framework that emphasized the importance the Union's perpetuation. American nationalism proved difficult to overcome. The conversations that took place in the convention intentionally remained a secret – "I am permitted to say nothing," Otis wrote his wife, Sally – but it seems clear that they never seriously considered the radical option of secession. While one particularly ominous resolution mentioned the possibility of disunion, it emphasized that "if the Union is to be destined to dissolution," such an action should only be "the work of peaceable times, and deliberate consent," rather than during the tumultuous period of war. This was not a decision to be rushed. Hartford Convention delegates did not aim to use the present conflict for leverage.

[46] Gouverneur Morris to Harrison Gray Otis, November 8, 1814, HGOP. Joseph Lyman to John Treadwell, December 14, 1814, in *The Life and Letters of Harrison Gray Otis, Federalist, 1765–1848*, ed. Samuel Eliot Morison, 2 vols. (Boston: Houghton Mifflin, 1913), 2:187.

Any push to such a "sudden decision" would not only be foolish but detrimental. The issues were complex and the solutions were far from simple. If "blind passions" had brought the war upon the nation in the first place, then proposals based on similarly rash emotions would make the problems worse. "It does not," the convention urged, "consist with the respect and forbearance due from a confederate State towards the General Government, to fly to open resistance upon every infraction of the Constitution." They refused to press any solutions that "might unfavourably affect [war activities]," or even any that "should embarrass the Administration." They proposed seven constitutional amendments that they believed would help the country, but gave no ultimatum and made no threat. Their list of grievances and proposals were to be understood as sincere, if earnest, pleas from fellow citizens still committed to the American cause.[47]

The convention's official report reveals much about how they imagined the balance of national and sectional interests. It constructed a declension narrative and emphasized that the Constitution was not only central to the nation's success, but still malleable enough to produce different results when in the hands of corrupted men. Some might believe, they claimed, that the problems in the republic were based in "intrinsic and incurable defects in the Constitution," yet they posited that "the evidence upon which [such a hypothesis] rests is not yet conclusive." They firmly believed that the Constitution – and, indeed, the American nation – might still be saved through the management of wise leaders and a correction of priorities. Indeed, when the right managers were at the helm, the Constitution had "proved itself competent to all the objects of national prosperity, comprehended in the views of its framers." The problems arose from the "natural offspring of bad Administration[s]," a problem that could be found "in all ages and countries." The American government was not unique in its difficulty to balance interests and liberties. It was a problem that pervaded all governments and empires. In traditional Federalist tradition, the report pointed to "the example of France," which had "shown that a cabal of individuals assuming to act in the name of the people, may transform the great body of citizens into soldiers, and deliver

---

[47] Harrison Gray Otis to Sally Foster Otis, December 18, 1814, HGOP. *Public Documents, Containing Proceedings of the Hartford Convention of Delegates; Report of the Commissioners, While at Washington; Letters from Massachusetts Members in Congress* (Boston: Published by Order of the Senate, 1815), 4, 5, 9, 19; for a detailed reconstruction of the debates and issues during the convention itself, see Banner, *To the Hartford Convention*, 229–345.

them over into the hands of a single tyrant." America threatened to go
down a similar path. It was under the direction of Jefferson and Madison
that a "new system" of government was introduced, and "the declension
of the nation has been uniform and rapid" as a result. But the losses were
not irretrievable. The United States as an idea, the Constitution as
a governing document, and the Union as an organizational structure
were all worth saving.[48]

But America's priorities had to be realigned if the nation were to be
redeemed. A consistent theme throughout the report was the importance
of balancing two ideas: the nation was to assess and inform the interests of
all states, and the government worked best when it acknowledged that
New England's interests were intrinsic and important to the broader
republic. The misdiagnosis of America's true interests had been accomplished through several mistakes. First, the government made the mistaken priority "to achieve the conquest of Canadian territory" by using
New England men, which left the Eastern states vulnerable even though
such an expansion was not in the state's "interests." Misplaced interests
also led to the embargo and trade restrictions in the years leading up to the
war. These measures crippled the economy and placed the priorities of
other states over those in the New England region. "Experience has at last
shown," the convention argued, "that [New England trade] is a vital
interest in the United States, that its success is essential to the encouragement of agriculture and manufactures, and to the wealth, finances,
defence, and liberty of the nation." However, the manufacturing states
often found themselves attacked by other regions and neglected by the
national government. As a result, "this [crucial] interest is always exposed
to be harassed, interrupted, and entirely destroyed, upon pretence of
securing interests." A union could never be "durably cemented" when
the "great interest" of the nation "does not find itself reasonably secured
against the encroachment and combination of other interests."
A government must balance the interests of its many constituents and
not lose sight of those that are most important.[49]

Besides war and trade, another problem hovered over the current
debate. The convention's resolutions went further than merely identifying
the nation's failure to manage interests during that particular time, but
were especially worried about one particular threat: western expansion.
This was understood to be a driving focus in Congress and a prime reason

[48] *Proceedings of the Hartford Convention*, 4, 5, 9, 13.
[49] *Proceedings of the Hartford Convention*, 10, 17.

for the war with Britain. It further promised to change the country's character, priorities, and power dynamics. "The admission of new States into the Union," the convention explained, "has destroyed the balance of power which existed among the original States, and deeply affected their interests." Indeed, one of the convention's proposed amendments, which they deemed "highly important, and in fact indispensable," was to "restrain the constitutional power of Congress in admitting new States." When the nation was founded, they explained, there existed "a certain balance of power among the original parties" which allowed them to maintain balanced interests. But through the admission of new states, with different people, societies, and cultures introduced into an expanding nation, "that balance has been materially affected, and unless the practice be modified, must ultimately be destroyed." This was not merely a New England problem, either, for while "the Southern States will first avail themselves of their new confederates to govern the East," eventually "the Western States, multiplied in number, and augmented in population, will control the interests of the whole." In this sense, "the Southern States will be common sufferers with the East, in the loss of permanent advantages." None of the original states, north or south, "can find an interest in creating prematurely an overwhelming Western influence." The nation worked best when limited to the space and population as originally envisioned. Attempts to alter that arrangement – including the attempted expansion through the War of 1812 – threatened the ideals and character upon which America was built.[50]

While this appeal to stop westward expansion has traditionally been interpreted as a last-ditch effort by a state worried about losing political power, which was certainly part of the issue, there was a deeper ideological reason for this anxiety. The incorporation of new western states did indeed threaten material priorities for the state – the convention's report mentioned both the commercial constraints and militant aspirations that an increasingly land-centered government might impose on the remaining

[50] *Proceedings of the Hartford Convention*, 15–16. Peter S. Onuf has written on the importance of western expansion to cultivations of national belonging prior to this period. See Onuf, *The Origins of the Federal Republic: Jurisdictional Controversies in the United States, 1775–1787* (Philadelphia: University of Pennsylvania Press, 1983); Onuf, *Statehood and Union: A History of the Northwest Ordinance* (Bloomington: Indiana University Press, 1987); Onuf, "Federalism, Republicanism, and the Origins of American Sectionalism," in Edward L. Ayers, Patricia Nelson Limerick, Stephen Nissenbaum, and Peter S. Onuf, *All Over the Map: Rethinking American Regions* (Baltimore, MD: Johns Hopkins University Press, 1996), 11–37.

seaboard communities – but an expanding American empire also grated against the imagined nationalism that many in Massachusetts had constructed. If a "nation" was meant to be composed of people with the same background, culture, interests, and even ethnicity, and if a national government was supposed to construct its laws and society on those shared principles, how could an overextended empire encompass so many diverse interests? Therefore, one of the problems the convention identified as leading to the nation's ills was the "easy admission of naturalised foreigners" that diluted the common American character and shared culture. Even though the original republic's thirteen colonies seemed disparate in many ways, there remained enough overlap and shared purpose to form a valid nation. Faced with these new issues, the report claimed, even "the Southern Atlantick States" were coming to the realization that "the great and essential interests of the people, are common to the South and to the East." There was still time for the states to unite in order to prevent future national problems.[51]

The call to end further expansion and the addition of new states was radical but consistent. Such a perspective led politicians like Governor Caleb Strong to believe that "the territory of the U.S. is so extensive as to forbid us to indulge the expectation that we shall remain many years united." Similarly, John Lowell Jr. wrote that a nation could only function in limited settings, because "where general opinion governs, it is necessary that the people should be less extended, and more enlightened, and that there should be some similarity in their manners, habits, and pursuits." Minister William Barrows warned that the extension of the nation would lead to the government becoming "humble satellites, revolving [a]round this grand luminary of the nation." Further, "the energy of government," Barrows explained, "would be lost, in its travel to the frontier of so mighty an empire." The republic would "become such an unwieldy monster, as infallibly to be crushed with its own weight." America's problems were based in altering its national character and the dilution of its national structure, both through the importation of people who did not share its culture and the expansion of states that did not share its interests. America had overgrown its borders.[52]

---

[51] *Proceedings of the Hartford Convention*, 5, 15.
[52] Caleb Strong to Timothy Pickering, February 7, 1815, Pickering Collection, MHS. John Lowell Jr., *Thoughts in a Series of Letters in Answer to a Question Respecting the Division of the States* (Boston: s.n., 1813), 34. Barrows, *An Oration*, 10–11, 14. For the Federalists' concern over western expansion, see Banner, *To the Hartford Convention*, 110–114.

The Hartford Convention's report closed on an optimistic note. "Our nation may yet be great," it assured readers, and "our union [proved] durable." But only if the government heeded their counsel. They delegated commissioners in January to take their proposals to state and federal governments and hoped they would receive a welcome hearing. Though there were rumors of peace, some feared their message might still be seen as too radical. "The proceedings of the Convention," Otis wrote his wife Hannah, "are adapted rather to appease than produce excitement." Yet their proposals arrived around the same time as word of Andrew Jackson's victory in New Orleans and news of the peace treaty in Europe. The resolutions, no matter how moderate, were now seen as pointless with the conflict over and America seemingly victorious. The mid-Atlantic states – Pennsylvania, New York, and New Jersey, who were the primary audience for the convention's resolutions – summarily dismissed the proposed amendments, and neither Madison nor Congress seriously considered them. Success in the war reaffirmed the emerging nationalist vision of conquest and expansion, and the limited republic envisioned by Massachusetts's nationalists was left behind. America was indeed to be an empire.[53]

Bad timing and an unwelcome political climate meant the sudden death of the Hartford Convention's proposals. The state governments of New York and New Jersey swiftly rejected the resolutions without explanation, but Pennsylvania was the only state to provide a long and substantive reply. They credited the convention for its critical engagement, but after "mature consideration" they could only "offer a reluctant dissent to all of [the proposals]." They could not see the harm in western expansion, as the recent addition of states had not affected Pennsylvania's "relative importance" at all, nor did they expect it to in the future. They scoffed at the idea that the congressional structure privileged Southern states, as they believed "the Senate," where New England wielded great strength, "is in fact the primary depository of the national power." (Indeed, they claimed it was the "large middle states" that suffered from lack of just representation.) Most importantly, they took offense at the idea that naturalized foreigners caused ill effects to the nation. People from different backgrounds brought "experience [that] may be useful,"

---

[53] *Proceedings of the Hartford Convention*, 20. Harrison Gray Otis to unidentified person, January 21, 1815, HGOP.

IMAGE 3.1 "The Hartford Convention, or Leap No Leap," Library Company of Philadelphia, Philadelphia, PA. Published in the wake of the War of 1812, where the battle's conclusion made the Hartford Convention's demands appear treasonous, the New England states – here represented as politicians from the convention – appear treasonous to the American cause. King George III urges on "my Yankey boys" to jump into his arms. Several of the states are reluctant, but Massachusetts urges them on.

the legislature explained, and provided a "deliberate voice" that was beneficial to a republic. For the Pennsylvania legislature, a nation was composed of an expanding number of people from many backgrounds, encompassing many states, extending across new territory, and working toward the same democratic goals. The expansive and diverse empire feared by Massachusetts was embraced in Pennsylvania.[54]

The Hartford Convention quickly became the object of scorn. One Philadelphian artist sketched a political cartoon that captured a prominent feeling about Massachusetts's cultural treason (Image 3.1). Titled "The Hartford Convention, or Leap No Leap," the states of Massachusetts, Connecticut, and Rhode Island were shown debating whether to leap off the American cliff and into the waiting arms of

---

[54] "Report of the Pennsylvania Committee," appendix in *Proceedings of the Hartford Convention*, 36, 37, 39, 40, 46.

British royalty. "O' tis my Yankey boys!," declared the portly king, "jump in my fine fellows, plenty molasses and codfish, plenty of goods to smuggle; honours, titles and Nobility into the bargain." Connecticut is one of the few states frightened of the jump, and begs the opportunity "to pray and fast some time longer" – a jab at the large number of Fast Day and thanksgiving sermons preached in New England. Massachusetts is presented as the lead instigator of the perilous action. "We must jump Brother Conn[ecticut]," he declared. The appeal of honors, titles, and nobility – all representative of the aristocratic accusations often thrown at the state – were what perceivably drove Massachusetts to consider leaping from the Union and removing itself from the American republic. The state was the head of a regional conspiracy against the nation.

Those in the middle states were not the only Americans to respond to Massachusetts's activities. Bolstered by Jackson's military victory, many Southern states rejoiced in the nation's success and couched their achievement in nationalist terms. To them, triumph over the mighty British Empire reaffirmed the strength of the republic and vindicated the direction that Jefferson, Madison, and other republicans had taken the government. They emphasized the fact that the war's largest losses came in the North, while the biggest victory came in the South. For Southerners, it was *their* patriotism, *their* devotion, and *their* strength that held the nation together, and they rejoiced in a national victory that identified their states as leaders in the emergent American empire. Even more, they believed that their success proved false the Northern claims that slavery had sapped Southern society of power, piety, and true patriotism. Perhaps it was the Northern states that had lacked patriotic allegiance. The soon-to-be governor of Virginia, Wilson Cary Nicholas, claimed, "if the New England men wou'd now do their duty, Canada to the woods of Quebec wou'd be ours." Another Virginia politician, Philip Barraud, denounced the "never-to-be-forgotten turpitude & traitorous conduct of the Eastern portion of our nation." A patriotic realignment in America's sacred geography had commenced.[55]

This new political framework was quickly trumpeted in public settings. A year after the war had ended, South Carolinian William Lane used the Fourth of July to place recent events within a nationalist context and argued that the conflict was both the parallel and culmination of the

---

[55] Wilson Cary Nicholas, quoted in Taylor, "Dual Nationalisms," 84. Philip Barraud to St. George Tucker, February 14, 1815, and February 22, 1814, Tucker Coleman Papers, Special Collections, Swem Library, College of William and Mary. See Taylor, "Dual Nationalisms."

American Revolution. If Madison and his administration were like
Washington and his generals, then the "traitors" in Massachusetts in
1814 were like the Tories of New York in the late 1770s. Lane juxtaposed
valiant citizens in the state of South Carolina to "the pusillanimous
Hartford Convention organized under [their] peculiar emergencies, for
objects if not traitorous, were so viewed by the enemy." Surely their
actions would be remembered "as an indelible stigma on the character
of the times." Their primary sin was placing their own interests over those
of the nation, and Lane feared that "the *mere idea* rendered familiar by
factious intrigues, of a separation of these states, scandalised our fair
name." But the triumph of the nation reaffirmed an important lesson:
"*This Republic stands alone in the universe.*" To maintain that exceptionalist blessing, however, America must always remember that "the impene-
trable armour of our national independence is UNION – union is the
brand on whose preservation depends the life of [the nation]." Lane's
oration embodied the firmly nationalist vision of many South Carolinians
in the wake of war and the dawn of expansion.[56]

Massachusetts and her sister states were now seen as wayward siblings
in need of reform. As a combination of their military prowess, their
disgust with what they believed to be a lack of support in New England,
and their ever-persistent anxiety over Northern abolitionism, some in the
South took the occasion to warn against Northern dissent with the threat
of a civil war. The *National Intelligencer* declared, "our brethren of the
eastern states cherish *union* as their true rampart against subjection.
Independence would be, for them, short and nominal. They would fall
beneath the sword of the south and west." Joel Campbell similarly warned
Northern citizens, "if you raise the standard of rebellion, your green fields
will be wash'd with the blood of your people and your country laid
desolate by the flames of civil discord! If you attempt to pull down the

[56] William Lane, *An Oration, Delivered on the Fourth of July, 1816, in St. Michael's
Church, S.C. By Appointment of the '76 Association* (Charleston, SC: Southern Patriot,
1816), 20–21. Similarly, Henry Laurens Pinckney, in a Fourth of July sermon two years
later, argued that the war had solidified the importance of unified interests and that "the
tree of liberty has not only expanded its foliage, but confirmed its roots": Henry
Laurens Pinckney, *An Oration, Delivered in St. Michael's Church, Before an
Assemblage of the Inhabitants of Charleston, South-Carolina; on the Fourth of July,
1818. In Commemoration of American Independence; by Appointment of the '76
Association, and Published at the Request of that Society* (Charleston, SC:
W. P. Young, 1818), 21–22. See also Marc D. Kaplanoff, "Making the South Solid:
Politics and the Structure of Society in South Carolina, 1790–1815," (Ph.D. diss.:
University of Cambridge, 1979).

pillars of the Republic, you shall be crush'd into atoms." The War of 1812 reaffirmed Southern nationalist pride, and they were willing to lash out against those regions in the nation that lacked the commitment they believed was required for the new and expanding American empire. Indeed, the end of the War of 1812 allowed South Carolina, along with other Southern states, the chance to gloat about their nationalist zeal. They, not their neighbors to the North, were the true patriots. This enabled them to cultivate a strong sense of national identity, even as states like Massachusetts had questioned the parameters of theirs.[57]

The war also vindicated America's westward march, and was celebrated as such by many who lived outside the original thirteen states. Henry Clay was especially enthusiastic. Speaking to fellow Kentucky residents in the October following the final battle, Clay exulted that "the effects of the war are highly satisfactory" because the nation's "character ... is raised to the highest point of elevation amongst foreign observers." A few months later, Clay further reflected on the war's influence on the nation's "character": "A nation's character is the sum of its splendid deeds. They constitute one common patrimony – the nation's inheritance. They awe foreign powers. They arouse and animate our own people." To Clay, the victory over the British, which cemented America's destiny to move west, heralded an apotheosis for the nation's character. The westward movement of not only America's borders but also America's interests solidified its grand future.[58]

This development posed great significance for nationalist imaginations as well as national borders. Along with the vindication of westward expansion came the death of New Englander's wish for a closely contained American society. Far from restricting the admission of new states, as the Hartford Convention asked, the postwar period witnessed an explosion of statehood extension. Within six years, Indiana, Mississippi, Illinois, Alabama, and Missouri were added to the Union. (Maine, carved out of Massachusetts, would also be added, but the New England power gained by its admission paled in comparison to these new Western interests.) In response, people in Massachusetts were forced to reconceptualize

---

[57] Joel Campbell to David Campbell, quoted in Taylor, "Dual Nationalisms," 84. *National Intelligencery*, quoted in ibid.

[58] Henry Clay, "Speech Delivered at a Public Dinner at Lexington, Given in Honor of Mr. Clay, October 7, 1815," in *The Works of Henry Clay: Comprising His Life, Correspondence, and Speeches*, ed. Calvin Colton, 10 vols. (New York: G.P. Putnam's Sons, 1904), 6:52–71, p. 73. Clay, "Speech on the Direct Tax, and the State of the Nation after the War of 1812, January 1816," in *Works of Henry Clay*, 6:90–91.

their nationalist visions and put them more in line with the rest of the expanding country. The westward movement, and the evolving notion of America along with it, was there to stay.

The War of 1812 and the Hartford Convention also inaugurated a new tradition of political discourse in America: the discourse of states-focused interests within a federal union. By arguing for more state sovereignty at the expense of federal supremacy, which was at the heart of the Hartford resolutions, New England Federalists laid the groundwork for nationalist visions that prioritized regional identities and issues and paved the way for a political philosophy of states' rights. They would quickly disassociate themselves from this position as they became ardent nationalists over the next two decades, but they provided the seeds that would find fertile soil in the area that originally denounced such treasonous ideas: the American South.

War, as always, proved an instigator for political thought and belonging. While the Napoleonic Wars swept across Europe and forced numerous communities to reconsider patriotic affiliation, America was once again in transition over the nature, purpose, and relevancy of their national union. Even if war did not shift geographic boundaries, the resulting westward expansion transformed the American empire. As the nation's borders moved, would the nation's interests transform as well? And as the country experienced an increasing sense of regional distinctions within their expanding geography, especially with regard to the type of free/unfree labor systems, would sectional politics come to dominate nationalist discourse?

Thomas Jefferson, reflecting from his retirement in Monticello, understood the tensions of these questions, even if he only approached them from one particular direction. Writing to Lafayette, he described the Hartford Convention as a "game for disorganization" that was being played by "the Marats, the Dantons, and Robespierres of Massachusetts." Jefferson flipped the script of Atlantic comparisons, casting those in New England as the individuals sowing the seeds of discord. These Federalists, Jefferson mused, "are in the same pay, under the same orders, and making the same efforts to anarchise us, that their prototypes in France did there." Even Jefferson saw these political debates during the War of 1812 within a much more Atlantic context, mere particulars in a larger political dialogue taking place in America and Europe.[59]

---

[59] Thomas Jefferson to Lafayette, February 14, 1815, in *Thomas Jefferson: Writings*, ed. Merrill D. Peterson, ed. (New York: The Library of America, 1984), 1364.

But while Jefferson viewed the New England Federalists' actions as treasonous and worthy of a death sentence under any other political system, he thought the American nation was strong enough to withstand their dissent. "We might safely give them leave to go through the United States recruiting their ranks, and I am satisfied they could not raise one single regiment," he told Lafayette. "The cement of this Union is in the heart-blood of every American." To Benjamin Waterhouse, Jefferson explained his satisfaction with letting the Massachusetts traitors go without punishment: "We let them live as laughing stocks for the world, and punish them by the torment of eternal contempt." The "eternal" description might have been a dig at the Congregationalists' belief, but the note of contempt was real. Jefferson knew where to look for the future of America's nationalist debates: "The emigrants from the Eastern states are what I have long counted on." And with this westward expansion came new questions concerning how American would balance regional interests – most especially, slavery.[60]

---

[60] Ibid. Thomas Jefferson to Benjamin Waterhouse, October 13, 1815, *National Archives: Founders Online*, http://founders.archives.gov/documents/Jefferson/03-09-02-0063 (accessed February 2015).

4

Liberty, Slavery, and the Rise of Sectionalism

WHEREAS our ancestors (not of choice) were the first successful cultivators of America[, we] feel ourselves entitled to participate in the blessings of her luxuriant soil, which their blood and sweat manured.

–Gathering of Philadelphia's Black Community, 1818[1]

This momentous question, like a fire bell in the night, awakened and filled me with terror. I considered it at once as the knell of the Union. It is hushed indeed for the moment. [B]ut this is a reprieve only, not a final sentence. [A] geographical line, coinciding with a marked principle, moral and political, once conceived and held up to the angry passions of men, will never be obliterated; and every new irritation will make it deeper and deeper.

–Thomas Jefferson, 1820[2]

Slavery had always been a central, if often unspoken, element of early America's nationalist imagination. Among the elites who sought to imagine a novel form of nationalism for the young empire of liberty during the country's first two decades, very few publicly grappled with the presence of those who were enslaved within its borders. Even while slavery was gradually abolished in Northern states, it was only strengthened in the South as the cotton boom proved its profitability and expanded its reach. Those who expected the practice to die a natural death failed to intervene during the institution's most fragile moment in the 1780s and early 1790s. This resulted in a slaveholding republic. The division of slave states in the

---

[1] *Resolutions and Remonstrances of the People of Colour Against Colonization on the Coast of Africa* (Philadelphia: s.n., 1818), 3–4.
[2] Thomas Jefferson to John Holmes, April 22, 1820, Library of Congress Online Exhibit, www.loc.gov/exhibits/jefferson/159.html (accessed January 2014).

South and free states in the North challenged conceptions of a united nation and forced individuals to confront the limits of both cultural symmetry and federal alliance. Could a nation remain linked while being geographically and ideologically divided on such a foundational principle? This was a global problem. Just as America sought to address the issue through a topographical division, Britain solved the issue with immediate abolition in its Caribbean territories. As both nations attempted to solve the problem of slavery in an Age of Revolutions, questions of national union remained paramount. This chapter traces these issues through the first three decades of the nineteenth century, particularly in Pennsylvania where a growing population of free blacks posed a unique challenge to traditional conceptions of racial belonging.

Like Thomas Paine before him, Thomas Branagan had not been in America long before he attempted to reform the nation. Born in Dublin in 1774, raised by a harsh father, and introduced to a life at sea at the age of 14, Branagan worked in the Atlantic slave trade, explored inland African villages, and served as a plantation overseer in Antigua. While in the Caribbean, he converted to Methodism, denounced slavery as wicked, and then moved to Philadelphia in 1798. Once there, he served as a missionary, married, and witnessed the births and deaths of three children. While most of his time was spent preaching the gospel, working with the poor, and helping "the needy, the halt, the maimed and the blind," his attention soon turned to the institution of slavery. "It was in my mind," he later wrote, "to bear testimony against slavery, from the press, as well as the pulpit." Though he claimed "little school learning, less natural capacity, and scarcely common sense," he maintained a firm belief that "the Almighty generally makes use of such poor, ignorant, destitute creatures" when striking down the "wisdom of the wise ... and mighty." He did not take his new calling lightly. From 1804 through 1814, Branagan proved more prolific than almost any other author in early America. He produced no fewer than eighteen volumes (most totaling more than 200 pages) on the topics of American slavery, morality, and religion. These books were written in both poetry and prose, presented in a (purposely) rough dialect, couched in a religious framework, and, importantly, steeped in a nationalist discourse. Branagan had a lot to say about the nature of American union.[3]

---

[3] Thomas Branagan, "A Beam of Celestial Light," in Branagan, *The Charms of Benevolence, and Patriotic Mentor; or, The Rights and Privileges of Republicanism, Contrasted with the Wrongs and Usurpations of Monarchy* (Philadelphia: Johnston and

Much of Branagan's rhetoric was tethered to a particular understanding of a national identity and character. In his 1805 pamphlet *Serious Remonstrances, Addressed to the Citizens of the Northern States*, he directed his remarks not only to the "true friends of Liberty," but "particularly the Agricultural, Mechanical, and Commercial Citizens of the northern States of America," whom he classified as "the bulwark of our Nation, and the pillars of our Constitution." The Northern states had earned this title, he explained, due to "their distinguished exertions in advocating the rights of man," by which he meant the abolition of slavery. He believed his message "imperiously demands the attention of the patriotic citizens of America," and that it was "essentially connected with their interest, and the prosperity of their children, and their children's children." His plea was one of "irritation" because, though he had only been in the nation for eight years, he feared for the country's direction. He was "astonished at the stupidity of our citizens" in allowing "the tyrants of the South [to] gain an ascendency over the citizens of the North" by promulgating a nationalist vision based on African slavery. The Southern states, which Branagan believed were "bent on [their] own ruin," possessed a completely different mindset from the rest of the nation and no longer deserved association: "our prospects and politics are as different from theirs, as light is from darkness." The time for debate was past, as "it would be absurd to reason with them." Words would no longer serve, and outright action was the only available option. To be a true American meant waging battle with Southern despots and severing the connection with slaveholding states.[4]

Branagan was not the first American, or even the first Pennsylvanian, to declare rhetorical war on competing states over slavery. But very few were as persistent, outspoken, or prolific in the cause. He was part of a growing anti-slavery movement that presented a radical new nationalist discourse which disrupted traditional understandings of political belonging. This was especially the case for Branagan's new home in Pennsylvania. For the early period of the union, primarily through the War of 1812, the state's emphasis on balancing divided interests, incorporating pluralist political

Patterson, 1813), 221–360, p. 296. For a helpful background on Branagan, see Lewis Leary, "Thomas Branagan: Republican Rhetoric and Romanticism in America," *Pennsylvania Magazine of History and Biography* 77 (July 1953): 332–352.

[4] Thomas Branagan, *Serious Remonstrances, Addressed to the Citizens of the Northern States, and Their Representatives; Being an Appeal to their Natural Feelings & Common Sense: Consisting of Speculations and Animadversions, on the Recent Revival of the Slave Trade, in the American Republic* (Philadelphia: Thomas T. Stiles, 1805), 3, 11, 13, 23.

cultures, and tolerating divisive nationalist visions served as a mediating presence in American print culture. Their heterogeneous society provided tools with which to conceive of a pluralistic nation. The first decades of the nineteenth century, however, witnessed an increase in prescriptive nationalist arguments that precluded the practice of slavery and, either explicitly or implicitly, denied the right of Southern states to claim a role in American nationality. These tensions, in turn, forced states like South Carolina to respond with more earnest proslavery arguments that vindicated their slaveholding interests.

As Branagan's background highlights, this debate had regional, national, and international contexts. Having been born in Britain, worked in Africa and the Caribbean, and lived in Pennsylvania, Branagan embodied the Atlantic connections that framed the anti-slavery crusade. America's discussions concerning slavery and regional division took place against the backdrop of the closing of the Atlantic slave trade as well as the victory of anti-slavery advocates in the United Kingdom. While America strengthened the slave institution, British politics succeeded in presenting a national vision centered on abolition. These anti-slavery advocates provided both an example and a threat to slaveholding nations. In America, free blacks and runaway slaves petitioned for citizenship and inclusion in the face of slave apologia and colonization. The nation's vision of a unified nation was coming apart at the seams. Americans, in the North and South, were forced to respond to these developments. This resulted in the rise of consciously divergent nationalisms, often cultivated in direct opposition to each other, as well as explicitly divisive cultural foundations that necessitated sectional jealousy and federal intervention.

Many in Pennsylvania questioned whether slavery could be reconciled with their view of nationalism even before the American Revolution. Quakers like John Woolman and Anthony Benezet, for instance, developed anti-slavery arguments that were based on both Christian and political principles. Benezet even flirted with the idea of reparations and argued that blacks should be given land in the western area where, under the direction of overseers, they could be industrious through free labor. In this way, "the Negroes, instead of giving just Cause of fearful Apprehensions, and weakening the internal strength of the Government where they reside, as they certainly must in their present Condition," he explained, "would become interested in its Security and Welfare." Later, he declared that until this national "sin" of slavery was eradicated, the British Empire and her North

American colonies would remain "obnoxious to the righteous judgments of the Lord." They could expect catastrophic divine punishments as a result. Others, of course, believed that these critiques, especially at a moment of political transition that required continental harmony, would only introduce instability and anxiety. Most prominently, Benjamin Franklin devised a rhetorical framework that, while maintaining that slavery was wrong and anachronistic, blamed the British for the slave trade and exonerated Southern states as merely dealing with what was forced upon them. The region possessed a mixed legacy.[5]

Yet the anti-slavery sentiment in Pennsylvania only grew louder during the revolutionary period. In 1773, Benjamin Rush wrote that, though a limited number of Quakers had previously "stood alone a few years ago in opposing Negro slavery in Philadelphia," it was now the case that "three-fourths of the province as well as the city cry out against it." (Rush's ownership of a slave highlighted the common paradox of many early anti-slavery agitators.) Accusations concerning the dangers of slavery and its harmful presence in a nation of liberty became key tenets of Pennsylvania's nationalist discourse. Indeed, a focal point of debate during the ratification convention was whether the Constitution did enough to constrain slavery. One anti-federalist worried that, if the document passed, "SLAVERY will probably resume its empire in Pennsylvania." In response, James Wilson assured citizens that, under the new constitutional contract, "slaves will never be introduced" into either new states or states that had already relinquished the practice. While the question of immediacy was debated, and most hesitated to intervene in Southern slavery, many in Pennsylvania could agree upon immediate action on the slave trade. "Nothing of consequence," Rush wrote, "can be done here till the ax is laid to the root" of slavery. The time had come for change.[6]

[5] Anthony Benezet, *Memoirs of the Life of Antonymn Benezet*, ed. Robert Vaux (New York: Burt Franklin, 1817), 30–31. Benezet, *The Case of Our Fellow-Creatures: The Oppressed Africans, Respectfully Recommended to the Serious Consideration of the Legislature of Great Britain, by the People Called Quakers* (1760; Philadelphia: James Phillips, 1784), 14. For the Quaker critique of slavery, see Maurice Jackson, *Let This Voice Be Heard: Anthony Benezet, Father of Atlantic Abolitionism* (Philadelphia: University of Pennsylvania Press, 2009); Brycchan Carey, *From Peace to Freedom: Quaker Rhetoric and the Birth of American Antislavery, 1657–1761* (New Haven, CT: Yale University Press, 2012). For the response to these Quaker critiques, see David Waldstreicher, *Runaway America: Benjamin Franklin, Slavery, and the American Revolution* (New York: Hill and Wang, 2004), 193, 213–214.
[6] Benjamin Rush to Granville Sharp, May 1, 1773, in Roger Bruns, ed., *Am I Not a Man and a Brother? The Antislavery Crusade of Revolutionary America, 1688–1788* (New York: Chelsea House, 1977), 270. William Findlay, quoted in *American Museum*,

As a result, citizens began to cultivate a new anti-slavery message that was founded upon their appeal to nationality. These local tensions were introduced to the national stage in early 1790 when a petition that originated in Pennsylvania, and signed by Benjamin Franklin himself, asked Congress to abolish the slave trade. This was prompted by a case in New York in which the state legislature, in response to another petition from local Quakers, claimed that only the federal Congress had power to end the trade. The recently formed Pennsylvania Society for the Abolition of Slavery therefore requested the Senate and House of Representatives to use that very power. The Pennsylvania petition claimed that "a just & accurate Conception of the true Principles of liberty, as it spread through the land" prompted Americans to relinquish their unfortunate attachment to the slave trade. Importantly, they argued that their impulse stemmed not only from the "Christian Religion" but also from "the *Political Creed* of America." Vanquishing the immoral institution was crucial "for removing this Inconsistency from *the Character* of the American People." Abolition was crucial for the nation's morality. While tolerance of competing interests was, of course, crucial to many nationalist visions in postrevolutionary Pennsylvania, a growing number came to question the elasticity of those boundaries. This was especially the case with practices like slavery that supposedly contradicted the moral fiber upon which the nation was built.[7]

This petition was a direct challenge to Southern states. It was received in the House of Representatives on February 12 and quickly sparked contentious debate. South Carolina congressman Thomas Tucker feared that the very discussion of such a petition "would be a very alarming circumstance to the Southern States," and that his constituents "would become very uneasy under the Government" as a result. The petition was nothing more than a "mischievous attempt" that was "signed by a man [Benjamin Franklin] who ought to have known the Constitution better." He warned Congress that emancipation, which he felt was the ultimate

November 1787, APS. James Wilson, speech, December 3, 1787, in Jonathan Elliot, ed., *The Debates in the Several State Conventions on the Adoption of the Federal Constitution as Recommended by the General Convention at Philadelphia in 1787*, 5 vols., 2nd ed. (New York: Burt Franklin, 1787), 2:451–453.

[7] "Memorial of the Pennsylvania Society for Promoting the Abolition of Slavery to the Senate and Representatives of the United States," February 3, 1790, HSP. (Emphasis added.) See also William C. diGiacomantonio, "'For the Gratification of a Volunteering Society': Antislavery and Pressure Group Politics in the First Federal Congress," *Journal of the Early Republic* 15 (Summer 1995): 169–197.

design behind the Abolition Society's motion, "would never be submitted to by the Southern States without a civil war." Similarly, Aedanus Burke, another South Carolinian, "was certain the commitment would sound an alarm, and blow the trumpet of sedition in the Southern States." Burke and Tucker worried that the democratic revolution sparked a misconception in which the "people" of the North believed they could make abolition a reality.[8]

What ensued was a harsh, and telling, debate. While most Southern congressmen were hesitant to give more than constitutional reasons for their objection to the petition, Georgia representative James Jackson declared that "there never was a Government on the face of the earth, but what permitted slavery." This pronouncement caused a stir. In response, Pennsylvanian Thomas Scott argued that, though the Quaker petition was framed as a religious protest, he did "not stand in need of religious motives to induce me to reprobate the traffic in human flesh." Even if there were no God, Scott reasoned, he would still oppose slavery "upon the principles of humanity, and the law of nature." While much of the debate, at least from Southern congressmen, focused on the constitutionality of the slave trade rather than its moral foundation, a deeper fissure concerning nationalist imagination became apparent. There was a fundamental division between those who held anti-slavery sentiments and those who believed the nation was dependent on slave labor. For Tucker, Burke, and other Southern representatives, not only was slaveholding necessary for national prosperity, but a nation emboldened and empowered to strike at that very system was a betrayal of the federal contract. Their nationalist imagination was centered on the slave institution.[9]

The longest and most systematic defense of Southern slavery on this occasion was given by William Loughton Smith. A lawyer from Charleston, Smith later served as the United States Minister to Portugal. The mere debate over this issue was a serious mistake, Smith warned, because "in the Southern States, difficulties had arisen on adopting the Constitution" due to fear "that Congress might take measures under it for abolishing the slave trade." It took all the energy the Federalists could

---

[8] For the quotes from Tucker and from Burke, see AC, 1:1240–1241. For more context, see Richard S. Newman, "Prelude to the Gag Rule: Southern Reaction to Antislavery Petitions in the First Federal Congress," *Journal of the Early Republic* 16 (Winter 1996): 571–99; Christopher L. Brown, "Empire Without Slaves: British Concepts of Emancipation in the Age of the American Revolution," *William and Mary Quarterly* 61 (April 1999): 273–306.

[9] AC, 1:1241–1242.

muster to convince their fellow citizens that such was not the intention of Congress, he cautioned. No matter how calm or reasoned any debate on the legality of the slave trade, it would "create great alarm" in South Carolina and be seen "as an attack upon the palladium of the property of our country." If South Carolinians had been aware that Northern states aimed to intervene in local affairs, they would have never ratified the Constitution. This discussion over the Society's petition, then, was a betrayal of the spirit upon which the Union was supposedly based. South Carolinians were not meant to "learn morals from the [Northern] petitioners." If Southerners wished an "improvement in their moral system," they could get it from "home," not from meddling Northerners. For Smith, these conflicts would lead to jealousies and secession. He accused the Northern states, especially Pennsylvania, of judging Southern actions and interfering with Southern property. While Smith's words were political threats, they also served as a form of nationalism, embodying how he understood a nation's limits. "A gentleman can hardly come from [the South] with a servant or two," he groused, but "there are persons trying to seduce his servants to leave him." Northern states were not only exploring legal ways to disrupt Southern life, but they were conspiring to do so through secretive and unconstitutional means. This was a nation divided.[10]

The discussion had become too heated and was quickly ended. Scott privately declared his amazement at hearing "at this age of the world" an "advocate for slavery, in its fullest latitude." James Madison, who during the Constitutional Convention had similarly declared the slave trade compromise "dishonorable to the American Character," declared that "the debate has taken a serious turn" that threatened to "alarm" Southerners. Congress, with the unanimous support of all middle and Northern states, voted for a committee to explore the petition – most Southern states, including every representative from South Carolina, voted against the action – yet the resulting committee report merely reaffirmed that Congress could do nothing concerning the slave trade until the constitutionally mandated date of 1808. The time for the threatened civil war had not yet come.[11]

---

[10] AC, 1:1243–1244. For background on Smith, see George C. Rogers, *Evolution of a Federalist: William Loughton Smith of Charleston, 1758–1812* (Columbia: University of South Carolina Press, 1962).

[11] Thomas Scott, speech, March 22, 1787, in *A Necessary Evil?: Slavery and the Debate over the Constitution*, ed. John P. Kaminsky (Madison, WI: Madison House, 1995), 226. James Madison, speech, August 25, 1787, in Kaminsky, *A Necessary Evil*, 63. AC, 1:12,

Yet even if the immediate crisis was averted, deep fissures were exposed. Two concerns reflected the heart of the issue. First, could slavery be reconciled with America's "character"? The Society for Abolition's petition implied it could not, which in turn necessitated federal intervention. But Southern congressmen set that particular problem aside and addressed the second, if related, question: did America as a nation, and the Constitution as a governing document, allow federal intervention in local institutions? This was a political question that cut directly to the nationalist imagination. South Carolina congressmen argued that such a constitutional intervention went explicitly against their federal compact. In the end, it was the political context that brought the debate to a close: Northerners required Southern congressmen to agree to consolidating national debt, which necessitated that the North acquiesce on the slave trade question. The wound brought by fractured sectionalism, briefly exposed, was quickly covered and left to be dealt with another day.

News of the discussion, despite its anticlimactic conclusion, caused consternation in Charleston. The South in general, and South Carolina in particular, became even more entrenched in its defense of slavery following the Revolution, in part thanks to the growth of the cotton industry. One Charleston resident believed it would "be more safe for a man to proclaim through this city that there was no God, than that slave-holding was inconsistent with his holy law." This new environment required a cultural defense that included both constitutional and moral justification. Slavery, they argued, was crucial to the societal structure in which they believed and with which they had thrived. This in turn led them to be suspicious about any federal authority that could potentially cause problems for their local practices. The "property in slaves," lectured one South Carolinian, "should not be exposed to danger under a Government instituted for the protection of property." This increasingly hostile environment, created in response to anti-slavery agitation, led over 1,000 Quakers to flee South Carolina during the first two decades of the nineteenth century.[12]

But slaveholders were not only responding to tensions within America's borders. The Revolutionary period witnessed a rise in anti-

---

12 46. See also Matthew Mason, *Slavery and Politics in the Early American Republic* (Chapel Hill: University of North Carolina Press, 2006), 21–24.

[12] "Extract of a Letter from a Gentlemen in Charleston, S.C., to his Friend in New-Jersey, Dated March 31," *Freeman's Journal*, August 11, 1790, LOC. Charles Cotesworth Pinckney, speech, July 12, 1787, in Kaminsky, *A Necessary Evil*, 53.

slavery agitation throughout the Atlantic world. Even as congress debated Pennsylvania's anti-slavery bill, a slave uprising in the French colony Saint-Domingue incited broader political commotion. The call to liberty throughout the Americas and Europe signaled that pro-slavery institutions could no longer be taken for granted. An onslaught of slave narratives, like the immensely popular memoir by Olaudah Equiano, inaugurated a print network that connected agitators across the nations. "May the time come," wrote Equiano, "when the sable people shall gratefully commemorate the auspicious era of extensive freedom." Only then could the British Empire "be named with praise and honour" for standing "forth in the cause of humanity, liberty, and good policy." These publications from black witnesses added human details to the long-told tales of the Middle Passage and forced labor. They encouraged more imminent action to alleviate the suffering of black bodies and reform particular nations and empires. This literature of abolition became a hallmark of intellectual debates, and even elite slave-owners like George Washington followed along with their development. Abolitionist ideas provided more tools for nationalist ideals.[13]

Britain constantly provided a threatening voice to America's slave institution. Even before the revolution, a batch of anti-slavery activities, court decisions, and abolitionist rhetoric convinced Southern colonists that there was a conspiracy to end the slave institution. Despite the overblown nature of these fears, there was a growing anti-slavery sentiment in some spheres of British politics. In the wake of losing thirteen of their North American colonies in a battle over "freedom," many in Britain sought to redeem the empire's image through a clarion call for abolition. Evangelicals especially saw anti-slavery efforts as a way to reaffirm their national idea of liberty. Politicians like William Wilberforce sought to implement those principles into policy. Though far from a majority, these conceptions of a British empire centered on interracial liberty shifted nationalist discourse in novel ways. A new wave of Evangelical politicians

---

[13] Olaudah Equiano, *The Interesting Narrative of the Life of Olaudah Equiano, Written by Himself, With Related Documents*, 3rd ed., edited by Robert J. Allison (Boston: Bedford/ St. Martin's, 2016), 198–199. See also David Richardson, "Through a Looking Glass: Olaudah Equiano and African Experiences of the British Atlantic Slave Trade," in *Black Experience and the Empire*, ed. Philip D. Morgan and Sean Hawkins (New York: Oxford University Press, 2004), 58–85; François Furstenberg, "Atlantic Slavery, Atlantic Freedom: George Washington, Slavery, and Transatlantic Abolitionist Networks," *William and Mary Quarterly* 68, no. 2 (April 2011): 247–286; Janet Polasky, *Revolutions Without Borders: The Call to Liberty in the Atlantic World* (New Haven: Yale University Press, 2015), 75–110.

used their social standing to decry the slave trade as antithetical to imperial interests. Anglican minister James Ramsay exemplified this loud chorus through works like his *Inquiry into the Effects of Putting a Stop to the African Slave Trade*, which argued that emancipation was both an economic and moral priority. "From our having been the most forward in this scandalous traffick," he reasoned, "it becomes us to be the first to labour in effecting a reformation." Abolition was a critical piece for refashioning British nationalism.[14]

Events in the French Atlantic accelerated these appeals. The French Revolution, dedicated to dissolve traditional boundaries of freedom and dependence, backed its way into questions of racial liberty. Delegates to the 1789 National Convention debated whether the "Declaration on the Rights of Man" meant the abolition of slavery in their Caribbean colonies. The creation of the Society of the Friends of Blacks energized more antislavery action in the midst of revolutionary tumult, as they accused the nation of hypocrisy for breaking "the chains of feudalism" while refusing to recognize the "political rights" of blacks and the tragedy of slavery. The question was eventually solved, of course, through the actions of the black colonists themselves. Saint-Domingue's rebellion forced the National Convention to declare slavery abolished. Revolutionary Pierre Gaspard Chaumette claimed that slavery was "like a vast cancer cover[ing] the entire globe with its venomous ramifications, poisoning now one now another hemisphere." He was proud that France supplied the "sacramental words" that sanctified its national mission: "*slavery is abolished.*" This enthusiasm would wane, of course, after Napoleon's conquest and attempt to re-enslave Haiti, but the question of racial liberty in an Age of Revolutions would continue to be debated.[15]

---

[14] James Ramsay, *An Inquiry into the Effect of Putting a Stop to the African Trade: And of Granting Liberty to the Slaves in the British Sugar Colonies* (London: J. Philips, 1784), 19. For British anti-slavery beliefs, see Deidre Coleman, *Romantic Colonization and British Anti-Slavery* (New York: Cambridge University Press, 2005); Christopher Leslie Brown, *Moral Capital: Foundations of British Abolitionism* (Chapel Hill: University of North Carolina Press, 2006), 333–450.

[15] Society of the Friends of Blacks, "Address to the National Assembly in Favor of the Abolition of the Slave Trade," in Liberty, Equality, Fraternity: Exploring the French Revolution, George Mason University, https://chnm.gmu.edu/revolution/d/290/ (accessed September 2016). "Speech of Chaumette Celebrating the Abolition of Slavery," in Lynn Hunt, ed., *The French Revoultion and Human Rights: A Brief Documentary History* (Boston: Bedford/St. Martin's, 1996): 116–119, p. 118. For the French Revolution and the Haitian conflict, see Laurent Dubois, *Avengers of the New World: The Story of the Haitian Revolution* (Cambridge: Harvard University Press,

These Atlantic developments served as the backdrop for the founding decades of the United States. America's strident perpetuation of the slave system, then, should be seen in tension with these broader debates over the morality of enslaved laws and governing nations. Many directly responded to these events, especially the insurrection in Saint-Domingue. Connecticut abolitionist Abraham Bishop linked the Haitian Revolution to America's conceptions of rights, asking "is not their cause as just as ours?" Bishop firmly believed that *"The Universal Father seems now demonstrating that of one blood, he has created all nations of men, that dwell on the face of the earth."* Several others posited a nationalist vision predicated upon free labor in which the union would be cleansed of its national sin, slavery. In 1806, at the first public celebration of free black people, Absalom Jones hoped that "the shores ... of the United States" would no longer "witness the anguish of families, parted ... by a public sale." The addition of black voices only heightened anti-slavery rhetoric, and the deep fissures between states over the place of African Americans and slavery within the imagined American community continued to widen. More and more activists identified the disjuncture between America's principles and its government.[16]

Success came slowly. The first step in the anti-slavery movement, the abolishment of the Atlantic Slave Trade, was finally achieved on January 1, 1808, the earliest date allowable under the American Constitution. This was seen as a victory for many as it theoretically ceased the harvesting and transporting of free individuals from Africa. But Southern states were also anxious to acquiesce to this action given it increased the value of the slaves already held as American property. Indeed, by 1806, South Carolina was the only state that allowed the importation of slaves. But to many in Pennsylvania, this was merely another step in the direction of abolition. Increasingly cognizant of and outspoken about sectional differences on the issue of slavery, many posited a more energetic national project of reform that both stemmed from

---

2004); Jeremy D. Popkin, *You Are All Free: The Haitian Revolution and the Abolition of Slavery* (Cambridge: Cambridge University Press, 2010).

[16] *The Argus* [Boston], November 22, 1791, LOC. (Emphasis in original.) *Aurora* [Philadelphia], December 13, 1806, LCP. For more anti-slavery nationalism in Philadelphia during the period, see selections in James G. Basker, ed., *Amazing Grace: An Anthology of Poems about Slavery, 1660–1810* (New Haven: Yale University Press, 2002), 636–683. For American responses to the Haitian Revolution, see James Alexander Dun, *Dangerous Neighbors: Making the Haitian Revolution in Early America* (Philadelphia: University of Pennsylvania Press, 2016).

and reaffirmed the nationalist principles upon which they believed the country to be built. This would inaugurate an energetic battle over nationalist principles that would continue for some time.[17]

Thomas Branagan was one of many Philadelphians in the first decade of the nineteenth century to present a public and strenuous opposition to slavery. Having been a former slave-trader himself, he felt he was in an authoritative position to denounce the practice. "Few have had the opportunity," he prefaced in his epic poetical work, *Avenia*, "of gaining the practical, as well as theoretical information on this subject, which Providence has put in my power." Yet much of Branagan's own background is unverifiable beyond the reminiscences scattered throughout his writings. Indeed, his life's narrative conspicuously matched the dominant themes of his carefully crafted message: a broken childhood home in which he was separated from his loving mother, lacked a sympathetic father, and was punished by a cruel (school)master. This echoed his critiques of slavery, which he believed engendered "continued acts of barbarity" that divested men "of their natural feelings" – both the abusers as well as the abused. It was barbarity in the form of a mugging that caused Branagan's "awakening" to Christianity, the violence of slavery that caused him to renounce the slave trade, and, when he traveled to America in 1798, it was the hostile environment of the South that caused him to move to Philadelphia, which he "preferred" due to the city's opposition to slavery. He felt called to a new mission.[18]

But regardless of his backstory's veracity, his message struck a chord in Philadelphia. Though there is no written or published record left by him during his first seven years in the United States, Branagan soon became a prolific author and his community provided an eager audience. Most of his books went through at least two printings and usually boasted large sales. Many later editions, like the third printing of *Flowers of Literature*,

[17] For the abolition of the Atlantic Slave Trade, see Mason, *Slavery and Politics in the Early American Republic*, 132–135.
[18] Thomas Branagan, *Avenia: Or, a Tragical Poem, on the Oppression of the Human Species, and Infringement on the Rights of Man* (Philadelphia: Silas Engles, 1805), viii. Thomas Branagan, *The Guardian Genius of the Federal Union; Or, Patriotic Admonitions on the Signs of the Times, in Relation to the Evil Spirit of Party, Arising from the Root of All our Evils, Human Slavery* (New York: For the Author, 1839), 7, 19–20. See Beverly Tomek, "'From Motives of Generosity, as Well as Self-Preservation': Thomas Branagan, Colonization, and the Gradual Emancipation Movement," *American Nineteenth Century History* 6 (June 2005): 121–147, p. 124.

noted that while 3,000 copies had just been published the previous year, excessive sales necessitated another print run of 3,000 copies. While some of this was certainly salesmanship, Branagan never had a shortage of potential printers. His popularity was by design. One of the most poignant elements of Branagan's corpus was a carefully constructed, rough writing style that not only made his work resemble, according to one literary scholar, the "plain" rhetoric of Thomas Paine but also exemplified a "strategic anti-eloquence, distinguished by a rejection of systematic composition." What made one historian refer to Branagan as a "literary cripple" was a potent attempt to disrupt literary flow and encourage a slow and careful reading. And considering the number of publishers who jumped at the opportunity to print his work, both his tone and his message were regarded as a success.[19]

Central to Branagan's work was a devout and outspoken commitment to the idea of American nationalism. While only recently an immigrant, he was fascinated by the American republic. "By contrasting the despotic governments of Europe with our federal government," he mused, "I saw the supreme and superior excellency of the last, and became passionately enamoured with liberty and America." It was this aspect of his writings that Branagan claimed was the true reason for his success. He believed that "if [Robert] Burns or [Robert] Bloomfield had made their literary appearance in this commonwealth, neither of them would have found a single patron." Americans had become so stalwart in their support of national authors that they would refuse to recognize genius when coming from foreign writers. Yet Branagan believed that slavery was not only an ill fit for the land of liberty, he also feared it would prove to be a "deadly wound" for democracy. Slavery was a moral travesty due to the physical and moral violence inflicted on black human beings. He claimed that "interested, mercenary, avaricious persons" had invented the idea of black inferiority as a "desperate expedient [to] cover their own" nefarious activities for monetary gains. Whites were not the only people degraded by the practice. Branagan explained that Africans were "part of the Human Species, capable of intellectual, moral, and religious

[19] Thomas Branagan, *The Flowers of Literature; Being an Exhibition of the Most Interesting Geographical, Historical, Miscellaneous and Theological Subjects, in Miniature* (Philadelphia: P. Ward, 1810), 2. Christopher N. Phillips, "Epic, Anti-Eloquence, and Abolitionism: Thomas Branagan's Avenia and the Penitential Tyrant," *Early American Literature* 44 (Fall 2009): 605–637, p. 609. Marcus Wood, *The Poetry of Slavery: An Anglo-American Anthology: 1764–1865* (New York: Oxford University Press, 2003): 425.

Improvement." He looked forward to the day when anyone who had "set their feet on the American shore" would find "an asylum from tyranny and oppression." Only such a standard could fulfill the nation's promise. Slavery, indeed, "is in itself so inconsistent, that it seem strange it ever should have a defender," especially in America. In *Avenia*, he emphasized this cultural paradox by highlighting hypocritical American Christians reaping slave bodies from Africa:

> Sing how these poor, unhappy dames
> Are violated at their rural games;
> How Africa's sons surrounded with alarms,
> Die in the cause of liberty, in arms;
> How with their bloody scourge the Christians go
> To Africa, dread ministers of woe.[20]

Throughout his work, Branagan cultivated a vision for the nation that would abolish slavery and engender a strong national character based on liberty. Yet each text was written from different angles and for different purposes. *Preliminary Essay* and *Avenia* were meant to be wide in scope and broad in conclusions, and were designed to highlight the hypocrisy of America's appeal to liberty while at the same time enslaving Africans. Branagan viewed the slave system as injurious to the entire country, not as merely a sectional issue, and that the federal government had an obligation to rid itself of the institution. "When you wink at the barbarous crimes of individuals, you make them national crimes," he explained, "and national sins are, and only can be, punished in this world; national characters and civil distinctions being unknown in the eternal world." Later, in his *Rights of God* (1812), the fullest explanation of his political theology, he noted that "it is very certain that national sins have been punished with national calamities," which he posited as the reason for the country's current conflict with Great Britain. This was not, of course, a singular idea in America. New England Federalists had long declared slavery the national sin, and even Benjamin Rush had stated that "national crimes require national punishments." Yet Branagan was much more systematic with his critiques and solutions. In his *Penitent Tyrant* and, more especially, *Serious Remonstrances*, Branagan focused

---

[20] Branagan, *Guardian Genius*, 20. Thomas Branagan, *Political & Theological Disquisitions on the Signs of the Times, Relative to the Present Conquests of France* (Trenton: For the Author, 1807), 12. Branagan, *Serious Remonstrances*, xiv. Thomas Branagan, *A Preliminary Essay, on the Oppression of the Exiled Sons of Africa* (Philadelphia: John W. Scott, 1804), 94, 126, 230. Thomas Branagan, *The Penitential Tyrant: or, Slave Trader Reformed* (1805; New York: Samuel Wood, 1807), 2. Branagan, *Avenia*, 15.

on how to implement his vision of an America based on principles of
universal freedom. He imagined a nation that would succeed or fail
together.[21]

Branagan was worried about a growing slave power that would dominate national interests. "It irritates me," he wrote, "when I remember that
the tyrants of the South, gain an ascendency over the citizens of the North,
and enhance their paramount rights of suffrage and sovereignty."
The political direction of the nation, led by a string of Southern presidents
and powerful slave states, threatened to change America into something it
was never meant to be. Yet while he worried about citizens in South
Carolina who lived "in a state of almost uninterrupted solicitude, anxiety,
and misery," a society which cultivated a people who were not fit to
participate in a democratic government, he was more concerned that
African Americans would one day rise up and annihilate white civilization. "Every slave ship that arrives at Charleston," he reasoned, "is to our
nation what the Grecian's wooden horse was to Troy." Worried about the
example of Haiti's revolution, Branagan warned South Carolinians that
their slave system would lead to an open and bloody rebellion: "as slavery
began with a vengeance," he cautioned, "it will assuredly end (as in
St. Domingo) with a vengeance." He believed that whites and blacks
could never live together in peace. In his telling of world history, every
empire, even "the most popular and prosperous nations of antiquity," had
fallen "through the instrumentality of vassals and the insurrection of
slaves." Due to this threat of insurrection, coupled with the broken
covenant of human liberty that revoked divine protection, America was
headed toward destruction unless it shifted course. This, Branagan
argued, could only be done through the immediate abolition of slavery
and, equally important, the removal of free blacks from white society.
Avoiding this potential demise was especially important to those invested
in nationalist ideals.[22]

There were limits to this anti-slavery vision. The contrast of Branagan's
detestation of slavery with his refusal to share society with free blacks has
led to mixed interpretations of his abolitionist message. Some historians
ignore his strong emphasis on colonization and disgust toward black

[21] Branagan, *Avenia*, 356–358. Thomas Branagan, *Rights of God, Written for the Benefit of Man; or, the Impartiality of Jehovah Vindicated* (Philadelphia: Johnson and Cooper, 1812), 9. Benjamin Rush, quoted in Davis, *The Problem of Slavery in the Age of Revolution*, 283. For New England ministers and the "national sin" of slavery, see Mason, *Slavery and Politics in the Early American Republic*, 13.

[22] Branagan, *Serious Remonstrances*, 13, 15–17. Branagan, *Penitent Tyrant*, 51, 215.

culture in order to emphasize his abolitionist views and herald him as one of the nation's earliest and most devout defenders of black freedom. Others have concluded that much of Branagan's abolitionist rhetoric was primarily a means to expedite the removal of blacks from Pennsylvania society. Gary Nash, for instance, identified Branagan as an example of the conservative backlash against Philadelphia becoming "a center of abolitionism and benevolence," and that his work was designed to "heighten white anxieties at all levels of society." Branagan therefore either serves as the epitome of liberal hypocrisy in early America or the omen for later abolitionist efforts.[23]

Yet this tension at the center of Branagan's nationalist imagination exemplified the fraught nature of racial thinking at the time. On the one hand, national ideas of universal freedom led him, and many others, to denounce slavery as antithetical to America's character; on the other, a trenchant belief in nations being constructed through ethnic homogeneity meant that racial exclusion was necessary. For many white citizens during the early republic, the irreconcilability of those principles – antislavery and anti-integration – drove them to conceive forms of national belonging that extradited non-white bodies. Even for some who supported the slave system but worried that an insurrection might destroy civilization, deportation was a tempting prospect. Thomas Jefferson, in his *Notes on the State of Virginia*, argued that there were biological differences between the races and that a racially mixed society would "divide us into parties, and produce convulsions which will probably never end but in the extermination of the one of the other race." Colonization, or the removal of freed slaves from the nation, was the only solution.[24]

---

[23] Gary B. Nash, *Forging Freedom: The Formation of Philadelphia's Black Community, 1720–1840* (Cambridge: Harvard University Press, 1988), 179.

[24] Thomas Jefferson, *Notes on the State of Virginia*, ed. William Peden (1785; Chapel Hill: University of North Carolina Press, 1996), 138–139. For the principles paradox of antislavery and segregation, see Nicholas Guyatt, *Bind Us Apart: How Enlightened Americans Invented Racial Segregation* (New York: Basic Books, 2016). For the colonizationist movement in general, see Claude Clegg, *The Price of Liberty: African Americans and the Making of Liberia* (Chapel Hill: University of North Carolina Press, 2004); Eric Burin, *Slavery and the Peculiar Solution: A History of the American Colonization Society* (Gainesville: University of Florida Press, 2005); Beverly C. Tomek, *Colonization and Its Discontents: Emancipation, Emigration, and Antislavery in Antebellum Pennsylvania* (New York: New York University Press, 2011); Matthew Spooner, "'I Know This Scheme is from God': Toward a Reconsideration of the Origins of the American Colonization Society," *Slavery and Abolition: A Journal of Slave and Post-Slave Studies* 35 (December 2014): 559–575. For the racial construction of social

Branagan's devotion to colonization was an important aspect of his nationalist imagination. Like many other whites during the period who wished to see the end of slavery but refused to share a society with Africans, removal – either forced or voluntary – was the only tenable solution. Following the example of Britain, which had established Sierre Leone as a colonization haven, Africa was a popular destination. Yet it was not the only option. For instance, Virginian St. George Tucker explored the possibility of gradual abolition and geographic relocation within the expanding American empire. The vast western territories seemed ripe for forced migration and would provide enough geographic distance. Thomas Jefferson, who oversaw the Louisiana Purchase, was also intrigued. When the Missouri Crisis shook the nation and threatened to divide the states, he proposed "diffusion," or black settlements in the western regions, as a possible solution. Yet a majority of colonizationists still insisted on Africa as the primary destination for freed blacks. They desired geographic distance to match racial difference.[25]

Branagan's particular approach to American-based colonization was a quixotic blend of nationalist vision, ideals of liberty, cultural anxiety, and political necessity. He believed that returning blacks to their "home-land" – that is, Africa – would be "both unjust and cruel." "Cruel" because the journey was treacherous and, based on his experience as a slave trader, he knew that there were few areas they could settle and be out of harm's way. "Unjust" because, as many African Americans were born on American soil, they were rightful inheritors of America's promises and America's land. Branagan's solution to the problem of a free black population was designed to be a political compromise. He believed the Louisiana Purchase, which most middle and Northern states feared would be used to extend slave-state power, was the solution. After the addition of this broad swath of land, Branagan proposed allowing free blacks to settle a large portion of western territory. This accomplished two purposes. First, it would provide freed slaves the land with which they could culti-vate their own community under the umbrella of American Freedom. The "fertile country [of] Louisiana," Branagan explained, had a climate

contracts, see Charles W. Mills, *The Racial Contract* (Ithaca, NY: Cornell University Press, 1997).

[25] St. George Tucker, *A Dissertation on Slavery: With a Proposal for the Gradual Abolition of it, in the State of Virginia* (Philadelphia: Mathew Carey, 1796); Tucker, *Reflections on the Cession of Louisiana to the United States, by Sylvestris* (Washington, DC: Samuel Harrison Smith, 1803). Thomas Jefferson to John Holmes, April 22, 1820, Monticello Online Library, www.monticello.org/ (accessed January 2014).

that would prove "congenial to [the Africans'] natures" – a belief entrenched in the scientific views of race during his period. And second, this compromise would also halt the extension of slavery beyond the states in which the system was already in place. Such an outcome would simultaneously disentangle whites from the menace of slavery while also preventing a mixed-race society.[26]

Branagan's colonization solution also reflected an assumption concerning cultural belonging and national construction. "Every nation," Branagan explained, "which has existed for any length of time, has its own manners, is particular habits of thinking, its prejudices and its partialities." These elements constituted its "national character," and "its government will always be conformed to them, either in its first establishment or by subsequent alterations." But within that nation were to be "independent states" that would constitute "a separate and distinct society" prepared to establish laws and customs "best adapted to promote and secure its own interests." This was a model of national union and pluralist cohesion that had been a hallmark of America's middle colonies. Therefore, Branagan believed that America's national character was to be based on freedom, which could only be accomplished through racial separation. Just like the ideal situation of various communities in Pennsylvania – the Germans, the Quakers, the sea merchants – living in their own distinct communities yet working under a broad umbrella of a united state, so too did Branagan's national vision include race-based societies that could claim equal freedom.[27]

This national conception predicated on colonization became common for many white elites during the period. A decade later, the American Convention for Promoting the Abolition of Slavery proposed Branagan's idea to the government and asked Congress to "consider how far it may comport with the interests of humanity, and public policy, to set apart a portion [of the] extended territory owned by the United States, for the colonisation of legally emancipated blacks." While Congress considered the bill, a House committee feared that, if the black colony would "increase as to become a nation" – note, of course, the continued use of the term "nation" to refer to a state or society within the boundaries of America – it would lead to quarrels and "civil wars." The same reasoning was given when whites rejected a plan for free blacks to migrate to Haiti because, as one Southerner wrote, no American would want "a nation of

[26] Branagan, *Serious Remonstrances*, 17, 64.   [27] Ibid., 61–62.

negroes" that lived "within a few days sail of our southern states." If blacks were to be moved, they had to be moved further away.[28]

By the time the American Colonization Society was formed in 1816, Branagan's scheme had been set aside. A number of explicitly racist politicians were now in control of the project. Because of these colonizationists' commitment to reserving western land for white settlement, as well as their racial prejudice against allowing blacks to settle anywhere near white society, Liberia became the consensus location for black expatriation. This was a nationalist imagination more directly tethered to white supremacy and racial exclusion. Branagan's fraught compromise was no longer possible. These debates would have serious implications for nationalist discourse in the following decades, especially as the fate of these western states were debated.[29]

African Americans were not only the subject of nationalist imaginations, but they imagined their own forms of nationalism as well. Their mere presence in urban centers like Philadelphia raised significant questions. A census in 1810 claimed that there were 9,500 black residents in the city. (There could have been more: white residents who feared the growing black population complained that several thousand were not recorded in the census.) The state had passed its Gradual Abolition Act in 1780 that freed all African Americans born after that date once they had reached their twenty-eighth birthday, and most were freed before 1808. Runaway slaves who had escaped from their owners, either in Pennsylvania or from Southern states, gathered in Philadelphia and created one of the most vibrant black communities in the nation. Yet while the presence of free blacks both reaffirmed and extended the region's rhetoric about free labor and individual liberties, it also uneased white residents. This tension only intensified during the conflict with Britain as the embargoes damaged

---

[28] *Minutes of the Proceedings of the Fourteenth American Convention for Promoting the Abolition of Slavery, and Improving the Condition of the African Race* (Philadelphia: W. Brown, 1816), 32–33. For Branagan's influence on the convention, see Tomek, "From Motives of Generosity," 139–142. *Annals of Congress*, 30:939. *National Intelligencer*, October 24, 1820, LOC.

[29] For this shift in colonizationist principles, see Sylvester Johnson, *African American Religions, 1500–2000: Colonialism, Democracy, and Freedom* (Cambridge: Cambridge University Press, 2015), 185–187. For background on the tensions between abolition and colonization during the period, see Richard S. Newman, *The Transformation of American Abolition: Fighting Slavery in the Early Republic* (Chapel Hill: University of North Carolina Press, 2002); Paul Goodman, *Of One Blood: Abolitionism and the Origins of Racial Equality* (Berkeley: University of California Press, 1998).

Philadelphia's maritime trade, which meant the pro-administration city had to find a scapegoat. The black community – who were, according to many whites in the period, indolent and parasitic upon the state's economy – were identified as a problem. As one resident quipped, free blacks in the city could very well be used as cannon fodder against Britain because they were plentiful and "could be better spared than any other class of the population." At one point in 1813, the Pennsylvania legislature drafted a bill that required all black residents to register with the state and threatened the imprisonment of any who lacked credentials.[30]

Black residents were not willing to merely stand by. In response to this proposed legislation, one of the city's leading African American activists, James Forten, penned a series of letters that not only attacked the bill, but also defended an idea of an American nation that centered upon racial equality. Forten, born free to a family that had resided in Philadelphia for nearly a century, was a successful sail-maker and member of the emerging middle-class colored community in the city. He was a veteran of the Revolution, during which he had been captured and imprisoned – evidence, he argued, of his patriotic credentials. He also knew the power of the pen. He frequently wrote for racial liberties he felt were inherent within the Land of the Free. When Congress rejected a petition that pled for the redress of colored people in the city in 1800, he wrote to a congressman that "though our faces are black, yet we are men, and ... [we] have the feelings and the passions of men [and] are as anxious to enjoy the birthright of the human race, as those who, from our ignorance, draw an argument aganest [sic] our petition." The black community, he argued, was just as entitled to the heritage of freedom as any other social group within the state. Part of a larger African American movement that sought to redeem the nation from the sin of slavery and fulfill its divine covenant of freedom, Forten told the Pennsylvania Abolition Society that they were "attached to our race by the Tie of Sympathy." As historian John Ernest has explained, activists like Forten were "citizens of a nation

---

[30] *Democratic Press*, January 13, 1813, quoted in Ronald Schultz, *The Republic of Labor: Philadelphia Artisans and the Politics of Class, 1720–1830* (New York: Oxford University Press, 1993), 194. For the anti-black immigration bill, see *Journal of the Twenty-Third House of Representatives of the Commonwealth of Pennsylvania* (1813–1814), 388–389. For a broader context, see Nash, *Forging Freedom*; Gary B. Nash and Jean R. Soderlund, *Freedom by Degrees: Emancipation in Pennsylvania and Its Aftermath* (New York: Oxford University Press, 1991); Julie Winch, *Philadelphia's Black Elite: Activism, Accommodation, and the Struggle for Autonomy, 1787–1848* (Philadelphia: Temple University Press, 1988).

imagined but not yet realized." Their voice became crucial to a novel and more inclusive American nationalist discourse.[31]

The nationalism of black abolitionists was one of hope and optimism, even if their victories were few. They boldly contested the nationalist arguments of those who vied for racial exclusion. A decade after his first entrance into public debate, Forten once again defended his vision of the American nation in 1813 in response to the state's proposed exclusionary legislation. His argument was framed around a belief that political leaders failed to fully understand America's founding documents. The principle that all men, no matter what race, were equal in the eyes of God was "one of the most prominent features in the Declaration of Independence, and in that glorious fabric of collected wisdom, our noble Constitution." Policies that were "subversive of this inestimable privilege" were "in direct violation of the letter and the spirit of our Constitution" and not fit for the American character. Throughout the letters, Forten consistently interchanged the use of "we" and "our" to mean his particular family, the black community, the "People of Pennsylvania," and citizens of the United States. All of these populations shared the same national heritage and possessed the same rights. He addressed "patriotic citizens" and claimed "only [a] reasonable Republic" could embrace the "glorious sentiment" that was crucial to America's birthright. That birthright included universal freedom and interracial justice. It was impossible to conclude, he reasoned, that "the authors of our Constitution intended to exclude 'African Americans' from its benefits," because such hypocrisy would be a betrayal of the Revolution's purpose. African American liberty was part of the American promise.[32]

Patriotic pride and nationalist rituals were part of this anti-slavery message. Akin to Frederick Douglass's later emphasis on the irony of Independence Day celebrations for the "negro," Forten highlighted the contested and unfulfilled nature of national celebrations. He dared his

---

[31] James Forten to George Thatcher, 1800, in Cox-Parrish-Wharton Papers, HSP. "Pennsylvania Abolition Society, General Meeting, Minutes, 1800–1824," 26, HSP. John Ernest, *Liberation Historiography: African American Writers and the Challenge of History, 1794–1861* (Chapel Hill: University of North Carolina Press, 2004), 79. See also James A. Monroe, *Hellfire Nation: The Politics of Sin in American History* (New Haven, CT: Yale University Press, 2003), 133; Varon, *Disunion*, 49–50.

[32] James Forten, "Letters From a Man of Colour, on a Late Bill Before the Senate of Pennsylvania," Web Supplement hosted by *William and Mary Quarterly*, http://oieahc .wm.edu/wmq/Jan07/winch.pdf (accessed December 22, 2013). For Forten's life, see Julie Winch, *A Gentleman of Color: The Life of James Forten* (New York: Oxford University Press, 2002).

readers to either grant him and other black residents full rights or concede
that their nation's founders were liars and opportunists. Celebrations of
the Fourth of July were an especially poignant example of America's
current duplicitous nature, he reasoned, for even though blacks had
been allowed to hold their own festivals for several years, they often
experienced antagonism from fellow citizens. "Is it not wonderful,"
Forten wryly remarked, "that the day set apart for the festival of
Liberty, should be busied by the advocates of Freedom, in endeavouring
to sully what they profess to adore[?]" The rituals of American nationalism were empty and hypocritical, he argued, and served more as an insult
than a bond for the country's black population. He desired a new national
identity.[33]

Forten was not only critical of the nation in general, but Pennsylvania
in particular. The state, he believed, should be the leader of America's true
nationalist sentiment. While all inheritors of Washington's legacy were to
be blamed, the "descendants of the immortal Penn" were especially guilty.
Forten drew on the state's proud legacy of anti-slavery arguments and
boasted that Pennsylvania was "almost the only state in the Union
wherein the African have justly boasted of rational liberty and the protection of the laws." Compared to other states and regions, nobody could
claim the same tradition of "moderation and humanity" as Pennsylvania.
It had always been "a refuge from slavery," and many a "Southern black,
when freed, has flown [to the state] for safety." In summary, it would be
"vain" to form societies built on a hypocritical reading of the nation's
founding documents. America, if it was to accomplish its lofty goals and
emulate its powerful ideals, necessitated an integrated community of
whites and blacks. Anything less would be a betrayal of the traditions of
both the state and nation. Nationalism served as both an ideological
instigator as well as a political tool for those who argued for a new racial
order in America.[34]

Black authors were active participants in this broader discussion concerning racial integration within the nation. Indeed, the anti-immigration
bill was not the only racial activity that Forten protested in the 1810s. His
other major opponent was the American Colonization Society (ACS) that,
though theoretically anti-slavery, also hoped to expel all blacks from the
country. Ideas of colonization had circulated in America, and especially in

[33] Forten, "Letters From a Man of Colour." For the racial tensions of Fourth of July
celebrations, see Waldstreicher, *In the Midst of Perpetual Fetes*, 308–322.
[34] Forten, "Letters From a Man of Colour."

Pennsylvania, for decades, but the years immediately following the War of 1812 witnessed the growth of organized and energetic societies devoted to the cause. At first, Forten was interested in the possibility, perhaps because he grew tired of increased racial strife in Philadelphia. Colonization provided African Americans a chance at self-government, even if outside America's borders. Yet after the formation of the ACS and its takeover by explicitly racist politicians like Andrew Jackson, and after gauging the interest among blacks for the project, Forten concluded that it was yet another attempt by white Americans to renege upon the nation's promises to blacks. His vision for America's future was much more inclusive.[35]

Those who opposed colonization carefully couched their dissent in nationalist terms. In response to the ACS's founding and first nationwide outreach, Forten was instrumental in organizing a meeting for black Philadelphians. When the majority concluded to reject the society, Forten helped to write the group's resolutions that condemned colonization. "WHEREAS our ancestors (not of choice) were the first successful cultivators of America," the resolution declared, we "feel ourselves entitled to participate in the blessings of her luxuriant soil, which their blood and sweat manured." Colonization was a result of "the unmerited stigma attempted to be cast upon the reputation of the free People of Colour," and they abhorred the accusation "that they are a dangerous and useless part of the community." They professed never to "separate ourselves voluntarily from the slave population of this country," because all black Americans were "brethren by the ties of consanguinity, of suffering, and of wrongs." All African Americans, both slave and free, were owed the blessing of American freedom. They deserved to experience those blessings on American soil.[36]

Much of Forten's argument was based on a specific understanding of the American nation and its character. Soon after his first published attack on the ACS, Forten coauthored a more detailed plea to potential philanthropists in Pennsylvania that urged them to reject the society's activities. Rather than being forced to settle a new colony that lacked civilization and infrastructure, black residents instead deserved "the benefits which

---

[35] For the early support of colonization by African Americans like Forten, see Johnson, *African American Religions*, 180–184. See also Eric Burin, *Slavery and the Peculiar Solution*, 80–100; Tomek, *Colonization and Its Discontents*, 43–62. Nicholas Wood, "'A Sacrifice on the Altar of Slavery': Doughface Politics and Black Disenfranchisement in Pennsylvania, 1837–1838," *Journal of the Early Republic* 31 (Spring 2011): 75–106.

[36] *Resolutions and Remonstrances of the People of Colour Against Colonization on the Coast of Africa* (Philadelphia, 1818), 3–4. See Winch, *A Gentleman of Color*, 177–206.

industry and integrity in this prosperous country assure to all its inhabitants." They were afforded the same national promise as white citizens.
Though Forten appreciated some of the priorities of the ACS, he "humbly
and respectfully urge[d them] that [relocation] is not asked for by us."
This was because African Americans preferred to "share the protection of
the excellent laws, and just government which we now enjoy, in common
with every individual of the community." They were due the education
and civilization provided by the American nation, which Forten believed
was the part of the country's character. Beyond just freedom, freed slaves
deserved the "instruction and improvement" promised to all citizens so
that they could "become in some measure fitted for their liberty." Without
these "habits of industry," any black colony in Africa would soon
"become the abode of every vice and the home of every misery." Slavery
would be "rendered perpetual" because that black society could never
reclaim the national promises that were supposed to be theirs in the first
place. They were owed the blessings and safeguards of the American
nation.[37]

Without Forten's support, the colonization effort floundered in
Philadelphia for much of the next decade. His voice, as well as many
others, soon spread to other states. A letter written by "A Man of Color"
that appeared in the *United States Gazette*, possibly penned by Forten
himself, declared that, though he "cooly and deliberately investigated the
[ACS's] projected plan," he still believed "it is calculated to perpetuate
Slavery in this Land of Liberty." Yet Forten was far from the only black
voice that portrayed a competing nationalist vision in the postwar era.
Indeed, the period introduced many African American figures that made
an impact on the political scene. Others persuasively utilized patriotic
language in their arguments against colonization and declared America
"the most virtuous republic on earth" and "our happy country." One
group in Washington, DC, warned that the only way they would colonize
would be if it were a "territory within the limits of our beloved Union."
African Americans were anxious to craft a nationalism of their own. This
increase of rhetoric, in turn, heightened Southern animosity toward the
North, especially toward neighboring states like Pennsylvania who had

[37] James Forten and Russel Perrott, "An Address to the Humane and Benevolent Inhabitants
of the City and County of Philadelphia," in *Minutes of the Proceedings of a Special
Meeting of the Fifteenth American Convention for Promoting the Abolition of Slavery
and Improving the Condition of the African Race* (Philadelphia: Hall and Atkinson,
1818), 69–72.

previously served as mediators. As the racial elements of competing nationalisms grew even louder, then, it was inevitable that they would bleed into the political debates about America's expansion westward.[38]

Slavery became a much more divisive issue in American politics during the fractured climate of the 1810s. Concerned that westward colonization would lead to the expansion of slavery and slave states' powers, politicians in Massachusetts worried about the nation's future. One of the most outspoken anti-slavery advocates was Boston's Josiah Quincy, who feared that his posterity was "destined to be slaves, and to yoke in with negroes, chained to the car of a Southern master." He similarly warned in 1811 that "*the bonds of this union are, virtually, dissolved.*" If slavery were more firmly entrenched, Quincy argued in Congress, free states should no longer be tethered to those that practiced slavery, and it would be best "*to prepare definitely for a separation; amicably if they can, violently if they must.*" Such an accusation offended Southern politicians, of course, who called him to order. Yet Quincy's argument struck a nerve in his state, and he continually repeated his message of national degradation at the hands of the slave power. Indeed, his narrative was no longer merely one of declension, as he characterized the first two decades of the republic as "bad, and humiliating" for Massachusetts. Rather, now that "the principles of the constitution [had been] modified by usurpation," their condition had become "a hundred fold worse." Quincy was more radical than most, especially regarding his declining faith that the Union could be redeemed. But his sentiment resonated with many others. "The lordly tenants of the Southern palaces and villas, the inexorable masters of hundreds of poor enslaved Africans," wrote one Bostonian, "were not fit to be entrusted with the guardianship of" the nation. In the wake of the

---

[38] *United States Gazette*, January 21, 1817, LOC. Quoted in Herbert Aptheker, ed., *A Documentary History of Negro People in the United States, Volume 1: From Colonial Times Through the Civil War* (New York: Citadel Press, 1951), 67, 69. *Poulson's American Daily Advertiser*, January 10, 1817, MHS. For black patriotic rhetoric, see James Oliver Horton and Lois E. Horton, *In Hope of Liberty: Culture, Community, and Protest among Northern Free Blacks, 1700–1860* (New York: Oxford University Press, 1997), 177–202; Robert Pierce Forbes, *The Missouri Compromise and Its Aftermath: Slavery and the Meaning of America* (Chapel Hill: University of North Carolina Press, 2007), 59–65; Matthew Mason, *Slavery and Politics in the Early American Republic* (Chapel Hill: University of North Carolina Press, 2006), 107–113; Manisha Sinha, *The Slave's Cause: A History of Abolition* (New Haven: Yale University Press, 2016), 130–169.

Hartford Convention, Massachusetts politicians could reaffirm their patriotic loyalty through anti-slavery rhetoric.[39]

Crucial to this nationalist rhetoric was the belief that slavery could no longer be seen as a sectional issue, but rather as a problem that plagued the entire nation. One Massachusetts Federalist believed that Americans who had overlooked Southern slavery while declaring the nation's ideals of liberty were deluded and hypocritical. "Whatever we may imagine, our country is *not* 'the last and only refuge of the oppressed,'" he trumpeted. "We are *not* 'the only free people on earth.' Slavery, degrading slavery," he explained, "exists in the very heart of our political institutions." It was finally time to take action in the moral battle. Until slavery was vanquished, he declared, "Let the vaunters of our national glory be stilled!" Philadelphia editor William Duane similarly wondered, "Have we no magnanimous champion of freedom?" He mourned that there was "no Wilberforce, no Fox, no Sharpe, no Clarkson" in a country supposedly founded on freedom. America had fallen behind in the transatlantic cause. Duane claimed that those involved in America's horrible practice, both the slave-owners and the citizens who allowed slavery to exist in the first place, were "lost to all the fine feelings which are the substratum of ... the love of liberty." Northerners had been stagnant for too long, and it was time to take action and reclaim America's direction. As a result, states began to take small steps to eradicate elements of slavery found in their region. For instance, the Pennsylvania Supreme Court ruled in 1816 that children born in the state to runaway slaves were henceforth and forever free. These developments worried Southerners, who feared they were setting a later precedent that, if realized, would lead to war.[40]

These debates took place against the backdrop of anti-slavery discussions also taking place across the Atlantic in Britain. British abolitionist rhetoric had been more consistent and vociferous than what had taken place in America during the previous four decades. This was partly because slavery

---

[39] Josiah Quincy, *Speech of Mr. Quincy, Delivered in the House of Representatives, on the Bill Admitting the Territory of Orleans into the Union, January 14, 1811* (Washington, DC: s.n., 1811), 2. (Emphasis in original.) Josiah Quincy, *An Oration Delivered before the Washington Benevolent Society of Massachusetts, on the Thirtieth Day of April, 1813, Being the Anniversary of the First Inauguration of President Washington* (Boston: Lewis and Spears, 1813), 15. *Poulson's American Daily Advocate*, December 15, 1814, MHS. Quincy's latter speech was reprinted throughout the South as proof of New England's treason. For instance, Charleston's *Investigator* published the entirety of it in seven installments from February 4–13, 1813.

[40] *Columbian Centinel*, July 17, 1816, LOC. (Emphasis in original.) *Aurora*, January 14, 1819, LOC.

was not as deeply integrated into common culture and was consigned to imperial and business interests. But it was also because anti-slavery rhetoric buoyed national discourse in the face of imperial disunion. Leading enlightenment thinkers like Samuel Johnson and Adam Smith denounced the slave institution, as did religious figures like Granville Sharp and John Wesley. To many of these outspoken individuals, to be British meant supporting abolition. This rhetoric only escalated in the second decade of the nineteenth century, as loud voices for the British Empire believed it was their role to police the destruction of the Atlantic Slave Trade. This was an enthusiastic and vociferous appropriation of British nationalist rhetoric that worried slaveholders throughout the Americas.[41]

Vanquishing the Atlantic Slave Trade was a particular triumph for this patriotic action. "We were a people more favoured by Heaven than any other nation had been from the commencement of time," one British author declared in 1807 as debates over the slave trade reached fever pitch, "but we should beware how we forfeited the protection of Providence by continual injustice; for if we did not look in vain hereafter for the glories of the Nile and Trafalgar." Within this Protestant context, abolition was the only way to redeem the nation and reinstall the empire as the greatest in the world. This pressure only increased during the following decades. Anti-slavery groups produced 800 petitions that urged parliament to pressure France and America to forfeit slavery in 1814. Two decades later, in 1833, the House of Commons received 5,000 petitions that were signed by more than 1.5 million people. That was soon followed by a women's petition that stretched more than half a mile and included 187,000 signatures. Another contemporary petition featured almost half a million signatures and urged government to give full liberation to slaves. This all resulted in the end of the slave institution within their empire. Britain's abolition of their slave trade at a time when it was still enormously profitable has been heralded as a hallmark for Western civilization. It also marked a new age in their nationalist imagination.[42]

[41] See David Brion Davis, *The Problem of Slavery in the Age of Emancipation* (New York: Knopf, 2014), 261–277; Gerald Horne, *The Counter-Revolution of 1776: Slave Resistance and the Origins of the United States of America* (New York: New York University Press, 2014); Alan Taylor, *Internal Enemy: Slavery and War in Virginia, 1772–1832* (New York: Norton, 2013).

[42] Linda Colley, *Britons: Forging the Nation, 1707–1837* (1992; New Haven: Yale University Press, 2009), 358–368; David Brion Davis, *Inhuman Bondage: The Rise and Fall of Slavery in the New World* (New York: Oxford University Press, 2006), 231–249.

This transatlantic context placed added pressure on America, as they were forced to justify the continued practice of slavery even as every other civilized nation abolished the institution. They also faced new problems on their own continent. Though slavery was secured in many Central and South American nations, the revolutionary spirit that swept across the Americas opened new emancipatory possibilities. Independence movements in Latin America birthed new anti-slavery agitation. Slaveholding elites in America originally supported these revolts against European colonial rule, but once those new republics questioned the legality of slavery and proposed new forms of racial equality, those same American Southerners felt surrounded by threats to their entrenched institution. Under the direction of James Madison and James Monroe, General Andrew Jackson used military force to eradicate black communities in Spanish Florida. By 1826, the new Democratic Party proposed a more isolationist policy toward their Southern neighbors. Caitlin Fitz has noted that "as a white republic in a hemisphere full of darker-skinned radicals," slave-owners felt increasingly under siege. To address these threats, Southern politicians posted ambitious imperial and domestic projects to secure their slave interest. There was a continental context for these nationalist debates.[43]

The first imminent question regarding the domestic institution was raised in 1819 when Missouri appealed for statehood. Part of the expansive territory obtained through the Louisiana Purchase, the presence or absence of slavery in the new state would set a precedent for future expansion. The original bill's author, James Tallmadge of New York, added an amendment that forbade the introduction of new slaves to Missouri and required that all children born to slaves from that point forward would be freed at the age of twenty-five. The House committee incorporated the amendment into the bill and it was passed in February of that year. However, the measure stalled in the Senate, where it received no support from slave states, and was set aside until 1820. In the meantime, Alabama was admitted into the Union as a slave state, which equalized the number of free and slave states in the Union. The new version of the bill, crafted by another New Yorker, John Taylor, included three crucial "compromises" that were meant to quell, but in the end ignited, the

---

[43] Caitlin Fitz, *Our Sister Republics: The United States in an Age of Revolutions* (New York: Liveright, 2016), 10. See also Matthew Karp, *This Vast Southern Empire: Slaveholders at the Helm of American Foreign Policy* (Cambridge: Harvard University Press, 2016), 12–16.

slave question: Missouri was to be admitted as a slave state, Maine would also be admitted as a free state in order to maintain the nation's balance, and a geopolitical line that ran from the southern border of Missouri all the way to the western edge of American territory would demarcate all future states that would be free (to the north of the line) and those that would be slave (to the south). More than just assuring the presence and possible expansion of slavery in these Western territories, the bill successfully sectionalized the issue of slavery and highlighted the geographic division between nationalist imaginations.[44]

The negative reactions to the compromise from the North were swift and passionate. They highlighted how such a division betrayed their understanding of the nation. In 1819, public gatherings in both Boston and Philadelphia declared their belief that all future states should "be subject to slavery restriction" because they believed free labor was the nation's future and human bondage its past. A month after the compromise was approved, Pennsylvanians toasted "*Missouri and the slave states* – May they be as ready and willing to protect themselves against their slaves, without the aid of the North, as they have been willing to increase their danger." Others in Pennsylvania burned an effigy of their congressman, David Fullerton, who had voted in favor of the compromise. One Philadelphian wrote that anyone who desired to claim a revolutionary heritage was now expected to "summon all his energy to extirpate Slavery." On the Fourth of July, citizens in Massachusetts, after toasting "Massachusetts – Proud of her *freedom*, and proud that she holds no man a *slave*," also declared, "Slavery – Her last refuge from persecution is in *Republican America*." To many in Pennsylvania and Massachusetts, the Missouri Compromise was a diversion from the nation's ideals and set a dangerous precedent for America's future. Congressman John Sergeant asked Congress if "any one serious [had] considered the scope of this doctrine," because he feared it would lead "directly to the establishment of slavery throughout the world." The same reasoning that extended slavery into Missouri "will justify its extension to another," he argued, which would then create a slaveholding empire that

---

[44] For a general overview of the Missouri Compromise, see Forbes, *Missouri Compromise*; Wilentz, *Rise of American Democracy*, 218–253; Mason, *Slavery and Politics*, 213–238; William W. Freehling, *The Road to Disunion: Secessionists at Bay, 1776–1854* (New York: Oxford University Press, 1991), 144–161; Daniel Walker Howe, *What Hath God Wrought: The Transformation of America, 1815–1848* (New York: Oxford University Press, 2007), 147–160.

was a betrayal of the nation's founding ideals. The bill was odious to America's national character.[45]

Responses in New England were just as passionate. In Boston, minister Joseph Wheaton placed the controversy, and its implications for the nation's image, in a global context. Throughout the world, he argued, people "are separated into different nations, and cherish different local attachments." The primary mode of judging an individual nation's character and standing, however, was how it treated its residents. Even though the "capacities" of races diverged – and Wheaton maintained the theological distinction that blacks descended from Ham – that did not justify ill treatment. The equality of mankind was designed to be the central principle for any nation, and success depended upon fidelity to God's covenant of human freedom. Anything else would be based upon faulty assumptions and deserved divine wrath. "All nations" were to be given separate "tribunals," in which they are "separated according to their characters; and whether destined to a state of reward or punishment, the existence of all is to be continued without end." While judgment and punishment for individual sinners came at a person's death, the condemnation of wicked nations immediately followed degraded policies. Wheaton argued that even "the phrase *republican slave holder*" was a contradiction in terms. "The Emperor Nero whose despotism and cruelty have long been proverbial," he declared, "had as good a claim to be called a republican, as any man who traffics in slaves or unnecessarily holds them in bondage." If the political decisions of 1820 represented America's new nationalist persona, its violent end was nigh.[46]

The fact that citizens in Massachusetts and Pennsylvania believed the federal government not only should, but *must*, intervene in stopping the spread of slavery demonstrated an evolving sense of nationalism that privileged centralized power. It posited certain principles, like racial equality, as central to America's purpose and character, while muting others, like states' rights. This divide even shaped how Americans viewed the nation's founding documents. For those who wished to emphasize

---

[45] Mason, *Slavery and Politics*, 179, 186. *Niles' Weekly Register*, February 26, 1820, LOC. (Emphasis in original.) *Poulson's American Daily Advertiser*, July 18, 26, 1820, MHS. (Emphasis in original.) *Annals of Congress* 35:389. For the importance of toasts in nationalist celebrations during the period, see Waldstreicher, *In the Midst of Perpetual Fetes*, 272–276.

[46] Joseph Wheaton, *The Equality of Mankind and the Evils of Slavery, Illustrated: A Sermon, Delivered on the Day of the Annual Fast, April 6, 1820* (Boston: Crocker & Brewster, 1820), 3, 6, 9, 22.

equality as the nation's founding principle, the Declaration of Independence was the blueprint for the nation's character. One Pennsylvanian believed that "the Declaration of Independence[,] being anterior to the constitution, ought to be considered as the basis of the union." John Quincy Adams similarly stated that, "with the Declaration of Independence on their lips, and the merciless scourge of slavery in their hands, a more flagrant image of human inconsistency can scarcely be conceived than one of our Southern slave-holding republicans." For those who argued state sovereignty to be the governing ideal, on the other hand, the Constitution was presented as a defense for the extension of slavery. Federal intervention into how local citizens constructed their society would be a breach of the political compact made in 1787. These were more than mere rhetorical calculations designed to persuade, but also glimpses into the ambivalent nature of nationalist imaginations during a period of upheaval.[47]

Indeed, the Missouri Compromise demonstrated the deep divisions that had been in place since the founding but had been either overlooked or ignored. The imagined nationalism centered on cultural unity was shattered. South Carolina Congressman Charles Pinckney could not fathom "any question" that could divide the nation as much as "the one which respects slavery." Thomas Jefferson saw these implications immediately. He explained that the compromise struck him "like a fire bell in the night, awakened and filled me with terror." He feared that "a geographical line, coinciding with a marked principle, moral and political, once conceived and held up to the angry passions of men, will never be obliterated." Every new "irritation will mark it deeper and deeper." The end result, he warned, would be "the knell of the Union." James Madison similarly believed that "should a state of parties arise founded on geographical boundaries, and other physical and permanent distinctions which happen to coincide with them, what is to control those great repulsive masses from awful shocks against each other?" He likened the

---

[47] *Poulson's American Daily Advertiser*, November 8, 1820, MHS. John Quincy Adams, *Memoirs of John Quincy Adams: Comprising Portions of His Diary from 1795 to 1848*, ed. Charles Francis Adams, 12 vols. (Philadelphia: J. B. Lippincott & Company, 1877), 4:492–493. For the debates over which document was more crucial to America's character, see Mason, *Slavery Politics in the Early American Republic*, 199–201; Christian G. Fritz, *American Sovereigns: The People and America's Constitutional Tradition Before the Civil War* (Cambridge: Cambridge University Press, 2007), 277–278. For the creeping influence of an expanding federal authority, see Brian Balogh, *A Government Out of Sight: The Mystery of National Authority in Nineteenth-Century America* (Cambridge: Cambridge University Press, 2009), 53–150.

rift in the Union to an unhappy marriage in which the husband and wife were no longer on cordial terms, a fissure which stemmed from, appropriately enough, a black stain on the latter's arm from "a certain African dye." Even the strongest Virginian nationalists worried what these developments would mean for the unity of the United States.[48]

These competing versions of nationalist discourse continued to diverge. Many in the North emphasized a national obligation to cultural regeneration, including the containment of slavery, while those in the South responded by cultivating images of a state-based confederacy. In a shift from the Hartford Convention, Northern states emphasized the power and obligation of federal authority, and Southern states took up the mantle of states' rights. Though it took decades for observers to realize the depth of this division, it eventually framed political clashes. South Carolinian William Henry Trescot expressed in 1850 that all the nation's problems stemmed from the decisions of 1820. The Missouri Compromise, he explained, initiated "a broad declaration that in the American Union there are two people, differing in institutions, feelings, and in the basis of their political faith." It had become impossible for the government to legislate both bodies, and therefore "as to certain matters of political interest, they must, by an imaginary line, be separated." Trescot wondered if the geographic line had "become a real boundary and the two people, bidding each other a friendly but firm farewell, [should] enter upon their paths as separate and independent nations." Though this divisive fruit didn't grow for decades, the seeds were planted early on.[49]

With this deep division came increased sectional accusations. Many of these confrontations revolved around fears of provoking slave insurrections. In 1821, John C. Calhoun wrote that though "the Missouri question is

---

[48] *Annals of Congress*, 35:1320. Thomas Jefferson to John Holmes, April 22, 1820, LOC. James Madison, quoted in Robert E. Bonner, *Mastering America: Southern Slaveholders and the Crisis of American Nationhood* (Cambridge: Cambridge University Press, 2009), 14. For Jefferson's nationalism in general, and its impact on his interpretation on the Missouri Crisis in particular, see Peter Onuf, *Jefferson's Empire: The Language of American Nationhood* (Charlottesville: University Press of Virginia, 2000), esp. 109–146.

[49] William Henry Trescot, *Oration Delivered Before the Beaufort Volunteer Artillery* (Charleston, SC: Walker and James, 1850), 7. On the strict division of national imaginations during the period, see Robert E. Bonner, "Empire of Liberty, Empire of Slavery: The Louisiana Territories and the Fate of American Bondage," in *The Louisiana Purchase: The Emergence of an American Nation*, ed. Peter Kastor (Washington, DC: Congressional Quarterly, 2003), 129–138.

settled," he feared that "the excitement is not allayed" on either side of the divide. Northerners believed that the compromise entrenched slavery within the union, and many Southerners feared the resulting rhetoric in favor of liberty – which was built upon, extended, and intensified the nationalist rhetoric of freedom from the previous decade – brought more danger for Southerners. The fear of a slave uprising, what they called the "internal enemy," was exacerbated by this new strident discourse, especially now that middle states like Pennsylvania had joined the loud chorus of New England critics. During the debates over Missouri, South Carolinian William Smith claimed it was ignorant outsiders, like those in Philadelphia, who caused his state to be "in a constant state of alarm" and "in constant danger." The *National Intelligencer* accused the North of hinting, during the War of 1812, "to the British commanders the practicability of exciting an insurrection among the Southern slave population." This, they believed, was nothing less than treason. In response, Southerners were left to reconceive an aggressively pro-slavery nationalist argument.[50]

South Carolinian fears seemed to be realized in 1822 with the Denmark Vesey slave revolt conspiracy. Authorities claimed to have uncovered a plot that summer in which Vesey, a former slave who had been a carpenter in Charleston for two decades, planned an insurrection with hundreds of accomplices to kill their masters and escape to Haiti. The alleged date for the revolt – July 14, 1822, Bastille Day – was supposed to signify their connection to other Atlantic revolutions. For a state in which blacks out-numbered whites two to one, this seemed a fulfillment of Southerners' worst nightmare. It was only avoided through advanced confessions. In the end, 131 men were charged with conspiracy, 67 were convicted, and 35, includ-ing Vesey, were hanged. The official report concluded that Vesey was influenced by three things: familiarity with the Haitian Revolution, the closure of the city's African Methodist Episcopal Church, and, importantly, the excitement over the Missouri Compromise. While the reality and extent of the supposed rebellion are debated, the response to the conspiracy high-lighted the deteriorating relationship between South Carolina and the North.[51]

---

[50] *The Papers of John C. Calhoun*, ed. Robert L. Meriwether, 28 vols. (Columbia: University of South Carolina Press, 1959–2003), 6:329. AC, 35:267–270. *National Intelligencer*, April 30, 1813, LOC. For the fear of slavery during the period, see Alan Taylor, *The Internal Enemy: Slavery and War in Virginia, 1772–1832* (New York: W. W. Norton, 2013).

[51] See James O'Neil Spady, "Power and Confession: On the Credibility of the Earliest Reports of the Denmark Vesey Slave Conspiracy," *William and Mary Quarterly* 68

At the very least, South Carolinians took advantage of the incident to fight back against Northern states like Pennsylvania. Thomas Pinckney published an anonymous pamphlet that claimed that, after the "Example of St Domingo," the second most influential catalyst for the insurrection was "the indiscreet zeal in favour of universal liberty, expressed by many of our fellow-citizens in the States north and east of Maryland," which was "aided by the Black population of those states." It was no coincidence, Pinckney concluded, that the same decade that had witnessed an increase in abolitionist rhetoric in the middle states had also given birth to more slave revolts. The emphasis on race equality and abolition, especially from free blacks, destabilized his own state's carefully crafted society. Pinckney denounced the "injustice, impolicy, and indiscriminating cruelty of many citizens of the Northern States, who directly or indirectly instigate our Black population to such scenes as they lately meditated." This "injustice" was "a violation of the Federal compact." Pinckney interpreted the nation's agreement to mean that states could not intervene in the moral affairs of other states. Such actions threatened to "dissolve the Union."[52]

These allegations quickly spread. That same year another South Carolinian, Edwin Holland, wrote an inflammatory and accusatory pamphlet that similarly attacked Northern states for undermining South Carolina's authority, conspiring to revoke the state's rights, and perverting the nation's political purpose. The anti-slavery ideas presented in Congress, he explained, gave dangerous ideas of freedom to slaves. But politicians were not the only Northerners to blame. Holland also accused "the swarm of MISSIONARIES, white and *black*, that are perpetually visiting us." In vivid language, Holland claimed that these ministers were duplicitous in that they carried "the Sacred Volume of God in one hand," while spreading ideas "of discord and destruction, and *secretly* disperse among our Negro Population, the seeds of discontent and sedition" with the other. After stripping Christianity "of her pure and spotless robe," Northerners instructed slaves "to creep silently to the pillow of his unsuspecting gamester, and at one 'fell swoop' to murder *him* in the unconscious hour of sleep, prostitute the partner of his bosom, violate

(April 2011): 287–304; Michael P. Johnson, "Denmark Vesey and his Co-Conspirators," *William and Mary Quarterly* 58 (October 2001): 915–976; Robert L. Paquette, "From Rebellion to Revisionism: The Continuing Debate about the Denmark Vesey Affair," *Journal of the Historical Society* 4 (September 2004): 291–334.
[52] [Thomas Pinckney], *Reflections, Occasioned by the Late Disturbances in Charleston* (Charleston, SC: A. E. Miller, 1822), 7–8.

the child of his affections, and dash out the brains of his innocent and unoffending infant." Another Baptist minister in Charleston, Richard Furman, further argued that a "body of men" in Philadelphia had introduced the "perversion of Scriptural doctrine" which was meant to introduce "scenes of anarchy and blood" in the state. These were not light accusations. But more than murderous sedition, Holland believed that Northern states had "waged a perpetual and incessant war against the interests of the Southern and Western States," a war which had threatened South Carolina's safety, prosperity, and interests. If continued, the state would have no other option but to seek "a separation of the Union." These were acts of war.[53]

Holland's pamphlet exemplified how some South Carolinians, at this time of national debate, constructed an idea of the nation. States like Philadelphia that cried for abolition were not only being uncivil, but also unpatriotic. "Bound together as we are by one golden chain of affinity," he explained, America was a "sublime and beautiful spectacle of an immense empire, composed of different sovereignties, revolving hitherto, in perfect harmony under the controlling power of a confederated Republican form of Government." The American nation, to Holland, was an expanding empire of independent sovereignties tethered to an underpinning, if loose, central government. What held them together was both "affinity" with fellow American citizens – an affinity that was betrayed by the blunt abolitionist rhetoric of the North – as well as a common interest in an expanding empire. The "harmony" was not found in identical cultures, or perhaps even a shared morality, but broader economic benefits. Within this system, South Carolina could claim "constitutional rights and privileges" that, while perhaps eschewed by other regions, worked perfectly fine within its locality. The union was challenged and the harmony was deconstructed when "a system of legislation ... strikes at the root of all their interests," which is what Holland believed was taking place. The United States, while cultivating different state-based societies and cultures, "are *one* for national

---

[53] [Edwin C. Holland], *A Refutation of the Calumnies Circulated Against the Southern & Western States, Respecting the Institution and Existence of Slavery Among Them. To Which is Added, a Minute and Particular Account of the Actual State and Condition of Their Negro Population. Together with Historical Notices of All the Insurrections That have Taken Place Since the Settlement of the Country* (Charleston, SC: A.E. Miller, 1822), 11, 12, 36–37. Richard Furman, *Exposition of the Views of the Baptists, Relative to the Coloured Population of the United States in Communication to the Governor of South Carolina* (Charleston, SC: A. E. Miller, 1823).

purposes." Each state has "their appropriate and peculiar orbits, like the stars," and attempts to disrupt that orbit through intervening in slavery's affairs would cause catastrophic results. This Southern vision of nationalism allowed the slave institution to remain secure.[54]

In Holland's telling, it was not the South that compromised America's ideals, but rather the North. The Hartford Convention, for instance, had proven that New England could not be trusted to keep the nation's best interests at heart and should instead be regarded as a "scorpion nest of sedition and intrigue." Further, Holland argued that Northern states had forgotten that the American republic itself was based upon the slave system. While states like Massachusetts and Pennsylvania now denied it, they "were *at a very early period*, actively and industriously engaged in the very traffic to which is to be attributed the introduction and existence of the *sin* of which they have since so loudly and clamourously complained." Holland offered a long and detailed history of America's rise to power that placed slavery at the very center of its success. To be American meant to profit from the slave system. Therefore, while Northerners attempted to "denounce the 'inhumanity' of the [slave] trade," they at the same time "entered fully into it, and shared, from their immense amount of tonnage afloat, almost exclusively the posits of it." Even after they had abolished slavery in their state constitutions, the interconnected American market still reaffirmed their attachment to slavery's products. It was not South Carolinians who were hypocrites for worshiping American liberty while enslaving blacks, but Pennsylvania and other Northern states for reaping the benefits of the slave system while condemning it as immoral. There was nothing more central to American nationalism than the slave institution.[55]

These debates cemented new political realities. In the wake of rising anti-slavery rhetoric, South Carolinians observed that they could no longer assume the credibility of their nationalist attachments. Instead, they were forced to proactively formulate a patriotic defense for their state interests and priorities. Threats to the slave institution, both domestic and international, proved a dangerous foe. Anti-slavery agitation in Europe and the American continent necessitated a strong fiscal, naval, and political response, and Southerners worked to craft a concomitant foreign

[54] [Holland], *Refutations of the Calumnies*, 8, 9, 60. (Emphasis in original.)
[55] [Holland], *Refutations of the Calumnies*, 10, 23, 31. (Emphasis in original.) The increased strength of Southern nationalism at this point of American debate is outlined in Bonner, *Mastering America*, 3–23; Mason, *Slavery and Politics*, 158–176.

policy. Abolitionist efforts within America's own borders introduced a fear that their fellow citizens could not be trusted and that safeguards must be put in place to limit federal intervention into Southern affairs. Over the next decade, many Southerners worked to construct a nationalist vision that was simultaneously strong enough to protect the slave institution from foreign activists while also pliable enough to restrain seemingly anti-slavery states within their own union. Such a paradoxical form of nationalism was sure to be tested.[56]

While conflicts over slavery had always been present in early America, these debates took center stage in the 1810s and 1820s. Many states that had previously served a moderating function, like Pennsylvania, now conceived of a federal power committed to liberty, free labor, and abolition. Black voices, too, entered the fray and presented arguments about an American character that destabilized the nation's racial assumptions. These developments worried Southerners like those in South Carolina, as the legality and political credibility of their slave institution had previously gone unchallenged. As a result, national divisions became more apparent. The debates surrounding the Missouri Compromise in 1820, then, did not appear out of nowhere, but were the culmination of competing nationalist trends that had been antecedent and would continue. How could a national union remain stable with such deep discord over such a central principle? This controversy set the stage for the following decade when national attention turned to a single state, South Carolina, and its bold attempt to set itself up as a quasi-independent nation in defiance of a country that no longer prioritized its best interests.

---

[56] For Southern slaveholders' control of America's foreign policy, see Karp, *This Vast Southern Empire.*

5

The Nullification Crisis and the Fracturing of National Interests

The moral entity – the grammatical being called a NATION, has been clothed in attributes that have no real existence except in the imagination of those who metamorphose a word into a thing; and convert a mere grammatical contrivance, into an existing and intelligent being.
                                        –Thomas Cooper, 1826[1]

A great excitement has for some time prevailed in a portion of the Southern States of the Union.
                                        –Edward Everett, 1830[2]

The States as *States* ratified the compact. The People of the United States, collectively had no agency in its formation. There did not exist then, nor has there existed at any time since, such a political body as the People of the United States.
                       –South Carolina Nullification Convention, 1832[3]

Progress toward a centralized and coherent nation-state was far from determined. If anything, the idea of a nationalism and national interests merging with a federal body only became more vexed during the antebellum period. Nowhere did it face a more imminent threat, at least prior

---

[1] Thomas Cooper, *Lectures on the Elements of Political Economy* (Columbia, SC: Doyle E. Sweeny, 1826), 16.
[2] Edward Everett, *Remarks on the Public Lands, and on The Right of a State to Nullify an Act of Congress* (Boston: Gray & Bowen, 1830), 26.
[3] "Address to the People of South Carolina, by their Delegates in Convention," in *Documents. Ordered by the Convention of the People of South Carolina, to be Transmitted to the President of the United States, and to the Governor of Each State* (Columbia, SC: S. Johnston, 1832), 4. (Emphasis in original.)

to the Civil War, than during South Carolina's flirtation with nullification during the early 1830s. Once faced with a federal government that many believed did not reflect their local interests, some South Carolinians explored alternate models of sovereignty that rested upon novel conceptions of nationalism. While historians have traditionally identified the birth of Southern nationalist awakening to the mid-nineteenth century, the seeds were planted during these earlier cultural and constitutional conflicts. Aided by romantic ideas of belonging that were then percolating in continental Europe, especially in Germany, a number of politicians and intellectuals in South Carolina imagined revised boundaries for cultural and federal union. This chapter explores the debates that preceded, were incited by, and followed the crisis over South Carolina's threat of nullification in 1832. They exemplify the fissuring within America's nationalist visions. Was one's primary loyalty to the state or to the nation? How could a federal body balance the competing interests of such a divided population? The competing answers for these questions threatened to disentangle the nationalist foundation from the previous five decades.[4]

Thomas Smith Grimké knew that serious trouble was on the horizon as early as 1827. Grimké, a lawyer with a Yale education and nationalist sympathies, worried that his fellow South Carolinians failed to recognize the deep federalist ties that undergirded the Constitution and the nation it founded. In December of that year, in response to a series of tariffs passed by the federal government that increased taxes on imports, the South Carolina legislature declared, in part, that "the Constitution of the United States is a compact between the people of the different States with each other, as separate and independent sovereignties." This meant that any "violation of the letter or spirit of that compact by the Congress of the United States" could be overturned by the people of various states in order to "remonstrate against violations of the fundamental compact." This was the first of an increasing number of warning shots sent from South Carolina politicians.[5]

---

[4] For the later development of Southern, and especially Confederate, nationalism, see Drew Gilpin Faust, *The Creation of Confederate Nationalism: Ideology and Identity in the Civil War South* (Baton Rouge: Louisiana State University Press, 1990); Charles B. Dew, *Apostles of Disunion: Southern Secession Commissioners and the Causes of the Civil War* (Charlottesville: University Press of Virginia, 2001); Paul Quigley, *Shifting Grounds: Nationalism and the American South, 1848–1865* (New York: Oxford University Press, 2011).
[5] "Report and Resolution, December 19, 1827," in *The Statutes at Large of South Carolina; Edited, Under Authority of the Legislature, by Thomas Cooper* (Columbia: A. S. Johnston, 1836), 242.

These arguments did not convince Grimké. An ardent nationalist, he believed these threats of nullification were based on a faulty understanding of the national contract. The Constitution, rather than an agreement between individual sovereignties, was an "act of *the People* of the Union, and not of the people of each of the *thirteen* United States." A state threatening a nation would be akin to a son "unsheathing the sword against a father," or a brother seeking "to shed his brother's life." He argued that "nature, religion, public and private duty, [and] the social feeling" had established "irrevocable laws" against speaking ill toward the parent-nation. In short, national allegiance took precedence over provincial concerns. "Our government is pre-eminently the government of the people," he concluded, "the offspring of mutual concessions and common interests." Grimké republished a Fourth of July oration he had delivered in 1809 because it spoke "in favour of the wisdom and expediency of UNION, and against the folly and madness of DISUNION." He also regaled Charleston with a series of essays that denounced sectional rebellion. Grimké identified "jealousy of interest, and the jealousy of rights, of party spirit, and of ambition" as both the "causes" and "probable consequences" of disunion, and urged citizens not to let "the clamors of faction deafen you to the voice of your country." He urged his fellow citizens to let nationalism frame state discussion, and not the other way around.[6]

Grimké was not alone in his consternation. On November 18, 1831, as the tension between the state and the federal governments intensified, a group of "Citizens of Chester District," located in the northern part of the state, gathered to protest the proposed state nullification convention. They drafted, signed, and voted to disseminate resolutions "expressing the

---

[6] Thomas S. Grimké, *Speech of Thomas Smith Grimké, One of the Senators from St. Philip's and St. Michael's, Delivered in the Senate of South Carolina, in December 1828, During the Debate on Sundry Resolutions, of the Senate and House of Representatives, Respecting the Tariff* (Charleston, SC: W. Riley, 1829), 9–10, 20, 21. (Emphasis in original.) Thomas S. Grimké, *An Oration, Delivered in St. Philip's Church, Before the Inhabitants of Charleston, on the Fourth of July, 1809, by the Appointment of the South Carolina State Society of Cincinnati, and Published at the Request of that Society, and of the American Revolution Society* (Charleston, SC: Wm. Riley, 1829), 5, 26, 30. See also Thomas S. Grimké, *To the People of the State of South-Carolina* (Charleston, SC: J.S. Burges, 1832); Thomas S. Grimké, *Oration on the Principal Duties of Americans; Delivered before the Washington Society, and Other Citizens of Charleston; in the Second Presbyterian Church, on Thursday the 4th of July* (Charleston, SC: William Estill, 1833); Thomas S. Grimké, *A Letter to the Honorable John C. Calhoun, Vice-President of the United States, Robert Y. Hayne, Senator of the United States, George McDuffie, of the House of Representatives of the United States, and James Hamilton, Jr. Governor of the State of South-Carolina* (Charleston, SC: James S. Burges, 1832).

sentiments of the people of Chester Dist. on the present state of public affairs." Their first resolution proclaimed that "the people of Chester District are determined, at all times, under all circumstances, and at all hazards, to adhere to the Union of the States, and to their ancient rights and liberties under the same." They declared the threat of nullification "a novel and dangerous doctrine, hazardous to the peace, union and safety of the American Republic," and that severe factionalism between the United States would prove "the experiment of republicanism under the most advantageous circumstances has failed, and that men are incapable of self-government." Tired of the bold and extreme actions of their state politicians, these citizens decided that it was time for their own voices to be heard.[7]

These petitioners emphasized their commitment to a nationalist ideal. They argued that nullification "ought to be opposed by every lover of his country." Drawing from the power of patriotism, they noted "that this meeting has unbounded confidence in the ardent love of country" as well as "the sound judgment and patriotic devotedness of President Jackson." On the final page of the pamphlet, a "Note from the Publisher" added that the call for nullification was "a specious pretext for the sacrifice of national character, and the fabric of our liberties to the lust of ambition!" To these residents of South Carolina, allegiance to the United States was more important than the interests of the state, and the "character" of the nation was just as important as economic freedom of the state. It was this groundswell of support that, at least in part, contributed to state politicians forgoing the cause of nullification a couple years later.[8]

These were contested ideas in antebellum South Carolina. Grimké and Chester County residents were fighting against a perspective that was just as loud and bold, if not more so. A combination of lived experience, patriotic traditions, and economic realities led to conflicting ideas of nationalism and a combustible blend of divided interests. For those located in Chester District, the benefits of the international cotton trade, built on the backs of forced labor, were not as critical as a strong connection to inter-state commerce guaranteed through a strong federal government. For those located in plantation-based societies, on the other hand, the priorities were reversed. The debate over nullification was a disagreement over the proper balance of local, state, national, and international interests, and a discussion about how these competing allegiances worked within a patriotic framework that

<hr>

[7] *Proceedings of a General Meeting, Held at Chester Courthouse, November 18, 1831* (Columbia, SC: A. Landrum, 1832), 3–4.

[8] *Proceedings of a General Meeting, Held at Chester Courthouse*, 4, 5, 16.

touched all national dialogue. In important ways, it was a climax to the first
five decades of American nationalist imagination.[9]

This anxiety was far from new. The concept of "interests" – the question of whether national priorities took precedence over the local, and to
what degree state liberty was expected to be infringed upon in the name of
the American union – had been a crucial point of tension from the
country's beginning. To an extent, the same ideological debate was
a root cause for the states' separation from Britain as well as a primary
point of debate for the Constitution's ratification. But the stakes were
evolving. Previously, a superficial appeal to disinterestedness and the
fractured nature of American print culture hid, in part, the extent of
regional distinctiveness and competing interests. The plea to place the
survival of the nation over the interests of the state, coupled with the
ignorance of competing nationalist visions, enabled deep-seated sectionalism to be minimized for the first few decades of the nation's existence.
The contrast now appeared much clearer.

The Nullification Crisis of the early 1830s brought these tensions to the
forefront. Unlike the debates over the Constitution, when federalists,
pundits, and participants feigned a rejection of parochialism in favor of
national unity, the debates surrounding nullification proved a shift in
nationalist discourse: it was now taken for granted that individuals, states,
and regions would have competing interests. The question now concerned
how those interests were to be prioritized within the framework of state
and national authority. As a resident of an American state, where was
one's primary allegiance? While cultural fracturing had been occurring
since the Revolution, the events and arguments in the early 1830s served
to collapse many Americans' hopes for national unity and consolidated
interests. Among other legacies, it set the stage for later disunion.[10]

---

[9] For the divided geographic interests within South Carolina during the debate, see
Avery Craven, *The Coming of the Civil War* (Chicago: University of Chicago Press,
1940), esp. 65.

[10] For overviews of the Nullification Crisis, see William W. Freehling, *Prelude to Civil War:
The Nullification Crisis in South Carolina, 1816–1836* (New York: Harper and Row,
1966); Sean Wilentz, *The Rise of American Democracy: Jefferson to Lincoln* (New York:
W. W. Norton, 2005), 330–390; Richard E. Ellis, *The Union at Risk: Jacksonian
Democracy, States' Rights, and the Nullification Crisis* (New York: Oxford University
Press, 1987); Donald Ratcliffe, "The Nullification Crisis, Southern Discontents, and the
American Political Process," *American Nineteenth Century History* 1 (May 2000): 1–30;
Daniel Walker Howe, *What Hath God Wrought: The Transformation of America,
1815–1848* (New York: Oxford University Press, 2007), 367–373, 395–410.

The Nullification Crisis was the result of a number of events, personalities, and assumptions that climaxed in the winter months of 1832 and 1833. It was rooted not only in competing interpretations of the Constitution and state power but also in conflicting visions of the American nation itself. The immediate causes for the crisis are easy enough to identify. To bolster the manufacturing industry in the wake of an economic downturn, the federal government passed tariffs in 1816 and 1824 that protected American industry from British imports by increasing duties on cotton, iron, wool, and hemp. These tariffs disproportionately affected the Southern economy, and as a result, Southern politicians began to argue that they were unconstitutional. The Tariff of 1828, which came to be known as the "Tariff of Abominations," increased these taxes substantially and brought tensions to a boiling point. Southerners expected the tariff to be reversed after Andrew Jackson's election, especially since their own John C. Calhoun was his vice president. Yet when Jackson proved unwilling, South Carolina considered the constitutionality of the state legislature nullifying federal regulations.[11]

The cultural causes for the conflict in South Carolina were more complex. The proud state, which only decades earlier had boasted of its present power and future potential, was perceived to be dwindling in prestige. During the 1820s, the state lost 56,000 whites to emigration and another 76,000 in the following decade. They also witnessed the relocation of 30,000 and 50,000 slaves during the same decades, respectively, which depleted their standing as a slave power in the growing international cotton economy. The slave institution's center seemed to move westward. While the state's population continued to increase through reproduction, their increase lagged behind their neighbors. Further, South Carolina's economic woes led to many moving out of the state, but only a few moved in. By 1860, nearly 97 percent of people who resided in the state had been born there, and less than half of those who were native South Carolinians had ever lived outside its borders. These parochial conditions, however, existed simultaneously with their cosmopolitan ambitions as expressed through the global cotton market. These paradoxical tensions shaped their nationalist vision and engagement with federal policies.[12]

---

[11] For background to these tariffs, see Freehling, *Prelude to the Civil War*, 89–133; Forrest McDonald, *States' Rights and the Union: Imperium in Imperio, 1776–1876* (Lawrence: University Press of Kansas, 2000), 71–96; Wilentz, *Rise of American Democracy*, 287–309.

[12] For population numbers, see Tommy W. Rogers, "The Great Plantation Exodus from South Carolina, 1850–1860," *South Carolina Historical Magazine* 68 (1967): 14–21;

A substantial portion of Southern anxiety was linked to a fear that Northern states were plotting to abolish slavery. The Missouri Compromise reaffirmed a sectional divide between the states and sparked an anxiety to intellectually and politically defend the institution. The state's suspicions were seemingly confirmed after Charleston discovered a slave conspiracy in 1822 that brought the fear of the North's abolitionist rhetoric closer to home. An expansion of anti-slavery activities and the rise of individual abolitionist efforts like William Lloyd Garrison's *The Liberator*, first published in 1831, alarmed many Southern slaveholding politicians. Reactions to the tariffs were more than just an opposition to particular taxes; they were also a statement against a creeping federalism that could one day impact their primary economic practice. A government strong enough to enforce unwanted taxes could also be strong enough to abolish slavery.

The result of these tensions was a political culture that was concerned over domestic viability and frustrated with a nation they felt stole its profits while targeting its property. For many, it became increasingly difficult to offer allegiance to a nation while seemingly under siege. At the heart of the crisis was the very definition of American patriotism. As one observer noticed, the circumstances produced the birth of "two political parties" that "each claim[ed] to be faithful to the Constitution." Both for pragmatic purposes as well as lingering ideological attachments, those who argued for and against nullification tethered their rhetoric to a nationalist ethos. This in turn brought the fracturing of national interests into clearer view. Together, they acknowledged the fracturing of nationalism itself.[13]

The outcry against the 1828 tariff was not isolated to elite politicians. Many of the first responses were local districts that published memorials. Each claimed to speak for the general population. Some were more

William W. Freehling, *The Road to Disunion: Secessionists at Bay, 1776–1854* (New York: Oxford University Press, 1991), 254–255. Michael O'Brien argues for a more expansive and outward-facing South Carolinian culture in O'Brien, *Conjectures of Order: Intellectual Life and the American South, 1810–1860*, 2 vols. (Chapel Hill: University of North Carolina Press, 2004).

[13] J. S. Richardson, *To the People. An Address in Five Numbers, Originally Published in the Camden Journal, by "Jefferson." Republished by Permission of the Author the Hon. J. S. Richardson, Together with His Speech Delivered at the Stateburgh Dinner, in Opposition to Disunion, Convention and Nullification* (Charleston, SC: Irishman and Southern Democrat, 1830), 3.

despondent than others. The citizens of Colleton District, for instance, warned other South Carolinians that the national government refused to hear their protests and that "your Memorials have been considered by the Congress of these States … They sleep quietly upon their table." At the center of the issue was a misunderstanding concerning the national union. The Colleton residents believed South Carolina had entered the "confederacy" by choice and "retained" its sovereign powers, but that the federal government had broken its promise and that "the constitutional grounds upon which our fathers resisted the pretentions of the British crown" now paled when "compared with those upon which we now stand." While they had hoped separation from Britain would inaugurate a new era, "the history of the Constitution of the United States, is the old story of every Constitution that was ever devised by Man": a glimpse at liberty, the exponential growth of government, and the introduction of tyranny. Allegiance to the American nation was just as hollow as allegiance to the British crown. Only through radical reform, achieved through a return to the Constitution's "uncorrupted principles," could America be saved. Their rhetoric mirrored that of Massachusetts from two decades earlier.[14]

These events caused many to question their commitment to the nation. Thomas Cooper, president of South Carolina College and an adamant states' rights defender, warned, "We shall, before long, be compelled to calculate the value of our union," because "the South has always been the loser and the North always the gainer." Congressman, and later governor, James Hamilton Jr. declared to South Carolinians that the American government, "your task-master," would "soon be taken as a tyrant." The slavery reference was not incidental. Robert James Turnbull, writing under the name "Brutus," wrote that "the more *National*, and the less *Federal*, the Government becomes, the more certainly will the interest of

[14] *An Address of Sundry Citizens of Colleton District, to the People of the State of South-Carolina* (Charleston, SC: Broadside, 1828). More measured district memorials include *Memorial of Citizens of Chesterfield, Marlborough, and Darlington, Assembled at Cheraw, in South Carolina, Against A Further Increase of Duties on Imported Articles. February 4, 1828. Referred to the Committee of the Whole House on the State of the Union* (Washington, DC: Gales & Seaton, 1828); *Memorial of the Inhabitants of Barnwell District, in S.C. Remonstrating Against any Additional Duties on Imported Woollen Goods. December 24, 1827. Referred to the Committee on Manufacturers* (Washington, DC: Gales & Seaton, 1827); *Memorial of the Citizens of Laurens District, South Carolina, Against any Increase of the Tariff, &c. January 22, 1828. Referred to the Committee on Commerce and Manufactures* (Washington, DC: Gales & Seaton, 1828). These and other district memorials are housed together in the Nullification Memorials Collection, SCL.

the great majority of the States be promoted" and "the interests of the South be depressed and destroyed." In this new context, "federal," a potent political word that went through several evolutions during the early republic, was revised once more. Rather than referring to a centralized federal power, it was now shorthand for a "con*federacy*" of individual states with divergent priorities. Indeed, Turnbull believed that the interests of the rest of the nation had become "diametrically opposed" to those of the South, and governance had to react appropriately. Many others questioned the nature and future of their state's relationship to the nation, which in turn reoriented their notion of nation itself. While the first attempt at a nullification convention failed, an increasing number of voices called for a radical reconsideration of unionism's benefits. This was a battle worth fighting.[15]

The most explicit and systematic examination of the relationship between state and nation came from the country's vice president, John C. Calhoun. Invited by the South Carolina congressional delegation to prepare a report on the tariff, Calhoun, who previously held moderate nationalist sentiments, produced a 35,000-word manuscript titled "Exposition" that argued for a revised understanding of federal power. America, in Calhoun's offering, was comprised of individual state sovereignties loosely joined through a confederate compact. Though much of the manuscript dealt with economic matters, which remained central to his concerns, the essay revealed how Calhoun understood the national union. It was also a navigating act between, as one historian put it, "the Charybdis of Thomas Cooper's radical idea of state nationality" on the one hand, and "the Scylla of Henry Clay's Unionism" on the other. By seeking a middle ground between Washington moderation and South Carolinian extremism, Calhoun was both cautious and thorough. But the result was far from uncontroversial.[16]

---

[15] Thomas Cooper, Speech, July 2, 1827, in William W. Freehling, ed., *The Nullification Era: A Documentary Record* (New York: Harper & Row, 1967), 21. Hamilton, quoted in Freehling, *Prelude to Civil War*, 152. Robert James Turnbull, *The Crisis: Or, Essays on the Usurpations of the Federal Government* (Charleston: A.E. Miller, 1827), 9. Only four years previously, Cooper had claimed that "Every man called to the national representation is a national, not a local representative," and that their decisions were to be based on "the great interests of the nation." Thomas Cooper, *Examination of a Tract on the Alteration of the Tariff* (Charleston, SC: A.E. Miller, 1823), 23.

[16] O'Brien, *Conjectures of Order*, 2:827. For Calhoun's earlier nationalist sentiments, see Wilentz, *Rise of American Democracy*, 292–293. The published edition of "Exposition" featured numerous changes made by the South Carolina delegation to further align with the party's message. The original and revised versions are compared side-by-side in

Crucial to Calhoun's "Exposition" was a strict constitutional interpretation. The Constitution provided Congress powers to tax in order to pay debts, but not for protectionist duties. Yet his argument went further by claiming that sovereignty resided in the people as state political bodies rather than as a federal structure. As evidence for this perspective, Calhoun noted that it was state conventions that had adopted the Constitution, not the American people in general. Sovereignty therefore truly resided with "the people of the several States, who created it." This reasoning allowed Calhoun to insist that power belonged to the people while also maintaining individual state sovereignty. A South Carolinian and a Pennsylvanian might be equal in the eyes of the Constitution, he believed, yet their authority came from distinct, if parallel, bodies that reaffirmed state interests. Calhoun rested no hope in a nation of like-minded people, nor did he have faith in a federal union that balanced the priorities of different groups of people. Instead, he envisioned a confederation of states that, based on their respective communities, acted as quasi-sovereign nations through a mutually dependent contract.[17]

The direct competition of interests was central to Calhoun's constitutional critique. Because there was a "diversity of interests in the several classes and sections of the country," minorities were constantly at risk. Even "representation," he argued, "affords not the slightest resistance" once one portion of states sought to oppress the other. The actual mechanics of nullification were based in the hope that a supermajority of states could better delineate justice. If a national policy was deemed odious by one state, they could assert their sovereignty by enacting a state convention through which specially elected delegates could nullify federal laws. The decision would then be taken to a convention of states, where a three-fourths vote would be required to overturn nullification. This complex process signified several important principles. First and foremost was that individual states, through a nullification convention, could unite and exercise sovereignty over the federal government. However, even that process remained within the scope of a "national" system in that its fate could still be vetoed by the other states. This concession signified, on the part of Calhoun, a persistent commitment to federal affiliation. But most

The Papers of John C. Calhoun, ed. Robert L. Meriwether, 28 vols. (Columbia: University of South Carolina Press, 1959–2003), 10:444–534.
[17] John C. Calhoun, "Exposition," in Meriwether, *Papers of John C. Calhoun*, 10:490. See also O'Brien, *Conjectures of Order*, 827–829.

importantly, the dominant national mechanism was not a centralized federal authority, but a tribunal of states. This mechanism demonstrated Calhoun's attachment to the idea that citizenship and sovereignty were based on states' rights.[18]

This was a radical new version of nationalist imagination. Calhoun offered an even more rigorous defense of his understanding of the American government, as well as the impossibility of its classification as a "nation," in his "Fort Hill Address." Since this was the first publication on nullification that acknowledged Calhoun as its author, the oration definitively attached Calhoun to the ideas already located in his anonymous "Exposition." In the address, Calhoun identified a "dissimilarity of interests" as the root cause of national strife. The United States could never account for such a wide variety of cultures, he argued, and it was therefore left to the state to embrace and protect the "local and peculiar." Calhoun recognized "the great and leading principle" of American politics to be "that the General Government emanated from the people of several States, forming one aggregate political community." Nullification, then, was a necessary measure to protect those states whose interests did not match those favored by the federal government. Elsewhere, he termed this dynamic the "unlimited and despotic" power of nationalist intentions. The only appeal to a greater source of authority was to the federal government, not the nation in and of itself. Thus, when Calhoun's Fort Hill address argued that his ideas were "truly and emphatically *American, without example, or parallel*," he meant that they were steeped in the political principles of 1787, not that they were sentiments shared throughout a unified American culture. The latter construction, which had previously been the dominant model for understanding of nationalism, was in fact impossible. There was no such thing as an "American" character.[19]

Calhoun's revisionist framework for nation and state was based in a particular definition of the founding. Shortly after achieving independence from Britain, he explained, "the States unanimously called the General Government into existence." This federal organization was solely meant to temper jealousy and prevent wars, not to become an authoritative system in and of itself. Though based on the historical and

---

[18] Calhoun, "Exposition," in Meriwether, Papers of John C. Calhoun, 10:486, 490, 520–522.
[19] John C. Calhoun, "Fort Hill Address," in *John C. Calhoun: Selected Writings and Speeches*, ed. H. Lee Cheek, Jr. (Washington, DC: Regnery Gateway, 2013), 320–321. Calhoun to Frederick W. Symmes, July 26, 1831, in *Papers of John C. Calhoun*, 11: 436–438.

"conservative" principle that a diffusion of powers and interests throughout sovereign states was the only recipe for success, "a plan was adopted
better suited to our situation, but perfectly novel in its character."
Previous political bodies divided their power "in reference to classes,"
but America's was instead divided "geographically." The country was
therefore prepared for divergent and, at times, competing interests, since
there was no cultural and political homogeneity. To preserve this arrangement, the limits of the federal government were to be determined by the
states, not the other way around. "If those who voluntarily created the
system cannot be trusted to preserve it," he queried, "what power can?"
In short, states were "sovereign and independent communities," and the
federal government was merely "a compact between sovereigns ...
appointed to superintend and administer the interests in which all are
jointly concerned," nothing more. An injudicious nationhood flipped
sovereign priorities.[20]

These political principles were steeped in and were influential upon
notions of cultural nationality during the period. In Calhoun's estimation,
not only were the customs, habits, traditions, and interests of Americans
in their various states radically different, but they were also unbridgeable.
There were not enough commonalities within American society to justify
a strong, centralized federal authority. The attempt to create
a homogenous national culture was a misguided dream. Rather, the
loose federal system was designed to "*restrain*" competing communities
from harming one another, just as laws are to "restrain *individuals*."
The American "nation" was, at best, a figment of naïve imagination or,
at worst, a political tool used by majorities elsewhere to oppress those of
whom they wished to take advantage. Calhoun's nationalist vision
directly countered much of what had come before.[21]

Some of Calhoun's ideas were, either explicitly or implicitly, drawn
from James Madison's doctrine of state sovereignty. Madison had for-
mulated these views in 1798 in response to John Adams and the Federalist
Party. Partly an overcorrection to the centralization in the Constitution
and partly an example of the partisan excesses in the late 1790s,
Madison's ideas from the period appeared to emphasize states' rights
over national authority, and they were thus a popular resource for
South Carolina nullifiers. (Some even claimed the "Spirit of '98" in their
writings.) Yet Madison's doctrine of sovereignty was still based on
a nationalist framework that privileged a federalist system in which

---

[20] Calhoun, "Fort Hill Address," 321, 323, 327.   [21] Ibid., 319.

power would reside in an elite few who could be trusted to think continentally. Indeed, Madison loathed seeing his words used by the nullifiers, despised that some were threatening to weaken the federal union, and sought to publicly dissuade South Carolinians from taking drastic actions. Shortly before his death, Madison counseled, "the Union of the States [should] be cherished and perpetuated. Let the open enemy to it be regarded as a Pandora with her box opened," he warned, "and the disguised one as the serpent creeping with deadly wiles into Paradise." Those who fought for nullification, however, continued to invoke the name of Madison as well as Jefferson and other founding figures to bolster the credibility of their position. The memory and validity of America's founders were crucial to nationalist debates.[22]

Neither Calhoun nor many of the other pro-nullification advocates were consistent with their arguments concerning sovereignty. For many slaveholders in South Carolina and other Southern states, federal power was a malleable object that could fit whatever purposes strengthened the slave institution. Internationally, when it came to foreign policy, naval power, capitalistic expansion, all of which proved important in defending the slave power, Southerners constructed a robust nationalism based on federal strength. Domestically, when it came to laws regarding fugitive slaves and western expansion, they also posited images of national control. Yet in response to federal regulations that hurt the slave system, like with the tariffs that sparked the Nullification Crisis, many of those same Southerners imagined more nuanced structures of federal power. This paradoxical political tradition of state and federal sovereignty evolved at different rates throughout the South, as unified visions that came together to form a united sectionalism did not appear until the Civil War.

The warning signs were already apparent in 1830. Congressmen from Northern states quickly became alarmed at the broader implications of South Carolina's political threats. Tensions boiled over during a debate between South Carolinian Robert Hayne and Massachusetts senator Daniel Webster. On January 19, in the midst of debates over the tariffs as well as land appropriations, Hayne proposed a Southern and Western alliance in order to overcome what he saw the tyranny of the North. Webster took exception to this disdain for national power and delivered

---

[22] See Kevin Gutzman, "A Troublesome Legacy: James Madison and 'The Principles of '98,'" *Journal of the Early Republic* 15 (Winter 1995): 569–589, p. 569.

an address that emphasized federal allegiance over states' interests. "I am a unionist, and in this sense a national republican," Webster declared on January 20. In a rejoinder the next day, January 21, Hayne denounced the "unprovoked and most unwarrantable attack upon the South" by Webster and claimed it was only the most recent of the North's attempts to emasculate the South and its economy. Emphasizing the sovereign status of individual states, Hayne argued that "the very idea of a division of power by a compact" is absurd, because that would imply that "one of the parties can arbitrarily determine its limits." Rather, the Federal Constitution was based on independent sovereign states voluntarily agreeing to a compact but simultaneously maintaining their individual rights. Any argument that supposed the government to represent a national "people," Hayne reasoned, "rests on the idea of state inferiority," and should therefore be rejected. There was no such thing as an "American people." He explained that the phrase that prefaced the Constitution, "We, the people of the United States," could not relate to an American "people" because "the Federal Government was not then in existence." It was impossible for citizens to act "in any other character than as citizens of their respective States," and any citizen's first "allegiance" should be to their state authority. To base political arguments on a fictional allegiance between citizen and nation – that is, on nationalism – fell flat.[23]

Webster's response on January 26 became the most widely circulated political speech of the period. It proclaimed a nationalist foundation for any constitutional interpretation. Webster reassured Hayne that there was never a "disposition in the North to interfere with these interests of the South" because there were no such thing as regional interests. In New England, Webster explained, "we look upon the States not as separated, but as united." States from South Carolina to Ohio to Massachusetts were connected "under the same General Government, having interests, common, associated, intermingled." He insisted that they "do not place geographical limits to our patriotic feeling or regard." Any misunderstanding about the principles of national privilege was based on a "misconception as to the origin of this Government and its true character": it was "made for the People; made by the People, and answerable to the People." That

---

[23] Webster, quoted in Merrill Peterson, *The Great Triumvirate: Webster, Clay, and Calhoun* (New York: Oxford University Press, 1987), 173–174. Robert Y. Hayne, *In Reply to Mr. Webster, of Massachusetts* (Charleston, SC: A. E. Miller, 1830), 2, 8, 9, 10, 20. See also Howe, *What Hath God Wrought*, 369–373.

is, there was indeed such thing as an "American" body of citizens. It was not to the states, but to "our Federal Union" that the people owed first allegiance. Here, Webster sought to downplay Massachusetts's sectionalism of the past two decades, highlighted by the Hartford Convention, in an attempt to reassert the state's nationalist tradition and once again lay claim to federal loyalty. As a result, this speech laid the groundwork for the nationalist framework that dominated Union discourse in the lead-up to the Civil War. Abraham Lincoln declared it "the very best speech that was ever delivered."[24]

Webster was not alone in his nationalism. Another Massachusetts politician, Edward Everett, similarly noted that "a great excitement has for some time prevailed in a portion of the Southern States of the Union," and that the ferment "is considerably greater in South Carolina, than elsewhere." He rejected Hayne's argument that states could nullify federal law and stated that such faulty logic rested on the mistaken assumption that "the Union is a mere confederacy" or "treaty between friendly sovereigns." This was wrong, Everett reasoned, because the nation was much more than a political contract between independent sovereignties but "is itself the creature (as we say) of the people." The federal government was not made for the states, but "for the individuals," and was meant to represent "the greatest number of minorities" rather than a small number of larger political bodies. Thus, the interests of a single state did not take precedence over an entire nation of people, and Everett chastised Hayne for threatening disunion over "exporting a few thousand bags more of cotton." America's true interests were located elsewhere.[25]

That both Everett and Webster represented the state that was associated with the Hartford Convention was not a coincidence. Massachusetts's faltering reputation that resulted from their flirtation with disunion forced many to lead the charge for a more strident national

---

[24] Daniel Webster, *Speech of Daniel Webster, in Reply to Mr. Hayne, of South Carolina: The Resolution of Mr. Foot, of Connecticut, Relative to the Public Lands, Being Under Consideration. Delivered in the Senate, January 26, 1830* (New York: Elliott & Palmer, 1830), 10, 11, 20, 47, 61. Lincoln, quoted in David Donald, *Lincoln* (New York: Simon & Schuster, 1995), 270. See also Maurice Baxter, *One and Inseparable: Daniel Webster and the Union* (Cambridge: Harvard University Press, 1984), esp. 188; Harlow W. Sheidley, "The Webster-Hayne Debate: Recasting New England's Sectionalism," *New England Quarterly* 67 (March 1994): 5–29.

[25] Edward Everett, *Remarks on the Public Lands, and on The Right of a State to Nullify an Act of Congress* (Boston: Gray & Bowen, 1830), 26, 27, 37, 38, 57, 72. For Everett's political thought, see Matthew Mason, *Apostle of Union: A Political Biography of Edward Everett* (Chapel Hill: University of North Carolina Press, 2016).

belonging. Several years before the Nullification Crisis, Everett told students of Harvard University that a country must "embrace the most important springs of national culture." Yet unless elements of that character are implemented into law, he warned, they are "little better than fanciful speculation." America's potential rested upon its ability to construct a "civil society" that matched the nation's natural genius and reflected the priorities of the governed. While some might complain that a majority of the young nation's intellectual exertions were too political in nature, Webster cautioned that the "first efforts" of any nation were to cultivate a national identity upon which all arts and literature were to be based. This made nationalist thought a "necessity" for politics. Only through capturing "the peculiarity of our condition," he reasoned, would an American nation flourish like no other country before. Denouncing South Carolina provided the opportunity to prove the state's patriotism in the face of betrayal.[26]

The prodding from New England only made political division more apparent. Many in South Carolina disagreed with Webster's belief that a common character could be both defined and deployed in political settings. Langdon Cheves, a South Carolinian unionist who moderately sympathized with the nullification argument, attended a "state rights" dinner in Columbia in 1830 and noted that, in contrast to many in the North who assumed a "common public sentiment embracing the whole union," the states were actually "divided into western, eastern, middle, and southern sections." Further, "the south has thus a separate identity and a common public sentiment among themselves," which made cultural clashes inevitable. The people in his South Carolina "are one people – one in interest, in feeling, in suffering, in locality and in power." In Cheves's mind, South Carolina portrayed more of a nationalist culture than America did. To avoid nullification, it was necessary for the government to acknowledge fractured interests and handle the sections accordingly.[27]

This emphasis on competing interests and a fractured nation captured the new framework for nationalist imagination. There was a split even within South Carolina, let alone the rest of the Southern states. To some, a "nation" that comprised such distinct bodies would fail to produce the compromises required for political harmony. Democracy in a large and

---

[26] Edward Everett, *An Oration Pronounced in Cambridge, Before the Society of Phi Beta Kappa. August 26, 1824* (Boston: Oliver Everett, 1824), 6, 7, 11, 18, 25.

[27] *Niles' Register*, October 16, 1830, annotated copy located in Langdon Cheves Papers, SCL.

multivocal collection of populations, in this instance, was a failed experiment. Yet to others, a political union that promoted national belonging
possessed the mechanisms necessary to assure stability. To the unionist
Thomas Grimké, for instance, the nation required the "mutual concession" of "common interests." Similarly, Andrew Jackson's State of the
Union address in 1830 freely admitted that there were "diversities in the
interests of the different States" that were dependent upon "situation,
climate, population, and pursuits." But to him this entailed a strengthening of political power based on nationalist principles. The federal government served as a meditor. The sovereignty of the American populace – not
to mention the power of his own personal authority – was enough to
balance these competing claims. For some, the spirit of nationalism
entailed the sacrifice of interests; for others, the latter destroyed any
chance for the former.[28]

Nationality was a matrix of cultural assumptions. There were always
multiple allegiances that often overlapped, but they just as often came into
conflict. It was at these moments that citizens had to prioritize their
affiliation. Nationalism was not always necessarily attached to the nation-
state, and sectional and national interests were often indistinguishable.
A person who accused the government of malfeasance was not necessarily
renouncing national ideals, but was most often bolstering their own
national commitment. Sectionalism, then, was a form of nationalism,
for it was rooted in a particular understanding of how the nation should
function. Dissent was a patriotic practice. This was especially the case for
Southern states, as they did not think of themselves as a "region," which
presupposed the priority of the nation-state, until after the Civil War.
To them, their state-based mindset was a form of nationalist
imagination.[29]

These seemingly parochial debates had a broader Atlantic context.
The previously universalistic hue of nationalist discourse in European
thought took a more fractured tone in the wake of the Age of
Revolutions. Those South Carolinians who sought to create a novel
form of unique cultural belonging had plenty of intellectual sources at
their disposal. During the first few decades of the nineteenth century,

---

[28] Grimké, *Speech of Thomas Smith Grimké*, 20. Andrew Jackson, "State of the Union
Address," December 6, 1830, in *Messages and Papers of the Presidents*, ed. James
D. Richardson, 10 vols. (Washington, DC: Bureau of National Literature, 1901), 2:512–513.
[29] David M. Potter, "The Historian's use of Nationalism and Vice Versa," *American Historical
Review* 67 (July 1962): 930–932; Michael O'Brien, "Regions and Transnationalism," in
O'Brien, *Placing the South* (Jackson: University Press of Mississippi, 2007), 5.

Southerners consumed an increasing amount of European ideas in their quest to find order in a seemingly chaotic world. Romantic thinkers who promulgated frameworks in which to understand diversity, complexity, and identity were particularly influential. This included the work of German philosopher August von Schlegel, who wrote *A Course of Lectures on Dramatic Art and Literature* in 1808, which was translated into English less than a decade later. It became immensely popular in Southern intellectual circles.[30]

Von Schlegel provided an intellectual blueprint for political discord. He dismissed arguments for cultural universalism in favor of societal distinction – to accept, in other words, "the peculiarities of [different] ages and nations." There is no universal principle of society, but that which "is capable of dividing and diverging into opposite directions." Human culture was dependent upon both "harmony and contrast." Similarly influential was von Schlegel's teacher, Madame de Staël, whose ideas had a more direct connection to nationalist formulations. De Staël, a French author who was driven from her nation by Napoleon and became famous for her writings on politics and society, produced a number of texts on cultural nationalism that were widely read by Southern thinkers. The nation, she once wrote, was "a discovery of the eighteenth century." Political allegiances were based in "metaphysical ideas" which saturate the mind and must be based in cultural practices or else they have no presence in reality. Nationality was something that could be transformed. Just as European philosophies enabled Americans to structure national union during the founding period, they now provided the tools to tear it down.[31]

These abstract ideas had crucial implications when it came to cultural nationalism. They provided the intellectual building blocks for shifting primary allegiance from a broader political body to a smaller cultural community. Beginning in the 1820s, a growing number of South Carolinians drew extensively from these Romantic authors in their attempt to construct a cultural heritage. The region's most prominent literary outlet, the *Southern Review*, dedicated space in each issue to these European dialogues and explicated what they meant for their own

[30] For South Carolinians' increasing reliance on European thought, especially Romanticism, see O'Brien, *Conjectures of Order*, 1:90–161, 2:691–701.

[31] August von Schlegel, *A Course of the Lectures on Dramatic Art and Literature*, in *The Monthly Review* (London), October 1816, 114. De Staël, *Dix Années d'Exil* (Paris: 10/18, 1966), 188. See also Suzanne Guerlac, "Writing the Nation (Mme de Staël)," *French Forum* 30, no. 3 (Fall 2004): 43–56.

community. Charleston thinkers Hugh Legaré and Thomas Grimké, for instance, translated these ideas into political arguments for local sovereignty and cultural supremacy. They also laid a foundation for sectional frameworks. Grimké came to write about "Northern and Southern nations" within America that cultivated different versions of liberties and interests. These European philosophies provided intellectual justification for the growing wedge between South Carolina and the rest of the United States.[32]

These debates soon found a national stage. The disagreement between the two nationalist visions was captured in competing toasts offered at a Jefferson Day Dinner in 1830 by the president and vice president. Jackson, toasting first, proclaimed, "Our Federal Union: It Must be Preserved." Calhoun, defensively, answered, "The Union, Next to Our Liberties the Most Dear. May we always remember that it can only be preserved by respecting the rights of the states." These were more than opening salvos in a states' rights battle, but rather the culmination of competing nationalist ideas. Two years later, Jackson declared that the United States had an "aggregate character" that had preceded independence, shared national sovereignty, and was the foundation for government. Any argument that claimed America was a "league" rather than a nation, he believed, was misguided and divisive. Conversely, Calhoun came to understand nationalist principles as based on shared political documents but espoused by different nation-states, each of which protected their respective interests and priorities. To Calhoun, a citizen's true allegiance was to protecting those liberties and *not*, necessarily, to the governmental institution that claimed those liberties as its heritage. This perspective allowed a much broader understanding of both abstract notions of loyalty as well as concrete applications in policies. Facing the nationalist arguments of the North, many South Carolinians came to refuse prescriptive forms of American nationality and, as a replacement, understood devotion to their own state as a form of nationalism itself.[33]

This radical reformulation required innovative constitutional interpretations. Political validity still depended on the principles found in America's founding documents, which necessitated a revisionist

---

[32] Thomas Smith Grimké, "Origin of Rhyme," *Southern Review*, February 1829, SCL.
[33] The toast quotations are from Robert V. Remini, *Andrew Jackson and the Course of American Freedom, 1822–1832* (New York: Harper and Row, 1981) 233–236. Jackson, "Proclamation," 1832, in *Messages and Papers*, 2:1211. For Jackson's nationalist message, see Wilentz, *Rise of American Democracy*, 379–389.

understanding of the nation's origins. One South Carolinian author, Francis Wilkinson Pickens, argued that the idea of nullification had always been part of the nation's political tradition. America's finest political minds had believed it to be a "Safety Valve, (if I may so say), of the growing *Usurpations* of our General Government." Pickens's pamphlet included lengthy quotations from famous American politicians that proclaimed what the editor believed to be the "doctrine" of nullification, even if many of the passages were vague in application. This collection, framed as an encyclopedic argument, signified the rhetorical potency of nationalist discourse as well as the malleability and inchoate nature of early America's political tradition. It also captured the dynamic practice of nationalism itself. By positioning nullification at the center of the idea of America, it revealed what the individual understood the nation to be: an imagined national character based on the freedom to dissent and the right for state sovereignties to could voluntarily join, leave, and amend contracts with her sister sovereign states.[34]

The state was still split on nullification from 1830 through the early part of 1832. Those who opposed the principle were equally strong in rhetoric and equally vehement in their national allegiance. One pamphlet denounced nullification as merely a cover for "conspiring against the integrity of the Union." It compared the radical faction to "France [and] her doctors of political atheism, political economy, and political perfectibility." Another denounced the "Calhoun doctrine" as an affliction that led to "patriotism . . . degenerate[ing] into petty local partialities." Indeed, the pamphlet reasoned, any appeal to "local and state pride . . . is equally unpatriotic and unjust." With the ratification of the Constitution, America had become a united nation. The author defined that event as a "movement of one people." Even the name "United States" was not a reference to a confederation between "distinct States," but a singular noun, similar to England: America was not *"thirteen sovereign States*, but a common sovereignty of the whole in their united capacity." There was no sovereign but the national, no allegiance but the federal. "The fatal error of Mr. Calhoun's doctrine," the pamphlet concluded, "is the assumption that our union is composed of materials essentially opposed

[34] [Francis Wilkinson Pickens], *The Genuine Book of Nullification: Being a True–Not an Apochryphal–History, Chapter and Verse, of the Several Examples of the Recognition and Enforcement of that Sovereign State Remedy, By the Different States of this Confederacy, from 1798 Down to the Present Day. (As Originally Published in the Charleston Mercury.) To Which are Added the Opinions of Distingushed Statesmen, on State Rights Doctrines* (Charleston, SC: E. J. Van Brunt, 1831).

in interest." George McDuffie similarly proposed that "states, as political bodies, have no original inherent rights." The belief to the contrary, as espoused by a number of fellow South Carolinians, was "a false, dangerous, and anti-republican assumption, which lurks at the bottom of all the reasoning in favour of state rights." Many in South Carolina remained committed to a more federal sense of national belonging. Yet the debates were far from over.[35]

Those in South Carolina who sought validation for nullification faced stiff opposition outside of their state. Mathew Carey, a long-time Philadelphia resident and one of the primary architects of American nationalism during the 1780s and 1790s, was at the forefront of the Northern attack on Southern discontent in the early 1830s. Still an influential printer and newspaper editor with the resources to disseminate his ideas, Carey was a nationalist who took seriously any threat to what he perceived to be America's national character. His experience as one of the most outspoken critics of the Hartford Convention in 1814 provided the foundation for his anti-nullification stance. Indeed, he merely added "New" to the title of his 1814/1815 magazine, *The Olive Branch*, when he published another periodical that defended nationalism in 1830/1831: *The New Olive Branch: A Solemn Warning on the Banks of the Rubicon*. He was so confident and prepared that he claimed to have written the entirety of the essays, which totaled nearly 300 pages, "in the midnight hours of about 7 weeks." Carey, present at the founding of American nationalism, was ready to defend it once again five decades later.[36]

[35] *Prospects of Disunion. Part 1* (Charleston, SC, 1832), 3. *The Calhoun Doctrine, or State Nullification Discussed, Originally Published in the "Irishman and Southern Democrat." By a Democratic Republican* (Charleston, SC: Office of the Irishman, 1831), 3, 21, 23, 24, 28. (Emphasis in original.) George McDuffie, *National and State Rights. Considered by the Hon. George McDuffie, Under the Signature of "One of the People," in Reply to the "Trio," with the Advertisement Prefixed to It, Generally Attributed to Major James Hamilton, Jr., When Published in 1821* (Columbia, SC: Free Press, 1831), 7. For more nationalistic arguments in opposition to nullification, see R. Barnwell Smith, *Speech of R. Barnwell Smith, Delivered in the House of Representatives, of the State of South-Carolina; on Certain Resolutions Referred to the Committee of the Whole, Relative to the Tariff Laws, Passed by the Congress of the United States* (Beaufort, SC: Beaufort-Gazette, 1829); Joel R. Poinsett, *Substance of a Speech, Delivered by the Hon. Joel R. Poinsett, at a Public Meeting held at Seyle's, 5th October, 1832* (Charleston, SC: J. S. Burges, 1832).
[36] Mathew Carey Diary, 1830–1836, Volume 2, entry for August 12, 1831, in the Matthew Carey Collection, HSP.

The title of Carey's essays invoked two potent metaphors. The "olive branch" was a symbol of peace that represented both the desired brotherhood between states as well as the hope that the crisis would not escalate to violence. The second metaphor, "the banks of the Rubicon," however, implied that a peaceful resolution was not the only, or even the most likely, result. The phrase referenced Julius Caesar leading his army across the Rubicon River, which had been the designated border forbidden for troops, to capture Rome. While a common phrase used in multiple contexts during the period, Carey meant for it to be understood quite seriously: "you are now," he cajoled South Carolinians, "on the banks of the Rubicon." If they followed "the course recommended to you by some of your leaders," it "will infallibly lead to a dissolution of the union, and to the civil war, with all its horrors." South Carolinians leading their state to nullification were just like Caesar leading his men to a long and perpetual battle. The result would be war.[37]

Carey's nationalist framework demonstrated the connection, in his mind, between competing interests and federal allegiance. The latter must always take precedence over the former. "It behooves all those who feel an interest in the national honour, or in the security of the peace and happiness of our beloved country," he argued, "to contribute their efforts to ally the existing ferment." The nation's prosperity and success depended on the ability of states to sacrifice their own interests in favor of those that were federal in scope. "All insurrections and revolutions," Carey reasoned, "are effected by minorities, often by a tenth, a twentieth, or a hundredth part of the population of a country." What the rebellious minority lacked "in numbers they compensate by zeal, ardour, energy, and industry." Carey believed the biggest threat to the nation were marginal groups that overwhelmed the nation with their own parochial interests. These minority tyrants would lead America into being "divided into three or four confederacies, jealous of, and embittered against each other." The militant expression of divergent interests meant the fracturing of the Union.[38]

---

[37] *The New Olive Branch: A Solemn Warning on the Banks of the Rubicon*, July 24, 1830, LCP. For the classical context of early America, see Carl J. Richard, *The Founders and the Classics: Greece: Rome, and the American Enlightenment* (Cambridge: Harvard University Press, 1994); Caroline Winterer, *The Culture of Classicism: Ancient Greece and Rome in American Intellectual Life, 1780–1910* (Baltimore, MD: Johns Hopkins University Press, 2001), 10–43.

[38] *New Olive Branch*, July 24, 1830, LCP. Carey also argued that behind these national insurrections were "the machinations of foreign nations" that were jealous of America's prosperity.

The problems originated with misguided priorities. Carey claimed that South Carolina's refusal to embrace a nationalist mindset led not only to conflict with the rest of the country but also to the difficult financial conditions under which the South Carolinians operated. The problems afflicting the state did not originate with the tariffs, but rather with South Carolina's attachment to and love for the international market. Carey reasoned that cotton culture had given the South a taste for the foreign that surpassed common sense and economic concern. Even those involved in agriculture "had been led to support this suicidal policy by the delusive hope, confidently held out to them by the new school of political economists, of deriving great advantage" from international connections through commerce and trade. The South's supposed "sound system of political economy" failed to take into consideration the federal pact between agriculturists and manufacturers. Their political scaffolding collapsed as soon as they looked outside the country's borders. Just as South Carolinians heralded the international capitalistic marketplace that wholeheartedly welcomed their production of cotton, Carey declared that the rise of "cotton culture" was a pact with the devil that promised "a violent collision between your state and the United States." Their tragic wound was self-inflicted.[39]

The results could be dire. Carey believed the fracturing of interests would lead to, as he wrote in one essay, an "establishment of separate confederacies, viewing each other with jealousy, and liable to be excited, from time to time, to deadly hostilities, by the machinations of foreign rivals, or the intrigues of domestic demagogues." This revealed two crucial points in his nationalist vision. First, that a nation could not exist without a balance of interests and the subordination of local to federal priorities. And second, that if the various states *did* separate into individual confederacies, it would lead not to peaceful independent sovereignties coexisting but competing and jealous enemies who could not be trusted to maintain amicable relations. On the former point, Carey built upon a strong Pennsylvanian tradition of balancing mixed interests in order to retain a common goal. The clear political calculation of balanced interests is revealed in an image which Carey used in one of his essays: South Carolina's balancing mechanism was displayed as tipped in favor of

---

[39] *New Olive Branch*, August 16, 1830; November 17, 1830; August 11, 1831, LCP. See also *New Olive Branch*, August 9, 1831. For the growing international marketplace for the production of cotton, see Walter Johnson, *River of Dark Dreams: Slavery and Empire in the Cotton Kingdom* (Cambridge: Harvard University Press, 2013), esp. 280–302.

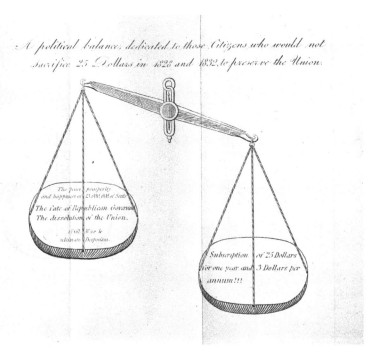

IMAGE 5.1 Mathew Carey, "The Political Balance" (1830), in Mathew Carey, *The New Olive Branch: A Solemn Warning on the Banks of the Rubicon*, no. 5 (August 16, 1830), 3–4, Library Company of Philadelphia, Philadelphia, PA. Taken from Carey's anti-nullification periodical, the image depicts "a political balance" between monetary gain and national peace. On the one scale is "The peace, prosperity, and happiness of 13,000,000 souls," the "fate of Republican Government," and the "dissolution of the Union." On the other scale is a mere "subscription of 25 dollars for one year, and 3 dollars per annum." In Carey's eyes, South Carolinians were risking national peace for a paltry sum of money.

"25 Dollars for one year and 3 Dollars per annum" over "the peace, prosperity, and happiness of 13,000,000s of souls," which equaled "the dissolution of the Nation, Civil War, & Ultimate despotism" (Image 5.1). The scales of justice were clear.[40]

Peril awaited those who failed to maintain the appropriate balance. The second of Carey's nationalist principles – that separate confederacies would only lead to perpetual war and bloodshed – was both a rhetorical trope and a sincere belief that national unity was the only chance for

[40] *The New Olive Branch: A Solemn Warning on the Banks of the Rubicon*, August 11, 1831.

continuous peace. On the one hand, this fear of war was a common threat during the period. One contemporary observer complained that "The *dissolution of the Union* is the standing scare-crow" of those demanding one section of the nation to forfeit its interest to another. Yet the image also represented a key element of Carey's political science. Carey had little faith in the natural character of humankind and believed Americans needed counsel and direction. The Constitution, then, and the federalism it represented, served to tutor and police a vulnerable citizenship. Nationalism was a regenerative mechanism that curtailed anarchy and fostered collaboration. Without it, all would fall to ruin.[41]

Carey was far from alone in highlighting South Carolina's failure to embrace a nationalist framework and accuse the state of betraying the nation. One Philadelphian's political cartoon, "The Demon of Discord," portrayed a "Nullification Column" that was based on treason and progressed from distrust to confusion, anarchy, and eventually to rebellion, murder, and death (Image 5.2). A banner waving in the front of the column urged readers to "Tremble Not at Disunion, Crisis, and Carolina Brutuses," and another assured citizens that "Nullification is a Peacefull Remedy." The description underneath identified the architect of the structure as Calhoun and the builders as "the Jacobin club" – a potent allusion in a nation that still defined political radicalism in terms of the "failed" French Revolution. Similarly, another large political cartoon from the period denounced those who sought to establish social hierarchies through parochial interests and skewered Southern slaveholders for seeking their own dominion over the democratic rights of citizens (Image 5.3). These were the biggest threats to America.[42]

This was a national debate. For many Northerners, especially those in Pennsylvania, the actions and beliefs held by South Carolinians struck at the heart of what they understood the American nation to represent: a democracy of individuals bound to a federal union and willing to balance competing interests. Their reactions to the Nullification Crisis were often couched in terms that both vindicated their ideas of nationalism and

---

[41] *The Emancipator*, May 5, 1836, LOC. For the use of "disunion" as both a rhetorical device as well as an acute representation of political thought, see Elizabeth R. Varon, *Disunion!: The Coming of the Civil War, 1789–1859* (Chapel Hill: University of North Carolina Press, 2008), esp. 31–124.

[42] For the use of the term "Demon of Discord" in the period, see *The Methodist Magazine and Quarterly Review*, April 1830, SCHS; John Blair, *To the Freemen of the Counties of Carter, Sullivan, Washington, Green, and Hawkins* (Washington, DC, 1833), 4; *Proceedings of the National Republican Convention, held at Frankfort, Kentucky, on Thursday, December 9, 1830* (Washington, DC, 1831), 15.

IMAGE 5.2 T. I. & P., "The Demon of Discord," [1832], in the Papers of Gaston, Strait, Wylie, and Baskin, South Caroliniana Library, Columbia, SC. Also known as the "Nullification Column," the rendition depicts the sequence of actions that would follow nullification from "distrust" and "confusion" all the way to "rebellion," "sacrilege," and eventually "death." Not all South Carolinians were in favor of the nullification mechanism.

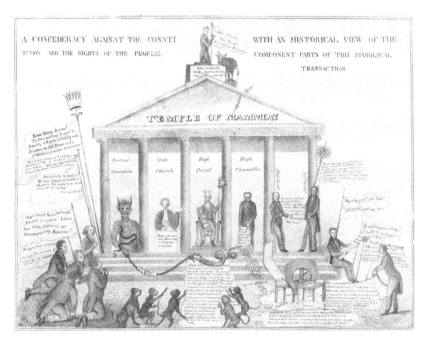

IMAGE 5.3 "A Confederacy Against the Constitution and the Rights of the People; With an Historical View of the Component Parts of the Diabolical Transaction" [1833], Library Company of Philadelphia, Philadelphia, PA. In this cartoon, Calhoun and his nullification views are grouped together with other social miscreants like plutocrats, tyrants, and the devil.

projected those nationalist assumptions across other regions. They believed South Carolina not only threatened the Union's stability, but also the Union's identity, character, and founding principles. The controversy of nullification may have inaugurated a dissident form of nationalism in South Carolina, but it only reaffirmed a more instigative and federalized framework for unionism for many in the North. The conflict both highlighted and expanded sectional divides over the very meaning of nation.

Tensions only escalated after 1831. South Carolina's States Rights and Free Trade Association, which had formed in Charleston the previous year, now extended its influence throughout the state. The organization aimed to raise support from all segments of the population, including the Charleston non-agricultural class, plantation owners, and non-slaveholding farmers. Their success was evident in the state elections of 1832 when nullifiers won an impressive victory at the polls. On October 20, the pro-nullification governor called a special session of the legislature with the purpose of calling for a nullification convention. The measure was passed by a thirty-one to thirteen vote in the Senate and a ninety-six to twenty-five vote in the House. In November, the Nullification Convention declared the tariffs of 1828 and 1832 to be unconstitutional and therefore nullified within the state of South Carolina. The governor then established a 25,000-man infantry and 2,000 mounted minutemen in order to defend the state from possible federal intervention. Nullification appeared triumphant.[43]

After deciding the terms and extent of their measures, the convention was left with an important task: explaining their actions to the federal government, to the people of South Carolina, and to the citizens of the United States. They separated these arguments into three distinct documents, each of which adopting a different tone and purpose. The three circulars were then bound together in a collection "ordered by the convention of the people of South Carolina, to be transmitted to the president of the United States, and to the governor of each State." In offering justification for their political actions, these texts imagined a new American union and political allegiance. Drawing from an enigmatic history of state and federal sovereignty, the authors boldly pronounced the failure of the American government system which was occasioned by the greed of the "manufacture" states and, importantly, the divergent cultural beliefs and practices of the nation's various regions. While one of these documents, William Harper's "Ordinance of Nullification," is usually noted by historians for its political arguments, all three pieces of propaganda are crucial evidence in examining how these nullifiers justified their political ideas through patriotic prose.[44]

Definitions were important. In the "Report of the Committee," the document that outlined the political reasons for nullification, the authors rejected even the notion that the United States was a "nation." It is "an egregious folly" to understand the United States as "one great nation," they reasoned. Such consolidation would necessitate "a people engaged in similar pursuits" and "having homogeneous interests." Only when all the people share "great interests," they countered, could a fair and balanced set of taxes, tariffs, and legislation be introduced. Instead, the United

---

[43] Freehling, *Prelude to the Civil War*, 224–260.
[44] *Documents. Ordered by the Convention of the People of South Carolina, to be Transmitted to the President of the United States, and to the Governor of Each State* (Columbia, SC: A. S. Johnston, 1832). Each document in this pamphlet was numbered individually, and some were published as separate documents on their own.

222 American Nationalisms

States entailed a much more loosely connected set of sovereigns that embodied its multifaceted nature:

> But it is the distinguishing feature of the American System, and one which stamps upon it the character of peculiar and aggravated oppression, that it is made applicable to a CONFEDERACY of twenty-four Sovereign and Independent States – occupying a territory upwards of 2000 miles in extent, – embracing every variety of soil, climate, and productions, – inhabited by a people whose institutions and interests are in many respects diametrically opposed to each other, – with habits and pursuits, infinitely diversified, – and in the great Southern section of the Union, rendered by local circumstances, altogether incapable of shame. Under such circumstances, a system, which under consolidated Government would be merely impolite, and so far, an act of injustice to the whole community, becomes in this country, a scheme of the most intolerable oppression, because it may be, and has in fact been, *so adjusted* as to operate exclusively to the benefit of a particular interest, and of particular sections of country, rendering in effect the industry of one portion of the confederacy, tributary to the rest.

Through the tariffs, the pamphlet argued, Washington, DC, had introduced "an entire change in the character of the Government." The term "confederacy" was now the desired description for a loose federal bond. It was a label that would only grow in popularity.[45]

While these arguments fit nicely within the tradition of fights over federal and states' rights in American government, they also revealed cultural tensions. Even in dissent, patriotic arguments were still expected to maintain some form of nationalist ideals. As early as the nation's independence, appeals to nationalist identities and other nationalist practices, as one historian has put it, "empowered Americans to fight over the legacy of their national Revolution and to protest their exclusion from that Revolution's fruits." Even decades after the eighteenth century, and even during debates over the nation's limits, the "continued politicization [of] nationalist rituals" maintained their "important meanings." In justifying their distaste for the nation, South Carolinian nullifiers were forced to distinguish nationalist meanings from the federal government. This was a narrative of declension rather than innovation. Even in nullification, nationalism still brought validity.[46]

---

[45] "Report of the Committee of Twenty One to The Convention of the People of South Carolina, on the Subject of the Several Acts of Congress, Imposing Duties for the Protection of Domestic Manufactures, with the Ordinance to Nullify the Same," in *Documents*, 5–6, 14.

[46] David Waldstreicher, *In the Midst of Perpetual Fetes: The Making of American Nationalism, 1776–1820* (Chapel Hill: University of North Carolina Press, 1995), 2, 7.

When the convention turned its attention to its fellow South Carolina citizens, it sought to reframe the state's sense of political allegiance. These debates were more than mere governmental practicalities, they assured South Carolinians. Rather, they had important ramifications for how citizens understood themselves. Most especially, there was no such thing as American nationalism when it came to a federal union. Because America "is a Confederacy," the pamphlet boldly declared, "it possesses not one single feature of *nationality*." The United States was only a compact between "*States*, and not of individuals." There was no such thing as "a political body as the People of the United States" – only "a citizen of South Carolina" bound together with citizens of other states "in the same *Social* Compact." This rejection of federal nationalism, and embrace of a "confederacy," was a rhetorical attempt to promote local allegiance over federal authority. It also rendered moot any patriotic attachment to American loyalty as the most important element in political discourse. By nullifying the priority of national over state citizenship, it forced South Carolinians to focus their attention solely on the interests of their state. "There is not, nor has there ever been any *direct* or *immediate* allegiance between the citizens of South Carolina and the Federal Government," the address concluded. National belonging at a federal level was a myth.[47]

In contrast, the nullifiers' appeal to the American nation at large focused on their shared heritage of revolutionary action. They claimed their actions were "impelled by the most sacred of all the duties which a free people can owe either to the memory of their ancestors or to the claims of posterity." It was those same principles which "animated your ancestors and ours in the councils and in the fields of their common glory" that "forbid us to submit any longer to a system of Legislation." Under the tariffs, South Carolina was "reduced to a condition of colonial vassalage" which is "more oppressive and intolerable than that from which our common ancestors relieved themselves by the war of revolution." In this way, the Nullification Crisis was merely the American Revolution reborn. This time, however, nationalist zeal led them to *dissent from* the United States rather than embrace its federal establishment. "South Carolina now bears the same relation to the manufacturing states of this confederacy,"

See also Carroll Smith-Rosenberg, *This Violent Empire: The Birth of an American National Identity* (Chapel Hill: University of North Carolina Press, 2010), 22–36.

[47] "Address to the People of South Carolina, by their Delegates in Convention," in *Documents*, 4, 14.

the convention reasoned, "that the Anglo American colonies bore to the mother country, with the single exception that our burthens are incomparably more oppressive than those of our ancestors." These were powerful words in a postcolonial nation that had, in the previous two decades, emphasized the romantic rhetoric of national union and shared interests.

With this radical form of nationalism came a tyrannical image of federal power. The American government was cast as the very "Oppression and Tyranny" it had previously vanquished, and the "CONSTITUTIONAL LIBERTY" upon which it was supposedly built was now being trampled upon. The appeal closed with a rhetoric reminiscent of that used during the Revolution: "We would infinitely prefer that the territory of the State should be the cemetery of freemen than the habitation of slaves." The irony of a slave state denouncing federal slavery was lost on the authors. Just as Jefferson – a figure whose name was, significantly, continually trumpeted as one who supported the principle of nullification – had declared independence from the tyrant King George III, the Nullification Convention was declaring independence from the tyrant President Jackson. This subversion of nationalist rhetoric was used to threaten the Union's dissolution by disintegrating the relationship between American principles and its current institutional embodiment. The nationalism of these South Carolinians no longer presupposed allegiance to the nation, but to the ideals upon which a degenerate government had trampled.[48]

The fact that they maintained nationalist rhetoric while threatening to separate from the nation-state demonstrates the potent nature of nationalism within early America's political framework. Their patriotism was not only based in dissent, but they believed their dissent to be the truest form of patriotism. Their sectionalism was not in opposition to nationalism – though it was in opposition to a federal authority based in nationality – but was an expression of nationalism in and of itself. They were not fully against federal power in total, just the federal power that contradicted their own interests. As those who participated in the Nullification Convention demonstrated, nationalism was not necessarily tethered to the nation-state, and could at times even be in competition with that political body. In proclaiming their disgust with the federal government's overreach, South Carolinians posited their own form of nationalism that was based in a distinct form of allegiance.

---

[48] "Address to the People of the United States, by the Convention of the People of South Carolina," in *Documents*, 3, 5, 11, 12, 16.

The anxiety over disunion and national discord was not limited to the political sphere. Indeed, worry concerning the political conflict spread throughout Southern culture. Caroline Howard Gilman, a native Bostonian who relocated to Charleston and in 1832 edited the juvenile weekly newspaper *Rosebud* (later named the *Southern Rose*), wrote to a friend that "our greatest apprehension is, that in the excited state of feeling which prevails, some inflammatory, though perhaps unintentional aggression, may cause the flame to burst out on either side." She was aghast at how a neighboring woman "would not own her son (a lad of 16) if he did not turn out against the Government forces." As the months wore on, the tension only grew more palpable. "To think, Louisa," Gilman wrote another acquaintance, "that we should live to see a Civil War! Our nullifiers are just as determined & the mass are as conscientious as the Whigs of '76." Gilman herself expressed these cultural anxieties through two memoirs, *Recollections of a New England Housekeeper* and *Recollections of a Southern Matron*, in which she blended an "exact a picture as possible of local habits and manners" with "imagination" in order to cultivate a coherent sense of domesticity across the regions. Literature seemed the most appropriate venue to capture their apprehensions. Fiction was the only way to narrate a peaceful solution.[49]

Perhaps the most potent example of literary sectionalism from the period was Algernon Sidney Johnston's *Memoirs of a Nullifier*. Self-published anonymously in 1832, the novel epitomized the didacticism of Southern literature. However, it was unique in format by including a love story, a pact with the devil, carnivorous demons, intergalactic travel, conniving Yankees, and, most importantly, an angel named "Nullification." The entire story was a grotesque if innovative satire of New England authors who were devoted to the literature of Dante, and much of *Memoirs* is a biting critique of the genre. For Northerners, the immense and dramatic scope of Dante's epic tale helped frame the grand cultural and national battle playing out before them. For Johnston, it provided a vehicle for antagonizing Northerners on their own turf. The sheer ridiculous nature of the narrative drew from novelistic tools many proto-secessionist authors used that expanded conceptions of the

[49] Caroline Howard Gilman to Mrs. A.M. White, Charleston, January 15, 1833; Gilman to Louisa Loring, Charleston, December 7, 1833, Carolina Gilman Collection, SCHS. Gilman, *Recollections of a New England Housekeeper* (New York: Harpers & Brothers, 1834); Gilman, *Recollections of a Southern Matron* (New York: Harpers & Brothers, 1838), 7.

"normal" and urged readers to consider new possibilities of American (dis)union. The gendered structure of the book – Johnston explained that he based the story around "a couple of constant lovers" so that he could "recommend his work to the more favourable regard of the gentler sex" – was meant to popularize the political message even more. By likening the American "union" to a marriage, the idea of nullification is no more radical than a divorce.⁵⁰

Johnston, a native of Virginia, boasted strong credentials. He edited Columbia's influential newspaper *Telescope* from 1828 to 1830, served as printer for the state's senate, and was the brother to future Confederate General Joseph Johnston. Yet while he had a background in print, he did not produce a literary masterpiece. The novel is redundant, pedantic, cloying, superficial, and lyrically choppy. It was virtually ignored for the first few years after publication, save for one parodied response from a Northerner, though it did appear in a handful of libraries. When it was finally noticed, it only attracted attention due to its cultural and political commentary rather than any literary virtue: the *North American Review* accused the book of making fun of the "simpletons of New England," to which the *Southern Literary Messenger* responded by claiming such a caricature was not off base. The novel was never serialized, never received a second printing, and the first time it earned substantial attention was when the *Knickerbocker* in 1859 presented it as an old relic newly relevant for a nation on the verge of war. Johnston's text, then, was more of a cultural artifact representative of its broader culture than it was a tool in fashioning a new cultural tradition. *Memoirs of a Nullifier* is important for the cultural context that created its narrative, rather than any cultural movement it inaugurated. As it acutely embodied many of the tensions from this period, it deserves close attention.⁵¹

---

⁵⁰ [Algernon Sidney Johnston], *Memoirs of a Nullifier; Written by Himself. By a Native of the South* (Columbia, SC, 1832). For the Northern preoccupation with Dante, see Joshua Matthews, "The Divine Comedy as an American Civil War Epic," *J19: The Journal of Nineteenth-Century Americanists* 1, no. 2 (Fall 2013): 315–337. For the Southern use of fantastic literature during the period, see Ian Binnington, *Confederate Visions: Nationalism, Symbolism, and the Imagined South in the Civil War* (Charlottesville: University of Virginia Press, 2013).
⁵¹ "Misconceptions of the New England Character," *North American Review*, January 1837, LOC; "The New England Character." *Southern Literary Messenger*, July 1837, SCHS. Background on Johnston is sparse. See the notice of his death in *Palmetto State Banner*, September 24, 1852, republished in *New York Daily Times*, September 29, 1852, LOC. Some have mistakenly assumed the novel's author was Thomas Cooper, Johnston's friend. For its appearance in local libraries, see *A Second Supplemental catalogue, Alphabetically Arranged of all the Books, Maps and Pamphlets, Procured by the*

The plot was straightforward, if quixotic. It follows an unnamed Southerner – heavily implied to be a South Carolinian due to his later commitment to South Carolina politics – who represents the ideal Southern citizen: a descendent of proud heritage with considerable wealth, a romantic who is set to marry his local town's prettiest woman, a capitalist willing to invest in the state (and national) economy, and an aspiring politician running for office on the same principles for which his father (in the War of 1812) and great-grandfather (in the Revolutionary War) had fought. Though he was raised in a "remote district" and attached to the nation's agrarian roots, he gained a considerable "knowledge of mankind" through "the pages of history, romance, and poetry." He soon learns his faith in humanity is misplaced. After being (deceitfully) told that New England mercantilists were "meritorious" and possessed a "wonderful character," he invests a large sum of money to develop a "Hooker's Patent Self Animated Philanthropic Frying Pan," only to learn the merchant had taken the money and fled north. The lawyer whom he hires to sell his family home had similarly taken "the road to New England, bearing with him my sixty thousand, and various other small sums with which he had been entrusted." And finally, he receives word that he had lost both the election and his fiancée. News of the latter came in the form of a note that merely explained, "Fate has decided that we must part." His life has taken a wrong turn.[52]

Without money, love, or a future, the protagonist cries out, "If Old Nick could now appear, he might certainly get my soul cheap." At this, Satan arrives and offers a deal of riches: in exchange for power, knowledge, and a personal demon named Kalouf, the South Carolinian merely

---

Charleston Library Society (Charleston: A. E. Miller, 1835), 362; *Catalogue of the Mercantile Library in New York* (New York: Baker, Godwin & Company, 1850), 267. For the rediscovery of the text, see "'Memoirs of a Nullifier': A Story of the Past," *The Knickerbocker*, March, 1859; "'Memoirs of a Nullifier': A Story of the Past Second," *The Knickerbocker*, April, 1859; "'Memoirs of a Nullifier': Part Third the Last," *The Knickerbocker*, May, 1859, LOC. The parodied response was Elnathan Elmwood, *A Yankee Among the Nullifiers: An Autobiography* (New York: William Pearson, 1833), and will be discussed below. *Memoirs of a Nullifier* never received a second printing, and was only available in archives until digital editions appeared in 2013. The book has not received much scholarly attention, save for brief engagements. See Avery Craven, *The Coming of the Civil War* (1942; revised edition, Chicago: University of Chicago Press, 1957), 175–176; Joshua Stevens Matthews, "The American Alighieri: Receptions of Dante in the United States, 1818–1867" (University of Iowa: PhD Dissertation, 2012), 32–40; Matthews, "The Divine Comedy as an American Civil War Epic."

[52] Johnston, *Memoirs of a Nullifier*, 5, 8, 9, 13, 16.

has to pledge that he will never marry. If the contract is broken, the devil could claim the young man's soul. The man agrees and lives an enjoyable few years until he meets a woman whom he wishes to betroth. But after learning about the pact from Kalouf, his fiancée fakes her own death to spare his soul. In grief, the protagonist constructs a gun-powder mechanism that shoots him into space so that he can search for his lost love in the stars. Due to a microscopic miscalculation, he misses heaven "by about fifteen inches." He then crashes into the universe's wall and is flung back to earth by an unidentified (and unexplained) giant, only to land in the northern section of the United States. Once back on American soil, the protagonist tours the American landscape, interacts with the people of New England (by whom, he remorsefully recounts, he is measured "against a big bible" and is "found wanting"), attends a congressional session in Washington, DC, (where he listens to the nation's "patriarch," Noah Webster), and eventually discovers his fiancée's ruse. Upon this last joyous discovery, he unites with his long-lost lover and they decide to marry despite the devil's warning. Things were looking up.[53]

But the happiness was not to last, as Satan returns a few years later in the early 1830s. He produces the original writ of agreement, which was housed in a packet of notable documents: contracts signed by the congressional committee "who drew up the tariff act of 1832," "three members from South Carolina who voted for said bill," as well as "the President of the United States, who threatened his native state with the bayonet, in case she attempted to defend her liberty." (The devil was well connected with the unionist circles.) However, Satan tells the man that he could be freed from the contract on one condition: finding twenty-five people willing to sacrifice their souls in his stead. Once the protagonist publishes an advertisement in the local newspaper proclaiming his interest in buying souls, he quickly discovers "several hundred persons" from New England eager to comply. When asked for a price, the Yankees gives lip service to "the worth of an immortal soul," the fact that "the blessed Saviour died to redeem it," and the importance of obtaining "joy in heaven," before concluding, "I will not take less than ten dollars in specie." The South Carolinian happily pays the requisite funds, gathers the twenty-five New Englanders into a room (where they persist in "trading with each other" until most were in debt), and waits for the devil to return so he can fulfill his revised deal.[54]

---

[53] Ibid., 17, 70, 73, 75.   [54] Ibid., 98, 101, 102.

Satan, however, rejects the offering for two reasons. First, he explains he could not buy "that which is my own property already," which implies his longstanding ownership of New Englanders. And second, New Englanders simply had "no souls." This he demonstrates by dissecting one Yankee and listing his ingredients:

Parts in a Thousand

Cunning	–	–	–	–	125
Hypocrisy	–	–	–	–	125
Avarice	–	–	–	–	125
Falsehood	–	–	–	–	125
Sneakingness	–	–	–	–	125
Nameless and numberless small vices			–	–	140
Essence of Onions, New England Rum,					
Molasses, and Cod-Fish		–	–	–	235
					1000

Crestfallen, the man and his wife await their fates, only to be saved by the devil being informed that he is needed at a "Unionist meeting" taking place in Charleston. Satan leaves in a hurry but promises to return the following day. The protagonist races to find a diabolist who has the knowledge and ingredients to free him from his bondage. Mixing together a combination of spiritual and patriotic elements, the "Angel of Nullification" appears to "nullify" the treaty. The story's hero is once again free.[55]

More than just a humorous text that harpooned Yankee culture, *Memoirs of a Nullifier* displayed the tensions of cultural disunion. The protagonist embodied the traditional South – noble, politically con- scious, and proud. Yet his downfall came at the hands of Northern influence: the speculating New Englander, Increase Hooker, represented the manufacturing industry that was constantly in debt and sought to fix problems through robbing the South; Mr. Phipps, the real estate lawyer who ran off with the South Carolinian's money, symbolized the conniving speculators who made their money off the "industry and enterprise in the South"; and the protagonist's loss at the polls came at the hands of a democratic zealot who promises "every man in the district ... a gold mine on his land, and a rail-road by his door, and that constables and sheriffs should be totally abolished." The threats to the story's hero were

[55] Ibid., 102, 103, 104, 105, 110.

the threats to Southern industry. The narrative presented a nation at odds with itself and doomed for conflict.[56]

Much of the critique was based on political economy and divergent fiscal interests. During a quick trip to hell taken by the protagonist half-way through the story (to attend a wedding, of all things), Northern mercantilists were depicted as depraved due to both their attachment to worldly goods as well as their nefarious mercantilist practices. When forced to leave everything behind at the judgment gate, a Yankee peddler has a particularly difficult time forfeiting his small collection of merchandise: "the separation of him and his peddling cart was infinitely more painful than that which had previously occurred between his soul and his body," the narrator explained. Even while traveling on the river of fire on the way to hell, the same Yankee jumps out of the water amidst a sea of monsters and creatures in order to grab "a large cooter" which he then whittles into "an elegant tortoise shell comb, and sold it, for a high price, to an old lady who had died of love." The demon in charge of judging human souls declares that these "new-England merchants" were the most common inhabitants of hell, and that they give him "more trouble than all the rest of the world put together." The only South Carolinians con-demned to hell were those convicted "for taking part with the General Government against his own State." Hell was filled with Yankees and those who sympathized with them.[57]

This humorous lampooning of New England's mercantilist spirit arose from a more serious conflict. Following the War of 1812, the Southern states witnessed an influx of Northern New England young men who partook in a peddling rage akin to the later California gold rush. One participant, Phineas T. Barnum, later famous for other cultural produc-tions, recalled that his "disposition was of that speculative character which refused to be satisfied unless I was engaged in some business where my profits might be enhanced." Another contemporary remem-bered that large groups of New Englanders would "start off South, in the fall season, and spend the winter in some of the Southern States, on trading expeditions, and return in the spring with the fruits of their industry and enterprise." More than just a consistent nuisance – the caricature "Damned Yankees" with their "tin-pedlars and wooden-nutmeg venders" were common staples in Southern literature – the presence of these salesmen reminded Southerners of the imbalanced trade between Northern and Southern states. These Yankee peddlers put a personal face on the nation's economic instability and growing cultural divide. A memorial published by rural South Carolina citizens in opposition to federal tariffs bemoaned the continued presence of "the manufacturers" who attempted to harvest Southern society for "their own benefit and emolument." They feared the government was supporting Northern commerce, though "in no part of the Constitution do we find the word manufacture used." Thomas Cooper described them as a "scheming, petitioning, memorializing, complaining, statement-making, worrying, teasing, boring[, and] persevering class of men." This cultural clash became a key staple of Southern literature, as "the Worthy Southron," who represented the traditional ideals of social and economic engagement, were ravaged by the "Demon Yankee" who sought to spoil their simple living through dangerous speculation.[58]

Beyond goading Northern mercantilists, *Memoirs of a Nullifier* jumped into the nullification debate through its various inept characters. While touring hell with Kalouf – this voyage is another caricature of the Dante genre, as the protagonist witnesses demons devouring a great number of New England politicians – the readers are introduced to the deranged leader of a renegade American army. He declares, "of all the discoveries which have enlightened or benefited our race," the greatest achievement was the nation's "Political Economy" that emphasized Northern manufacturing. This cut straight to the core of the political debate in early 1830s America, as citizens disagreed on the nation's economic priorities. For those in the Southern states, Northern politicians focused too much on New England-based manufacturing and punished Southern agriculture. This led to problematic policies like the tariff acts that proceeded the nullification debates. The "sublime science" that led to mercantilist dominion, the hellbound militia leader reasoned, was due to the "clearly established" truth that "two and two do not make four, but something

---

[58] P. T. Barnum, *Struggles and Triumphs or, Forty Years' Recollections of P.T. Barnum* (Buffalo, NY: Warren and Johnson, 1872), 18. Thomas Douglas, *Autobiography of Thomas Douglas, Late Judge of the Supreme Court of Florida* (New York: Calkins & Stiles, 1856), 25. *National Intelligencer*, June 18, 1829, LOC. *Memorial of Citizens of Chesterfield, Marlborough, and Darlington* (Washington, DC: Gales & Seaton, 1828), 3, 5. Cooper, Speech, July 2, 1827, in William W. Freehling, ed., *The Nullification Era: A Documentary Record* (New York: Harper & Row, 1967), 21. The "worthy Southron" and "demon Yankee" types are explored in Binnington, *Confederate Visions*, 70–92.

else, I have not yet exactly ascertained what." Policies that led to "the higher price of northern manufactures" and "the lower the price of cotton" were in the best interest of the nation, for it made the Northern states rich and the Southern states "economical," for "economy is one of the chief of the virtues." All of these principles, the oratory declared, were based on the writings of "the great Mathew Carey," whose pamphlets were bulging out of every militiaman's pockets. The Philadelphia author represented national discord.[59]

Johnston skewered the North's cultural colonialism by depicting a congressional session that was led by Noah Webster. Besides highlighting New England's hypocrisy – the Webster character proclaims "lofty strains of patriotism in praise of the Hartford Convention" as well as a rebuke of "the foul spirit of Southern disaffection" – Johnston attached New England's sense of cultural superiority to their political machinations. "It is easy to see that New England, always the chosen seat of the most spotless good faith, and of patriotism the most devoted and enlarged," Webster declares, "must become the 'magna parens' of taste, of learning, and of politeness, to all the less favoured regions of our land." It was time for the "elegant and profound genius of new-England" to be "emancipated from the sordid occupations to which it is too often condemned." This would enable them to "enlighten the rest of the nation." As a result, Webster introduces bills that enable New England scholars to educate the Southern states, make it law that all American children must learn from Webster's "American Spelling Book," and mandate the spread of New England "physical handicrafts." In an echo of the very threats that were in place while Johnston penned this story, Webster warns that the South's failure to follow these codes will result in the conviction of "treason" and necessitate the President to use "the Army and the Navy of the United States [that] are placed at [his] disposal." Cultural homogeneity was a serious matter.[60]

Memoirs of a Nullifier depicted a nation divided against itself. Whether through the implications of a lecherous North feasting on the honest work of the South, or the explicit invocation of "NULLIFICATION" as the solution to a demonic pact, Johnston's narrative ably captured the tensions that were percolating in early 1830s South Carolina. The nexus of the book's cultural clashes were competing notions of nationalism. At various points in the narrative, both the fictional Noah Webster in the North and the conjurer in the South explicitly summoned the heritage

[59] Johnston, *Memoirs of a Nullifier*, 50–52.   [60] Ibid., 75, 76, 77, 80, 84.

of the nation's founding moment for a defense of their cultural beliefs: the former's pious "patriotism" that dwelled on New England's revolutionary heritage, and the latter's use of Jefferson's writings and the "bones gathered from the battlefields of the Revolution." But more than that, Johnston's protagonist was an embodiment of what he believed to be the American spirit – honor, a political economy based on free-market capitalism, and an allowance for various states or regions to embrace what they found to be their best interests. The blundering characters of New England, by contrast, represented the greatest threats to those principles: a cultural colonialism that sought to consume Southern sociality, a political economy that privileged Northern manufacturers over Southern exportation, and a dependent Northern culture that sapped the energy and finances from Southern society. These anxieties drove a growing number of South Carolinians to declare their own cultural and political independence.

The book was not without its critics. One of the few responses to *Memoirs of a Nullifier* came from New Englander Elnathan Elmwood. A year later, Elmwood wrote *A Yankee Among the Nullifiers* as a fictional, and parodied, autobiography that cast South Carolinians as greedy hotheads who replaced reason with passion. The juxtaposition between the two novels could not be more stark. In Elmwood's hands, the nullifiers were so obsessed with "politics, State Rights, and Nullification" that they lacked the fortitude to understand tradition or consider long-term implications. As one blundering leader of the book's nullification party argued, "the value of *Union* may be calculated as well as the value of an *onion*, or any other given commodity." The commodification of something so foundational as constitutional belonging invited problems, and the book's tale ended with discord and blood. Elmwood's concern over underestimating the importance of union was also further highlighted in a political cartoon at the time, "The Union Pie," which placed the nullification debates within a context of international intrigue (Image 5.4).

South Carolina's arguments were so dangerous, according to the cartoon, that they might well have originated in Great Britain. The British were depicted as a portly John Bull character standing by, ready to devour the American states. "In '76 & '13 tho' thwarted in my pride," Britain rhymed, "If I cannot eat all now, I'll see it <u>divide</u>." To Elmwood and many in the North, South Carolina's cold calculation spelled the doom for the American nation for it acknowledged a cultural discontinuity too great for political union. Conversely, for Johnston and many in South Carolina,

IMAGE 5.4 "The Union Pie," Negative 35159, New-York Historical Society. Another anti-nullification cartoon, this artist depicted South Carolina's actions as the work of Britain. "In '76 & '13 tho' thwarted in my pride, if I cannot eat all now, I'll see it divide!!"

that calculation was a mere reflection of the reality: the nation's cultural fissures were too deep to justify political union.[61]

The debates over nullification heated up once again before a conclusion could be reached. In January, Charleston resident and later mayor Charles Macbeth wrote to his brother that "we are on the eve of a fight," and though they expected President Jackson to send troops, the city's residents were in no way "intimidated & they are preparing zealously their arms and ammunition." Though they might be outnumbered, Macbeth was confident that South Carolinians could "carry the loud spirit to the field

---

[61] Elmwood, *A Yankee Among the Nullifiers*, 14, 52.

which now animates them [and] it will be found that nullifiers are not easy to be beaten." The city was ready for a war.[62]

While citizens prepared for battle in Charleston, congressmen continued to argue in Washington. President Jackson declared they could still resolve the problem through "the prudence of the officers" and, especially, "the patriotism of the people." He believed the conflict invoked "the fidelity of the patriot and the sagacity of the statesmen" just as it did any subject that touched on national interests. Drawing further on nationalist sentiment, Jackson claimed a "rich inheritance bequeathed by our fathers" that made it his "sacred obligation of preserving [the Union] by the same virtues which conducted them through the eventful scenes of the revolution" – namely, the power of the democratic governance. Working together, the nation's politicians could once again prove "the *Union indissoluble.*" If a peaceful solution could not be achieved, however, a violent response would be necessary.[63]

Henry Laurens Pinckney, one of the most vocal nullifiers, interpreted Jackson's message as a call to arms. South Carolina "no longer looks to the opinions or feelings of the President," he announced. He and his colleagues now saw Jackson as "a Monarchist" with the "heart of a tyrant." Citizens of the state had an "oath of allegiance ... to sustain South-Carolina in a great and unequal conflict with the Federal Government." They were not violating the Constitution, but "maintaining its spirit, and resisting its infractions." Reaching back before the Constitution, Pinckney declared that these actions were justified because the Declaration of Independence had pronounced them "FREE AND INDEPENDENT STATES" and *not* "ONE PEOPLE OR ONE NATION." He accused Jackson of perverting the true nature of nationalism, for "allegiance is due *only to a sovereign.*" Whoever heard of "*citizens of America?*" he asked. Calhoun echoed many of the same principles on the Senate floor, and the constitutional crisis seemed destined for a bloody climax.[64]

---

[62] Charles Macbeth to Robert Macbeth, Charleston, January 26, 1833, Robert Macbeth Papers, SCHS.

[63] Andrew Jackson, *Message from the President of the United States, Transmitting Copies of the Proclamation and Proceedings in relation to South Carolina. January 16, 1833* (Washington, DC: House of Representatives, 1833), 1, 18, 19.

[64] [Henry Laurens Pinckney] *Remarks on the Ordinance of Nullification* ... (Charleston, SC: A. E. Miller, 1833), 4, 10, 15, 23, 38. See Charles M. Wiltse, *John C. Calhoun*, 3 vols. (Indianapolis, IN: The Bobbs-Merrill Co., 1951), 2:189–195, for Calhoun's final defense of nullification in the Senate.

Northerners refused to back down. Massachusetts's senator Daniel Webster accused Calhoun, and others who defended nullification, of having "no foothold on which to stand" and that "every thing beneath his feet is hollow and treacherous." Everything in their arguments, he claimed, merely embodied "the whole South Carolina doctrine" of state sovereignty and a weak federal union. Webster then noted the nationalist foundation upon which any constitutional argument must be based: "It is our own liberty, guarded by constitutions and secured by union; it is that liberty which is our paternal inheritance, it is our established, dear bought, peculiar American liberty to which I am chiefly devoted, and the cause of which I now mean, to the utmost of my power, to maintain and defend." Webster's argument included two important components: first, that America's liberties were secured by "union," and were thus not found outside of that compact; and second, that constitutional liberties were inherited through a patriotic lineage that had been "bought" by revolutionary heroes and bequeathed only through fidelity to a federal government. In short, constitutional rights were based on a connection to nationalist ideals.[65]

Webster believed that the nullifier's misunderstanding was even apparent in their language. The Massachusetts politician argued that Calhoun's grammar signified a fundamentally flawed idea of what the constitution, and the nation it founded, really meant. "I must say to the honorable gentleman," Webster reasoned, "that, in our American political grammar, CONSTITUTION is a noun substantive," meaning that it "imports a distinct and clear idea, of itself." Calhoun, on the other hand, had turned the word "into a poor, ambiguous, senseless, unmeaning adjective." Thus, Webster implied that the term was used to describe a relationship between sovereign states larger than the document itself, instead of the Constitution being both the means *and* the ends of government. "We will not give up our forms of political speech," Webster warned, "to the grammarians of the school of nullification." The Massachusetts orator emphasized that "the constitution of the United States is not a league, confederacy, or compact, between the people of the several States in their sovereign capacities." Rather, it is "a Government proper," and existed by "creating direct relations between itself and individuals," not through intermediary stategovernments.Nationalist devotion,

---

[65] Daniel Webster, *Speech of Mr. Webster, in the Senate, In Reply to Mr. Calhoun's Speech, on the Bill "Further to Provide for the Collection of Duties on Imports." Delivered the 16th of February, 1833* (Washington: Gales and Seaton, 1833), 4, 5.

patriotic heritage, and citizenship were bound together in the Constitution. Those committed to the Union worked to build up the nationalist identity; those who believed in such a thing as nullification were merely "architects of ruin." The nationalist schism was clearly apparent.[66]

The outcome of the Nullification Crisis served as a temporary stopgap even as it failed to produce any permanent solutions. Even while he continued to battle in the senate, Calhoun wrote a letter to nullification supporters in South Carolina urging them to consider reconciliation. He worked with Kentucky's Henry Clay to come up with a settlement that would avert military crisis. While the tax rates that resulted from the compromise were only marginally better for the following three years, the agreement did guarantee major cuts over the next two decades. The Compromise Tariff of 1833 was passed by Congress on March 1 with little trouble, and each side felt they could declare victory: unionists believed the revised tariff favored domestic manufacturing, and South Carolinians saw the compromise as a recognition by the federal government that it had overstepped its bounds. Calhoun raced back to South Carolina to make sure the Nullification Convention, set to reassemble in a matter of weeks, accepted the compromise. Jackson, for his part, was relieved that "Nullification is dead," yet still feared that the Southerners "intend to [now] blow up a storm on the subject on the slavery question." Indeed, Elmwood's *Yankee Among the Nullifiers*, the novel that critiqued Johnston's *Memoirs of a Nullifier*, posited that a race war with freed slaves would be the only logical end of the nullification controversy. Just days after the compromise, Jackson's second inaugural address warned that "the loss of liberty, of all good government, of peace, plenty, and happiness, must inevitably follow a dissolution of the Union." Problems clearly remained.[67]

---

[66] Webster, *Speech of Mr. Webster*, 6, 16, 48.

[67] John C. Calhoun to William Preston, [February 3, 1833], Washington, DC, in *Papers of Calhoun*, 12:37–38. (Emphasis in original.) Andrew Jackson to John Crawford, April 9, 1833, in *Correspondence of Jackson*, ed. John Spencer Bassett, 7 vols. (Washington, DC: Carnegie Institution, 1926–35), 5:56. Elmwood, *A Yankee Among the Nullifiers*, 120–137. Jackson, "Inaugural Address," March 4, 1833, in Richardson, *Messages and Papers of the Presidents*, 3:4. Over a month earlier, a regretful William Drayton, then serving as a South Carolinian congressman, came to the conclusion that "the majority of States will not permit South Carolina, *peacefully*, to secede from the Union," and thus suggested compromising. William Drayton to Joel Poinsett, December 31, 1832, Washington, DC, Joel Poinsett Papers, SCL. (Emphasis in original.) For an overview of

If the terms of the compromise were not as favorable to South Carolina as they had wished, many still interpreted it as a resolute victory. Pinckney, only months removed from his scathing accusations against Jackson and the federal government, delivered a Fourth of July oration that placed the state's attempt at nullification within America's proud nationalist tradition. Noting the particular relevance of celebrating America's independence due to "the important circumstances which have recently occurred," Pinckney pointed out that both South Carolina in 1832 and America in 1776 had witnessed their liberties being "trampled and crushed by tyranny" while struggling for their life "against the gigantic power" of a tyrannical government. Those who argued for nullification were not challengers to America's proud tradition, but rather its saviors: "Liberty has emerged from the ordeal, not only uninjured, but strengthened and refined. South-Carolina has not only gallantly sustained the shock, but restored and confirmed the Constitution and the Union." Pinckney was euphoric about the sacred connection between the revolutionaries of '76 and the would-be-nullifiers of '32:

We have not forgotten the precepts, or dimmed the glory, of our fathers. We have not deserted the standard, or disgraced the cause, of freedom ... Who more worthy to celebrate the deeds of the Whigs of '76 than the Whigs of '32? Who more worthy to call WASHINGTON their father, than those who approve his conduct by imitating his example? Who more worthy to eulogise JEFFERSON, than those who believe him that; "Nullification is the rightful remedy," and who, acting as he did in '98, have added fresh lustre to his fame by another signal triumph of his principles?[68]

Beyond placing their patriotism on par with those who founded the nation, Pinckney recast America's narrative of independence not as a story of disparate colonies joining together to build a "more perfect union," but an awakening to the global benefits of "the principle of free trade." The "discovery of America" centuries before, the "American Revolution" in 1776, and the "regeneration" of America's liberties in 1832 – all of these triumphs were based on an expanding capitalistic principle that transcended both state and nation, and each were most aptly described as a "war for commerce." The cause of America was now the cause for a global capitalism that was unfettered by state or

the Nullification Crisis's conclusion, see Freehling, *Road to Disunion*, 279–286; Wilentz, *Rise of American Democracy*, 385–390.
[68] Henry L. Pinckney, *An Oration, Delivered in the Independent, or Congregational Church, Charleston* (Charleston, SC: A. E. Miller, 1833), 3, 4, 5.

national boundaries. The nullification debates "achieved a glorious and decisive victory" by pointing toward "a great revolution, by which the character of our government will be purified, its policy enlightened, and its stability secured." Nationalism, to Pinckney, was not fidelity to a particular government or institution, but to the economic principles upon which he believed government should be built. Taken further, his nationalist vision expanded beyond national borders so that his allegiance could be tethered to the international market in which the cotton trade, supported by unfree labor, participated, and which the American government could not and should not oppose.[69]

Thomas Grimké could not enjoy the unionist victory for long. Only a year after Jackson's resolution, Grimké, along with James L. Petigru and Abram Blanding, argued a case before the State Court of Appeals in Columbia that became known as *M'Cready v. Hunt*. The case concerned the fate of a "test oath" passed during the tense months of late 1832 that had required members of the state militia to pledge "faithful and true allegiance" to South Carolina. The legislation was vague regarding how this pledge related to national allegiance and whether this oath took precedence over one's loyalty to the federal government. Governor Robert Y. Hayne, a staunch defender of nullification, along with State Attorney-General Robert Barnwell Rhett, defended the notion that, despite the uneasy compromise between the state and President Jackson, the oath still prioritized state above federal allegiance. But the Court of Appeals decided, in a two-to-one decision, that the oath violated both state and federal constitutions. When Grimké succumbed to cholera later that year, he died with the belief that his efforts vindicated federal sovereignty. However, those who supported nullification vowed revenge against a system they believed privileged federal over state authority, and the Court of Appeals was abolished the next year, not to be reestablished until the eve of the Civil War.[70]

---

[69] Pinckney, *An Oration*, 6, 9, 15, 27, 28, 33.

[70] See Lacy K. Ford, Jr., *Origin of Southern Radicalism: The South Carolina Upcountry, 1800 to 1860* (New York: Oxford University Press, 1991), 148–149; Ellis, *Union at Risk*, 180. For Grimké's argument for federal sovereignty in the trial, see his *Argument of Thomas S. Grimké Delivered in the Court of Appeals of the State of South-Carolina Before the Hon. David Johnson & Wm. Harper on the 2d and 3d April 1834* (Charleston, SC: J. S. Burges, 1834).

Ambiguity remained long after the debate's climax. Even before the nullification crisis was over, some recognized that their complaints concerning states' rights were destined to falter as long as the other Southern states failed to share their interests and purposes. Langdon Cheves, a former congressman and Speaker of the House who retired to his South Carolina plantation, was a proponent of state sovereignty yet refused to be swept up in the current fervor. He privately wrote to fellow South Carolinian David McCord that, though he believed "the oppression under which the South labours is one under which a free people ought not to suffer an hour longer than is necessary," circumstances were not severe enough to lead him to support nullification – at least not yet. "The metaphysics of *nullification*," he explained, "is the worst shape in which the bad principle of separate action can be embodied." His opposition was not based in theory – he agreed that the nation had failed to recognize and cultivate the interests of the South – but in practice: South Carolina lacked the requisite support of the neighboring states. "It ought first to be attempted and we should wait long and patiently before we separated from our sister states on the question," he reasoned. Until Alabama, Georgia, North Carolina, and other Southern states forfeited their toxic and unnecessary allegiance to the American federal government, little progress could be achieved. In the future, however, there would be a "body of common sufferers" which could then form a true union with shared interests by seceding from a nation that had become an impediment. Sectionalism would yet be triumphant.[71]

The fate of Algernon Sidney Johnston's *Memoirs of Nullifier* mirrored the fate of South Carolina's nullification dreams. Just as the nullifiers lost – or at least, failed to win – their battle against Jackson, so too did the novel lose its attempt at lasting influence. Johnston's work faded remarkably quickly from the public eye. It would be another Southern novel, penned four years later, which gained broader prominence. *The Partisan Leader*, penned in 1836 by Virginia politician Nathaniel Beverley Tucker, envisioned a group of Virginia rebels breaking away from the North to join other states, including South Carolina, in a new confederacy. Once the Civil War commenced, the book was republished in both the North (with the subtitle, "A Key to the Southern Conspiracy") as well as the South (with the subtitle, "A Novel, and an Apocalypse of the Origin and Struggles of the Southern Confederacy"). Tucker's text became the

---

[71] Langdon Cheves to David J. McCord, August 15, 1831, Langdon Cheves Papers, SCL. (Emphasis in original.)

much more famous secessionist novel. Where Americans were hesitant to adopt a vision of a single state nullifying the actions of the federal government through metaphysical means, they were eager to consume a vision of competing regional sovereignties – the "body of common sufferers" predicted by Cheves – that made war inevitable. Tucker's vision of secession and civil war that spread across the South carried much more currency than Johnston's nullification that remained centered in South Carolina.[72]

Indeed, the debates over nullification in the early 1830s proved restricted in geography and limited in scope. While some states' rights defenders from neighboring Southern states offered meager support, South Carolina remained isolated in cultivating a revised understanding of nationalism. And lacking broader regional backing, their complaints led to a temporary fix that left lingering and larger issues unresolved. In the coming decades, however, their vision of a nationalism steeped in agriculture, states' rights, global interests, and a slavery-based society became more prominently shared by neighboring states. By projecting their nationalist principles, now freed from the federal union, onto a newly constructed "nation" of like-minded, slaveholding states, they constructed a nationalist vision that posed a more direct threat to the American union.

Yet at the same time that South Carolina's faith in the Union was diminishing, elsewhere a strong nationalist vision was growing. The arguments of Andrew Jackson and of Daniel Webster foreshadowed the nationalist arguments of the coming decades. The Nullification Crisis proved a test case for unionist arguments and, though the dispute did not lead to war then, demonstrated how far people were willing to go to defend what they believed to be national interests. In the end, the most convincing arguments over the correct balance of state and national rights, and the correct understanding of the nation itself, was found not in polemical newspapers or combative state houses, but on the battlefields of the Civil War.

---

[72] Nathaniel Beverley, *The Partisan Leader: A Key to the Disunion Conspiracy* (1836; reprint, New York: Rudd & Carleton, 1861); Beverley, *The Partisan Leader: A Novel, and an Apocalypse of the Origins and Struggles of the Southern Confederacy* (1836; reprint, Richmond: West and Johnson, 1862). See Varon, *Disunion*, 120–121.

Epilogue

The Boundaries of America's Nationalist Imagination

Andrew Jackson's response to John C. Calhoun and the other South Carolina radicals signaled his commitment to national sovereignty. But there were limits to what he imagined a nation to entail. Even as he confronted the nullifiers, Jackson signed an Indian Removal Act that physically excised indigenous tribes from the political body. The fact that societies like the Cherokee were distinctly referred to as a "nation" implied that they were a people apart and did not match the interests and values of the American nation. "We have indeed fallen upon evil times," noted Cherokee author Elias Boudinot. He confessed his "utter ignorance" of how American politicians could be so misguided on "the rights of the Indians" and "the relation in which they stand to the United States." Despite the valiant effort of many indigenous actors, the Cherokee, along with a number of other tribes, were eventually forced West. Assimilation was deemed impossible. And Indians weren't the only problem. "We have never dreamt of incorporating into our Union any but the Caucasian race," bellowed John C. Calhoun after the Mexican-American War brought new land and bodies under American control. The thought of adding persons of Mexican heritage insulted Calhoun's sense of national belonging. "Ours, sir," he declared, "is the Government of a white race." This racial understanding of nationalism and political belonging would remain long after the Age of Jackson.[1]

---

[1] Elias Boudinot, in *Cherokee Editor: The Writings of Elias Boudinot* (Athens: University of Georgia Press, 1996), 118–119. *Congressional Globe*, 30th Congress, 1st Session, 98, LOC. See Theda Perdue and Michael D. Green, *The Cherokee Nation and the Trail of Tears* (New York: Viking, 2007); Steve Inskeep, *Jacksonland: President Andrew Jackson,*

Disagreements over the "nation" during the 1830s led to new political mobilization. Though the American Whig Party was formed around pragmatic opposition to Jackson's presidency, a robust nationalism was central to their vision. At their 1839 convention, James Barbour, governor of Virginia, proclaimed that the "personal predilections" of politicians and states must be "instantly ... surrendered as a ready sacrifice when that sacrifice is demanded by our country." The Whig Party, he explained, is "not here to promote any local object to acquire the supremacy of this or that state." Rather, the American political system "should embrace the whole Republic." But their failure to uniformly address the slave institution, among other problems, led to the party's collapse. It wasn't until the formation of the Republican Party in the 1850s, and the radical abolitionists within the movement took center stage, that a more radical and inclusive nationalist program was offered. Conversely, the Democratic Party, especially those from the South, developed sophisticated arguments for an American nation based on slavery and white supremacy. Could a nation be comprised of such disparate groups? Was cultural and political heterogeneity a recipe for disunion? Americans struggled to find an answer.[2]

Some of these questions would not be settled until the Civil War. Others remained unanswered long after the Confederacy's surrender. Even after the federal government became triumphant, and nationalism became permanently attached to the nation-state, nationalist imaginations continued to be racialized. Once African-Americans gained suffrage and flocked to the Republic Party, Democratic candidates warned of political degradation. "This is a white man's country," 1868 presidential candidate Horatio Seymour posited as his campaign motto, "let white men rule." Black citizens were not the only targets. The first Asian immigrants arriving to the West Coast led to the Chinese Exclusion Act, passed

Cherokee Chief John Ross, and a Great American Land Grab (New York: Penguin Press, 2015); Edward J. Blum, *Reforging the White Republic: Race, Religion, and American Nationalism, 1865–1898* (Baton Rouge: Louisiana State University Press, 2005); W. Paul Reeve, *Religion of a Different Color: Race and the Mormon Struggle for Whiteness* (New York: Oxford University Press, 2015).

[2] *Proceedings of the Democratic Whig National Convention, Which Assembled at Harrisburg, Pennsylvania, on the Fourth of December, 1839, For the Purpose of Nominating Candidates for President and Vice President of the United States* (Harrisburg, PA: R. S. Elliott, 1839), 13–14. For the Whigs, see Daniel Walker Howe, *The Political Culture of the American Whigs* (Chicago: University of Chicago Press, 1979); Michael F. Holt, *The Rise and Fall of the American Whig Party: Jacksonian Politics and the Onset of the Civil War* (New York: Oxford University Press, 1999).

in 1882, which forbade immigrants from China from coming to America. That policy lasted until World War II, only two decades after Native Americans finally received citizenship. In the mid-twentieth century, as African-Americans fought for civil liberties, black activists were once again seen as threats by institutional authorities like the FBI. Throughout America's story, there has been a persistent attempt to discredit discordant voices as legitimate participants in the American political body. The admission of new groups to America's national imagination has always been delayed and contested.[3]

The twenty-first century has witnessed yet another resurgence of nativism both inside and outside of the United States. In response to increased immigration, many Europeans and Americans have perpetuated a nationalism that decries diversity. The United Kingdom voted to leave the European Union in 2016 largely based on Euroscepticism, a move that radicals in other European nations sought to replicate. Months later, Donald Trump won the American presidential election based on a xenophobic and discriminatory campaign. "Make America Great Again," his slogan trumpeted, a clarion call to a mythical past when American culture was homogenous. One of Trump's key advisors, Newt Gingrich, claimed America must "defeat [the] left-wing mythology that you can be multicultural and still be a single country." Many critics have rightly called out these remarks, but have wrongly argued that they are alien to America's political history. If anything, these ideas reaffirm an entrenched political tradition within the country.[4]

---

[3] "Our Ticket, Our Motto: This is a White Man's Country; Let White Men Rule," Campaign Badge Supporting Horatio Seymour and Francis Blair, Democratic candidates for the President and Vice-President of the United States, 1865, New York Public Library Digital Collections, digitalcollections.nypl.org (accessed March 2017). See David W. Blight, *Race and Reunion: The Civil War in American Memory* (Cambridge: Harvard University Press, 2001), 98–139; Edward J. Blum, *Reforging the White Republic: Race, Religion, and American Nationalism, 1865–1898* (Baton Rouge: Louisiana State University Press, 2005); Kevin M. Kruse, *White Flight: Atlanta and the Making of Modern Conservatism* (Princeton: Princeton University Press, 2005); Khalil Gibran Muhammad, *The Condemnation of Blackness: Race, Crime, and the Making of Modern America* (Cambridge: Harvard University Press, 2010).

[4] "Newt Gingrich: We Must Defeat 'Left-Wing Mythology that You Can Be Multicultural and Still Be a Single Country,'" *Media Matters*, https://www.mediamatters.org/video/20 17/03/22/newt-gingrich-we-must-defeat-left-wing-mythology-you-can-be-multicultural-and-still-be-single/215786 (accessed March 2017). For this context, see, for example, "The New Nationalism," *The Economist*, November 19, 2016; Christina Pazzanese, "In Europe, Nationalism Rising," *Harvard Gazette*, February 27, 2017.

America's nationalist imagination has always been dynamic yet fleeting. Born during the Age of Revolutions, an era that posed new problems and possibilities for models of cultural belonging, it has never been coherent nor consistent. The relationship between an American "character" and the American "state," as well as the discourse surrounding nationalism itself, evolved in multifaceted and uneven ways between the constitutional debates in the 1780s and the Nullification Crisis in the 1830s – just as it has ever since. Whereas the dream of a unified culture governed by a representative federal power disappeared into the void, new and competing visions of culture, community, and nation took center stage. If "America" is just as much an idea as a polity, then it has always been a contested idea that was imaginatively constructed from divergent cultural tools, subtly influential in crafting political experience, and sufficiently malleable for competing purposes. These thoughts led, in turn, to new programs, policies, and even wars. Conceptions of the United States brought about everything *except* union.

Nearly two-and-a-half centuries after independence, Americans are still trying to imagine what the nation actually entails.

Index

Osgood, David, 104–105, 110, 141–142
Osgood, Samuel, 36
Otis, Harrison Gray, 117–118, 143, 144,
    149

Pacifism, 137–140
Paine, Thomas, 2, 97, 98–99
Parish, Elijah, 137–138
Pennsylvania Society for the Abolition of
    Slavery, 161
Pickens, Francis Wilkinson, 213
Pickering, Timothy, 126, 144
Pinckney, Charles, 187
Pinckney, Henry Laurence, 235, 238–239
Pinckney, Thomas, 190
Pluralism embrace of, 65–66
Political economy, 37–38, 216–217,
    231–232
Postcolonial Theory, 11–12, 14–15
Print culture, 14, 19, 48, 81–82, 131
Providentialism, 80–81, 85–88, 91–92

Quakers, opposition to slavery, 159–160
Quincy, Josiah, 181

Ramsay, David, 49, 54–55
Ramsay, James, 166
Regeneration, cultural, 38–39, 40–41, 83,
    208–209
Regionalism, 14–15, 35–36, 39–40, 59–60,
    81–84, 109–111, 121–123, 133–135,
    146–147, 186, 188–193, 209–210,
    216–220, 240–241
Religion, role in nationalism, 13–14, 20,
    62–64, 73–76, 88–89, 94–101, 105–106,
    137–138, 190–191
Rousseau, Jean-Jacques, 3, 29, 96
Rush, Benjamin, 28–29, 40, 54–55, 57–68,
    160

Saussure, Henry William de, x
Schlegel, August von, 211
Schlegel, Friedrich, 96
Scott, Thomas, 162–163
Scottish Enlightenment, 65
Sectionalism, *see* "regionalism."
Sentimentalism, cultural, 40–41, 141–142,
    211–212
Sieyès, Emmanuel, 38

Sinclair, Sir. John, 37
Slavery, x–xi, 19, 61–62, 112, 151,
    199–200, 206, 224, 241, 243; and the
    threat of violence, 171, 189–191;
    arguments for the abolition of, 164–167;
    congressional debates over, 161–163,
    184–185; Constitutional Convention
    debates over, 160; relationship with
    nationalism, 162, 172, 174, 176–177,
    191–193
Smith, Adam, 37, 65, 78
Smith, John, 140
Smith, William Loughton, 162–163, 189
Southern Review, 212
Spring, Samuel, 95–96
Staël, Madame de, 211
States' rights arguments, 21, 34, 121, 154,
    188, 209, 222–224, 241
Strong, Caleb, 136–137, 138, 143, 144, 148

Tappan, David, 87
Tariffs, national, 199
Thanksgiving sermons, 76–77, 79–84, 101,
    106–109
Trenchard, James, 55–57
Trump, Donald, 244
Tucker, Josiah, 35
Tucker, Nathan Beverley, author of
    The Partisan Leader, 240–241
Tucker, St. George, 173
Tucker, Thomas, 161–162
Turnbull, Robert James, 201–202

Vattel, Emer de, 4
Vesey, Denmark, 189–191

Washington, George, 79, 106–107, 113
Webster, Daniel, 207–209, 236–237
Webster, Noah, 2, 3, 29, 40, 58–68, 232
Webster, Pelatiah, 54
Westward expansion, 39, 42–43, 118–119,
    128–129, 134–135, 146–148, 153–155,
    173–174, 184–185
Whig Party, 243
Wilson, James, 50–51, 160
Winchester, Elhanan, 103
White, William, 103–104
Wollstonecraft, Mary, 97
Worcester, Samuel, 138–139

For EU product safety concerns, contact us at Calle de José Abascal, 56–1°,
28003 Madrid, Spain or eugpsr@cambridge.org.

www.ingramcontent.com/pod-product-compliance
Ingram Content Group UK Ltd.
Pitfield, Milton Keynes, MK11 3LW, UK
UKHW010038140625
459647UK00012BA/1460